Abbey Road

The story of the world's most famous recording studios

Abbey Road

The story of the world's most famous recording studios

Brian Southall
Peter Vince
Allan Rouse

FOREWORD BY
Sir Paul McCartney

PREFACE BY
Sir George Martin

OMNIBUS PRESS
LONDON · NEW YORK · SYDNEY

Copyright 1982, 1997 & 2002 EMI Records Ltd
First published by Patrick Stevens, Cambridge, 1982

This Edition Copyright © 2002 Omnibus Press
(A Division of Music Sales Limited)

COVER DESIGN
Pearce Marchbank

BOOK DESIGN
Lisa Pettibone

ISBN: 0.7119.9111.1
Order No: OP 48719

Exclusive Distributors
Book Sales Limited,
8/9 Frith Street,
London W1D 3JB

Music Sales Corporation,
257 Park Avenue South,
New York, NY 10010, USA.

Macmillan Distribution Services,
53 Park West Drive,
Derrimut, Vic 3030,
Australia.

To the Music Trade only:
Music Sales Limited,
8/9, Frith Street,
London W1V 5TZ, UK.

PHOTO CREDITS
Every effort has been made to trace the copyright holders of the photographs in this book but one or two were unreachable. We would be grateful if the photographers concerned would contact us.

FRONT AND BACK COVER PHOTOGRAPHS
Phil Dent

PICTURE RESEARCH
Allan Rouse and Peter Vince

The original text for this book was written by Brian Southall. It now contains four additional chapters written by Peter Vince and Allan Rouse who conceived the original idea and provided additional research.

Printed in Singapore.

A catalogue record for this book is available from the British Library.

Visit Omnibus Press on the web at www.omnibuspress.com

Contents

Foreword

I would just say that Abbey Road is the best studio in town; town being the world. I don't think I've ever been in a better studio although obviously there are much more modern studios, much more technological studios, places where you can park your car, but there's a lot of kinda nostalgia for me whenever I come back to the place. I met Sir Malcolm Sargent here and Sir Donald Wolfit on the steps outside and that illustrates the great depth of the place. It's not just a pop studio; you'll run into Daniel Barenboim downstairs, that kind of thing and that's great really; it's a bit of a number meeting all those guys. I love Abbey Road because it has depth, back up, tradition and all those things.

PAUL McCARTNEY
January 1982

Preface

Abbey Road Studios and I grew up more or less at the same time, although we were both in our arrogant twenties before we first met.

I well remember that day in 1950 when, barely protected from the November cold by my old Naval greatcoat, I cycled into the Abbey Road forecourt to begin my work as an assistant to the head of Parlophone Records. I have often reflected that the improvement in my personal transport kept pace with the standard of equipment within the studios, so that by the time we were using two-track tape, 10 years later, I had actually progressed to the luxury of a Mini.

In those early days we both treated each other with a certain reserve, but I quickly appreciated that, although she was marginally my junior in years, Abbey Road was able to teach me quite a thing or two. Our relationship flourished through respect into affection so that my leaving in 1965 to build an upstart rival in AIR Studios was a sad but inevitable pause in our lifelong affair. And today, when I return, I always get that tingle of warmth which is the feeling of coming home.

If you believe, as I do, that a house has atmosphere, and is capable of absorbing the personalities and emotions of its inhabitants, you will have no difficulty in appreciating the unique quality of Abbey Road. Countless performances of master-pieces by the greatest musicians and artistes in the world have been captured by her mikes and there is no need for the photographs on the walls to remind me of their presence. Not only the performers are there; one can sense the presence of the great engineers and producers of the past, long since gone. Names which may mean little to the average man, but great people such as Arthur Clarke, Dougie Larter, Bob Beckett, Charlie Anderson, Walter Legge, Charlie Thomas and my own dear mentor, Oscar Preuss, who taught me so much. These men flew the record industry in open cockpits by the seat of their pants, and paved the way for the modern, jetstream, computerised machine that today's young talents have to guide.

Dear Abbey Road – you demanded, and took, a great deal; but you gave much more back. I am very proud to have been part of you and I thank you and salute you.

GEORGE MARTIN
January 1982

1
The Album

An album, recorded over a five-month period in the summer of 1969, and a photograph, one of six shots taken during a 10-minute session, have become permanent tributes to a rather ordinary piece of 19th century architecture in North London and made it a building as internationally famous as any presidential address or royal palace.

As a possible final thank you, or perhaps because they could find no inspiration for a better title, The Beatles named the last album they recorded together, *Abbey Road,* after the studios where, for seven years, they made records which established them as the most successful pop group in the history of recording.

Since June 1962, when they were first invited to the studios of EMI Records at Number Three Abbey Road, The Beatles had become regular visitors to the elegant London suburb of St John's Wood, close to Lords cricket ground. They worked, played and even slept there as they forged their way to the very top of the pop music world. Although its official name was EMI Studios, it wasn't long before fans and the media were referring to the studios simply as Abbey Road (as did the musicians who had worked there) and making regular visits to the large white house with its imposing wrought iron gates and tall railings.

That final album by the four young men who had journeyed down from Liverpool, dreaming of success and stardom, has become the most successful made by the quartet affectionately known as the 'Fab Four'. The worldwide sales are a tribute to the skill, professionalism and, at times, patience of the people who worked hand in hand with John Lennon, Paul McCartney, George Harrison and Ringo Starr.

It was Paul McCartney who made the initial approach to George Martin, the man who had produced their records for so many years, and said that The Beatles, already involved in legal wrangling, wanted to make an album "the way we used to". Martin was cautious because of problems he had encountered in earlier albums and made it clear that if the album was to be "the way it used to be" then the four Beatles also had to be "the way they used to be". Paul was adamant that there would be no problems.

So, in April 1969, the four of them gathered with Martin for what were their last sessions at Abbey Road as The Beatles. They each broke off from the indi-

An Abbey Road crossing with a difference. Paul and Linda McCartney take their pony, Jet (named after the Wings' single), across the famous crossing (photographed by Denny Laine of Wings).

vidual pursuits which had become increasingly important to them as they strived to establish themselves as individual artists. John came from his peace campaign, Ringo left his recently established film career, Paul put off his planned trip out of London, George broke off his recording with the Radha Krishna Temple.

However, for all Paul's insistence that things would be "like they used to be", there were rows and disagreements. George Martin recalls that George was the first to become disenchanted with the idea of putting back the clock. "He really wanted more say in what was going on in the studio and for a long time had been asking for one of his songs to be considered as an A-side."

He was to get his way with the haunting 'Something', a song that has since become one of the great classics in The Beatles' catalogue. But the album best served to illustrate the musical rift which was growing between John and Paul. It has become common knowledge that John saw this last Beatles album as a collection of rock'n'roll songs, while Paul preferred the concept of a rock symphony. Reviewers saw the album as a carefully constructed blending of these two styles – but that was not how John Lennon saw it.

Speaking to Jann Wenner of *Rolling Stone* in 1970 he said, "I liked the A-side but I never liked the sort of pop opera on the other side. I think it's junk because it's just bits of songs thrown together. 'Come Together' is all right... that's all I remember. That was my song. It was a competent album like *Rubber Soul*. It was together in that way but *Abbey Road* had no life in it."

Paul McCartney, on the other hand, was pleased if not totally happy with the end result. "Looking back on it I suppose it was tense but at the time it didn't feel like a tense album. There were one or two tense moments but I was getting into a lot of musical ideas; the medley on the second side – I was really up on that."

One of the more tense moments no doubt came when Yoko Ono, still not accepted by the other three members of the group, brought a bed into the studios in which to rest following a car crash. Even when the album was finished John and Paul failed to agree on the type of press launch to be held for the new album. Paul wanted a few journalist friends while John wanted the underground press as well; in the end there was no party.

The final recording session on the final Beatles album took place on January 3rd 1970 when they recorded 'I Me Mine' which takes its place in history as the last song ever recorded by The Beatles (although John Lennon was on holiday in Denmark at the time). Abbey Road Studios had seen the beginning and end of a group which in seven years had taken the pop world by storm, changed the way the music business was run and achieved levels of success and adulation which are unlikely ever to be repeated.

The controversy surrounding the last Beatles album did not end with its release in September 1969. The cover shot created a whole new sensation as eagle-eyed, fanatical Beatles fans in America read all sorts of hidden meanings into the photograph of four young men striding purposefully across the zebra crossing just outside Abbey Road Studios. There in the middle of the photo-graph was Paul McCartney without shoes and parked to one side was a white Volkswagen 'Beetle' whose number plate read '28 IF'. To those with fevered imaginations these two seemingly unimportant and totally unrelated facts had the most bizarre meaning... Paul McCartney was dead!

Being barefoot is apparently a Mafia sign of death and the car's number plate indicated the age Paul would have been if he had lived – '28 IF' (actually he would have been 27). But it didn't stop there. The other three Beatles were in on it as well with John, in his white suit, representing the minister, Ringo, dark suited, was the undertaker and George, in denims, was the grave digger. If he was dead how could Paul be on the photograph? Easy, said the fans who had started and spread the rumour, he had a double who had undergone plastic surgery.

McCartney, surprised and sickened by the rumours of his death, explained all in an interview with Paul Gambaccini in *Rolling Stone* in 1974. "I just turned up at the photo session. It was a really nice hot day and I think I wore sandals. I only had to walk round the corner to the crossing because I lived pretty nearby. I had me sandals off and on for the session. Of course when it comes out and people start looking at it and they say: 'Why has he got no shoes on? He's never done that before'. Okay you've never seen me do it before but in actual fact it's just me with me shoes off. Turns out to be some old Mafia sign of death or something."

The man who took that photograph well remembers the day he was called to Abbey Road to take a picture of The Beatles. Iain Macmillan, who had worked with Yoko in the past and had met John previously, got the job to take one of the most famous photographs of all time. "It was a nerve-racking experi-

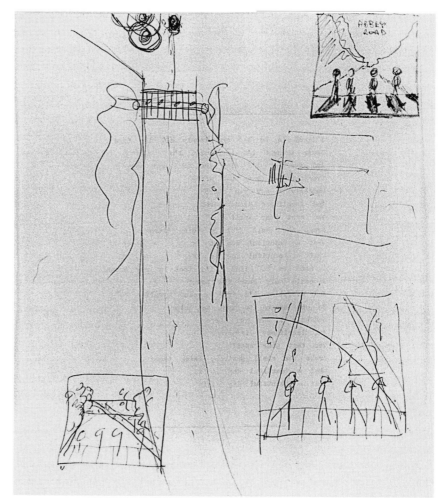

Paul McCartney's sketch showing just how he saw the Abbey Road album cover. In the top right-hand corner is photographer Iain Macmillan's more detailed drawing, and visible through the paper are some lyrics, presumably by Paul.

ence. I had never met all four Beatles together before that day. I had to climb up a step ladder in the middle of the road to take the shot and a friendly policeman held up the traffic for me. Surprisingly there was no great gathering of fans, most people hardly seemed to take any notice."

Macmillan also recalls McCartney's great interest in the photographs as it was he who had outlined exactly what the shot was to be and had drawn a rough sketch of how he saw it. "Paul turned up in his Oxfam suit and sandals and because it was a hot day he decided to do some shots with sandals on and some with sandals off. Paul checked all the pictures with a magnifying glass – I don't think the other three were particularly bothered. He chose the neatest shot with the legs stretched in almost uniform style and it was pure coincidence that it happened to be the one with his sandals off. I got the job through John but it was Paul's idea and I was given 10 minutes around about lunchtime to do it. They came out of the studios, where they were recording, to do it and I managed to take six shots in all. I've got to say that even now the final shot that was chosen still gives me a lot of pleasure."

However, that wasn't the end of Macmillan's involvement in taking pictures of the now famous Abbey Road crossing. "Years later I was asked to do the same shot again for an album by Hinge and Bracket and, as I was setting up to take the shot, which was a parody of The Beatles' cover, a white Volkswagen car drove up and parked in almost exactly the same spot as the one on the original cover shot. It was very weird but by the time I got around to actually taking the shot it had driven off again. But it was really strange."

In fact Macmillan's famous photograph, if the visitors to Abbey Road are anything to go by, has been reproduced in virtually every country in the world with innocent Japanese, excited Americans, determined Germans and embarrassed English fans all congregating on the world's most famous road crossing to take their own pictures. Journalist Adrian Hope was a visitor to Abbey Road some years back and recalls his first sighting of the crossing. "I had this bright idea of photographing the zebra crossing as it was featured on the *Abbey Road* cover. But I couldn't get a clear run at the shot because a Japanese gentleman with a necklace of cameras was busy trying to persuade four other Japanese gentlemen to stride in step, Beatle-fashion, across the crossing. I was told when I got into the studio that was I lucky that there was only one chap taking a picture as apparently most days there is a queue of photographers all taking the same picture."

Nor is the crossing the only much prized subject for the hungry photographers; there's also a City of Westminster sign announcing Abbey Road but this is not just a target for the photographers. The signs are prised off the wall and carried away as souvenirs as fast as the council can put them up.

The author found two young visitors to Abbey Road armed with cameras on a cold and windy October afternoon. Fifteen-year-old Sarah Ogan and Sally Barton had journeyed from Rickmansworth during the school half-term holidays. "We just wanted to take some pictures and see the place. We've taken

The famous road sign

pictures on the zebra crossing just like the *Abbey Road* sleeve and taken shots of the building and the road sign. We've also taken pictures with one of us on the wall like the ones with George Harrison on the wall, resting during the *Abbey Road* session."

One man who has more reason than most to remember the *Abbey Road* album and the historic photograph is Ken Townsend, now retired from his long standing position as general manager of the studios but at the time chief technical engineer. He firmly believes that, by naming their album after the studio in which they recorded for so many years, The Beatles have made many musicians and producers aware of the contribution that Abbey Road itself made to The Beatles' success story. "I'm sure that we got an awful lot of bookings and enquiries as a result of that album. We take it as a great compliment that The Beatles should choose to name what turned out to be their last album after our studio. At that time it didn't occur to us that it would be their last album together but as the album neared completion it was pretty obvious that a rift was developing between them."

In 1993 Iain Macmillan, Paul McCartney and Arrow came to Abbey Road to create this parody of the original.

Two other people who view the album as a significant factor in the history of Abbey Road are Sir Cliff Richard and Mickie Most, both of whom first got to know the studios in the late Fifties. Cliff sums it up like this: "The rock'n'roll scene put Abbey Road on the map and The Beatles album, of course, clinched it." Mickie Most says simply: "Abbey Road has remained part of the tradition of the record business and one of the best albums ever made was called *Abbey Road* and you can't get a better advert than that."

2
The Days of Whores and Artists

Although it was the work of four extraordinary young men from the North of England that made Abbey Road a household name, we have to go back five generations to trace the birth of the building that houses the most famous recording studios in the world. It was in the England of William IV that the story really begins. The ascension to the throne by the third son of George III in 1830 was the beginning of a seven-year reign which was not to pass without incident. During those years, until succeeded on his death by his cousin, Victoria, William IV saw the passing of the First Reform Bill; Faraday's invention of electromagnetic induction; the first British Factory Act passed through Parliament; the victimisation of the Tolpuddle Martyrs; the use for the first time of the word "socialism"; the granting of independence for Texas from Mexico; and, on a scale far less grand, the construction in North London of yet another house in the rapidly emerging select area of St John's Wood.

On a site originally listed as number 2 Abbey Road (it was promoted to number 3 in 1872) work began on a nine-bedroomed residence with five reception rooms, two servants' rooms, a wine cellar and a 250-foot garden. The first occupant of this "desirable" property, one Richard Cook, found himself living in an area which was fast becoming a fashionable neighbourhood in 19th century London. His neighbours during his 24 year stay in the house included artists, bankers and exiled Heads of State. Abbey Road had indeed come a long way from its humble beginnings as a footpath from Lisson Green to Kilburn Priory, also known as Kilburn Abbey, which dates back at least to the 12th century. From the lane leading to the Abbey eventually came the name Abbey Road.

Another enterprise which was to become a household name was opening in an even more humble way just up the road from number 3. In 1874, members of the Free Church of Abbey Road met in the Free Church Hall to form a fund for the benefit of the residents of Abbey Road. Money was collected from interested parties and put into a fund which was then used to purchase houses. These houses were then given to participating members on a simple lottery basis and the fund was given the title, The Abbey Road Building Society, a name it retained until 1944 when it merged with the National Building Society to become the Abbey National Building Society.

*Below: **This selection of money boxes and ash tray were early promotional items issued by The Abbey Road Building Society, whose foundation began in the church which is clearly visible in the background***

PARTICULARS
OF THE
VALUABLE UNRESTRICTED
Freehold Building Site
KNOWN AS
No. 3, ABBEY ROAD
ST. JOHN'S WOOD, N.W.8.

Opposite the junction of Grove End Road and Abbey Road, close to Lord's Cricket Ground and about six minutes' walk from St. John's Wood Road and Marlborough Road Stations (Metropolitan Railway) and a little over a mile from the West End.

The Motor Omnibus Services 53 and 153 pass the site and there are numerous other services within a short distance.

At present occupied by a Detached Residence containing : -

Nine Bed Rooms,   Bath Room,
Five Reception Rooms,   Kitchen,
Two Servants' Rooms, &c.

arranged as follows:—

ON THE SECOND FLOOR—
Two Attic Bed Rooms.

ON THE FIRST FLOOR—
Seven Bed Rooms, approximately 18-ft. by 15-ft.; 18-ft. by 15-ft. 6-in.; 24-ft. by 16-ft. 3-in.; 15-ft. 6-in by 15-ft.; 9-ft. 6-in. by 6-ft. 6-in.; 15-ft. 6-in. by 15-ft.; 16-ft. 9-in. by 15-ft. 3-in. W.C.
Bath Room on Half-landing.

ON THE ENTRANCE FLOOR—
Dining Room, about 23-ft. by 15-ft. with Service Lift to Lower Floor.
Handsome Drawing Room, about 39-ft. by 18-ft. with parquet flooring.
Library, about 15-ft. by 14-ft. 6-in.
Morning Room, about 23-ft. by 16-ft.
Study, about 15-ft. by 10-ft.
W.C.

IN THE HALF-BASEMENT—
Kitchen, Scullery, Servants' Hall, Pantry, Two Servants' Rooms, Larder, Wine Cellars, etc., W.C.

LARGE GARDEN AT REAR.

THE PROPERTY has a FRONTAGE of about 91-ft to Abbey Road, and a DEPTH of about 250-ft.

There is therefore an Area of approximately
22,750 Square Feet

and offers an exceptional Site for the erection of

AN IMPORTANT BLOCK OF RESIDENTIAL FLATS FOR WHICH THERE IS A STEADY and INCREASING DEMAND in the neighbourhood.

or alternatively

FOR STUDIO RESIDENCES, BIJOU HOUSES OR FOR A PRIVATE RESIDENCE or INSTITUTION, INCORPORATING THE EXISTING BUILDING.

The Building line will be defined by the London County Council upon submission of a Building Scheme.

Vacant Possession will be given upon Completion.

The estate agent's particulars circa 1929, of the house which was to become the most famous recording studios in the world.

The house changed hands in 1857 when one Joseph Hornsby Wright moved in and again in 1891 when William Todd purchased it. The Todd family retained the house until 1913 with Todd's cousin taking over residency. A descendant of the Todd family, Olive Westbrook-Todd, still recalls the days when peacocks strutted across the well laid out lawns of number 3 Abbey Road. With the outbreak of the First World War the Todd family sold the property and moved out of town. John Henry Cordner-James was the next owner and it may have been he who instigated the work which saw the grand old house converted into flats by the developers, Henry & Robert Eyre. This conversion brought to Abbey Road one of London society's most colourful and notorious characters.

John Arthur Maundy Gregory moved in and it was from his Abbey Road flat that he operated his business of selling "honours". For a mere £10,000 a knighthood could be purchased and for £25,000 Gregory would make you a baron. Allegations made at the time suggested that the income from these deals was split between Gregory and the Liberal Coalition government of Lloyd George, who strenuously, and not surprisingly, denied all knowledge of Gregory's activities.

Gregory's flat was in what had by now become known as Abbey Lodge and his great friend, Edith Rosse (the former music hall star, Vivienne Pierpoint) also lived in the house. They were both great music lovers, as if foreshadowing the developments that would occur in the old building in the years to come. They installed baby grand pianos in their homes and Gregory acquired a set of trap drums on which he accompanied the gramophone recordings of the Paul Whiteman orchestra.

Not surprisingly the law finally caught up with Gregory and he was arrested and convicted under the Honours (Prevention Of Abuses) Act of 1925 and sent to prison for two months. Just prior to his imprisonment, Edith Rosse fell ill and died in the Hyde Park Terrace flat to which she had moved. Her daughter suspected foul play and a three-month post-mortem followed (still one of the longest in police history) but there was no evidence to connect Gregory with her death, despite the suspicions of both the daughter and Chief Inspector Arthur Askew. On his release from prison, Gregory left the country with the police hot on his heels but he managed to reach France where he lived until 1941, dying bankrupt in a German prison hospital in Paris. There are those who have claimed that Abbey Road is haunted by an elegant lady ghost; if this is the case then it's likely to be Edith Rosse although she did not die there.

So ended the life of one of the most colourful characters ever to occupy number 3 Abbey Road. He is immortalised still in the catchphrase: "Lloyd George knew my father; Father knew Lloyd George", which were the words used by children in the Twenties when asked why their father had been honoured or promoted.

In 1929 the house was purchased by Francis Myers, a builder, who, within six months and at a handsome profit of £4,000, had sold it to The Gramophone Company Limited for the princely sum of £16,500. Thus, on December 3, 1929, one of the smartest residences in London took on a new lease of life as the home of recorded music.

The late David Bicknell was closely involved in the decision to purchase the house in Abbey Road and turn it into a custom-built recording studio. "When I joined the company in 1927 it was still The Gramophone Company, before it merged with the Columbia company which resulted in the formation of a new company called EMI [Electric & Musical Industries Ltd]. In those early days we had done most of the recording in a building in the Clerkenwell Road and then two new, but small, studios were built at Hayes when The Gramophone Company factory was opened there.

"The principal studio, however, was the small Queen's Hall, in Langham Place near Oxford Circus, and we rented the bigger Queen's Hall itself or Kingsway Hall for larger recordings of full orchestras. Even with these various alternatives there was an enormous pressure on the company for recording time and my boss, Trevor Osmond Williams, who was manager of the International Artistes Department and the Technical Recording Department, had the idea to build a studio of our own. This was at a time when no recording or broadcasting company anywhere in the world had a custom-built studio."

It was far from plain sailing as Williams and Bicknell sought an all-purpose recording centre, as Bicknell recalled: 'Osmond met with tremendous opposition to his plan and he was surprised when he discovered that the man most violently opposed to his idea was Fred Gaisberg, the artistic director of the HMV division of the company and the man who discovered Enrico Caruso. As a recording man himself, Osmond thought that Gaisberg would be one of his strongest supporters but instead he took the view that it was utter madness for recording companies to think of sinking large sums of money into such things as offices and studios."

Williams was undeterred, however, and ploughed on with his brainchild, calling on the chairman and founder of The Gramophone Company, Alfred Clark, and it was he who 'sold' the idea to the board. They saw it as a practical idea which would benefit the company in many ways. "Our next step was to look for a suitable building which could be converted into a recording complex. The first place we looked at was the old Embassy Theatre in St John's Wood, just off the Finchley Road but the acoustics were unsatisfactory and there was really no room for expansion. Osmond liked the idea of finding something in the St John's Wood area, not just because it was pleasant but also because he lived nearby and, finally, the company's property consultants came up with a house with large grounds in Abbey Road."

Bicknell recalled the visit he and Williams paid to 3 Abbey Road. "Osmond decided very quickly that it was the ideal place, even though it was by then nearly 100 years old. The house was purchased and plans drawn up including building over the gardens to create the big Number One studio." With his plans passed by the board and the property found and purchased, Williams was only a few short steps from his dream of a custom-built recording studio near the centre of London.

Sadly the man who fought to create Abbey Road studios never lived to see his dream come true. "He was struck down while on a trip around Europe and died of a brain tumour in Vienna at the age of 45 in the summer of 1930," recalled Bicknell. "It was one of the great tragedies of the music business. He was an immensely talented man. He was a director of Covent Garden and he revived the London Symphony Orchestra, becoming their director." Bicknell was on a fishing trip in Ireland when heard the news of the death of his boss and friend.

The work to convert a detached London residence into a recording studio took two years to complete and involved the development not just of 3 Abbey Road but adjoining land as well. Both the house and garden at 5 Abbey Road were purchased along with part of the gardens from houses in Alma Square and Hill Road. Inside the house, builders set about converting the comfortable rooms into offices, reception areas and lounges. Under the regulations laid down by the Borough of Westminster, no changes could be made to the exterior of the building.

A large block of buildings was erected in the garden which consisted of a studio, transfer or mastering rooms, workshops and listening rooms. At right angles to this, Studio Two was built and a garage was erected for the mobile recording unit. In just under two years 3 Abbey Road was transformed into the world's largest building devoted exclusively to gramophone recording – without

November 12, 1931 and Abbey Road studios are officially declared open. Sir Edward Elgar, on the podium, prepares to conduct the London Symphony Orchestra in the studios' first ever session with, seated on the steps, Sir Landon Ronald (left) and George Bernard Shaw.

the average passer-by even noticing the difference. It is interesting to note that, despite all the building and rebuilding which took place during those years, it wasn't until 20 years later that the original kitchen range in the basement and the saddle and harness hooks were finally removed.

By the time the studios were ready, the merger between The Gramophone Company and the rival Columbia company had taken place, so the new studios were opened by the new company – EMI. However the Abbey Road studios, the biggest and best of their kind in the world, were a long way removed from the early days of recording by The Gramophone Company in 1898. Some 27 years later the Western Electric Company of America introduced the first electrical system of recording, using microphones to pick up sound. The resulting flexibility enabled recording companies to use larger groups of artists and musicians, and this led to the use of larger studios and halls such as Queen's and Kingsway. It was exactly this new found freedom which had inspired Osmond Williams in his search for the perfect studio.

After all the hard work to create this prestigious building, it was fitting that the opening ceremony should be something truly special; and so it was. November 12 1931 was the day chosen and, following so closely on the merger between the Gramophone and Columbia companies, it served as a double celebration. Showing commendable flair, it was decided that a simple 'ribbon-cutting' ceremony was insufficient to reflect the importance of the occasion and that the best way to open a new recording studio was to make a recording.

With George Bernard Shaw, Sir Walford Davies and Sir Landon Ronald, musical director to The Gramophone Company since 1900, in the audience, Sir Edward Elgar stepped on to his conductor's podium, greeted the London Symphony Orchestra with a cheery, 'Good morning gentlemen. A very light programme this morning. Please play as if you've never heard it before', and set off conducting the historic recording of 'Land of Hope and Glory'.

The press release issued at the time by EMI was headed "London's Latest Wonder" and made the following observations: "Three studios have been built in order to accommodate the different categories of music which have to be recorded from day to day. The medium and large studios have formidable stages, the latter having a platform to accommodate 250 musicians, while the auditorium will accommodate 1,000 people.

"The walls of these studios are specially designed to give correct resonance to all sounds and to avoid any echo. A special system of air cleaning and ventilation has been installed in order that the atmosphere in each studio will ensure that artistes and musicians will be able to perform during any period of the year under the most comfortable conditions. The warm air is continually washed and purified.

"Just over four and a half miles of electric cable connect the three studios with the central control room. Six microphones can be used at any one time in each studio and each microphone has separate control. This will ensure that all records will be recorded with the correct balance of instruments and vocalists. There are waiting and retiring rooms for artistes and special departments for the scientific maintenance of the whole installation."

With the opening of the Abbey Road complex, the studios owned and run by the Columbia company in Petty France became obsolete. They were closed down in 1932. Ironically this decision was taken by the former head of Columbia, Louis Sterling, who was to become the first managing director of the new EMI company.

David Bicknell, although not at the opening ceremony which seems today to have been a terrible oversight on somebody's part, then set to work in the new recording studios as a classical producer working with Elgar, Beecham, Rubinstein and many other great artists. "Elgar was extremely fond of recording and was never troubled by it but he did go to great lengths to ensure that he worked with people he knew and respected. The leader of the London Symphony Orchestra, Willie Reed, was a life-long friend of his and was on nearly every Elgar session. It was appropriate that Elgar should have been chosen to open the studios; he was the grand old man of English music and a pioneer of recording."

Bicknell, so closely involved with Williams in the fight to get Abbey Road studios opened, looked back on their determination with great pleasure. "The opening of Abbey Road studios was a masterstroke in three ways. Firstly, it was the first custom-built studio of its kind anywhere in the world; secondly, it brought the greatest musicians in the world to the building in the nine years up to the war and they spread the word about this great studio in London and, thirdly, it was a great financial investment. It cost £100,000 to buy, build and equip and now must be worth many millions of pounds. It was extraordinarily ahead of its time. The music world didn't have recording facilities anything like Abbey Road and its opening led the way for many other companies to build independent studios."

With some satisfaction he reflected on what might have happened if he and Osmond Williams had not won the battle for a new studio complex in London. "Interestingly enough the Queen's Hall was blown sky high during the war and if Abbey Road hadn't been opened we would have been in a terrible panic. Without Abbey Road we would have presumably just carried on in the halls we had. Queen's Hall was our prime studio before Abbey Road. Its opening certainly made London the recording centre of the world."

Despite the fact that he was to work at Abbey Road for over 30 years, Bicknell did not remember his first working visit. "I can't recall my first session there although I'm pretty certain that at the time it would have been with a pianist. We had at least two dozen of the world's greatest pianists signed to the company; people like Horowitz, Rubinstein and Schnabel. They all recorded in Studio Three and I spent many weeks of my life with these people in that studio; it became almost a second home to me."

While EMI had gone to great lengths to construct the epitome of recording studios, they still realised the importance of being able to record their leading European artists in their native countries. Before Abbey Road had even begun to take shape in Osmond Williams' mind, the Lancia mobile unit, so called because it was built on a Lancia chassis, had travelled extensively, recording all manner of sessions. One of its earliest locations was the Temple Church in London where in 1927 a religious recital was recorded. Having a couple of waxes left over after the session, the engineer asked a choirboy to sing something "just to use them up". The boy was Ernest Lough and he chose to sing 'Hear My Prayer' and 'O For The Wings Of A Dove'. Within a matter of weeks the record was selling in huge quantities and, seventy years later, it remains a steady seller.

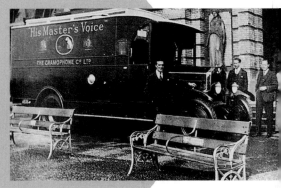

This mobile unit, which was eventually housed at Abbey Road, comprised a purpose-built body on a two-ton Lancia chassis equipped with a complete recording system, including two weight-driven lathes. A jacking system was used during recordings to support each corner and the power for amplifiers, suction and heating of the waxes came from the batteries which were continually being re-charged during periods off the road.

The famous old Lancia mobile unit which travelled the length and breadth of the country (from left to right) Jim Mays, Edward Buckley, Arthur Clarke and George Dillnott

The Abbey Road mobile became renowned for its versatility and in the competent hands of driver, Harry Hands, it flitted from the first Glyndebourne Festival in 1934 to La Scala in Milan to record Beniamino Gigli performing *Pagliacci* and *La Bohème*, and from bird calls recorded by Ludwig Koch in his series on British birds to the Aldershot Military Tattoo where recordings of the rehearsals were processed and brought back for sale before the end of the tattoo.

David Bicknell remembered the Lancia mobile and his first trip out in 1928. "We went to the Albert Hall to record Malcolm Sargent conducting a recording of *Elijah*. Because of the old wax machines it was difficult to record accurately and recording in front of a concert audience was particularly difficult. You couldn't stop the recording if anything went wrong and you had to make sure the whole thing started within a limited number of seconds in order to avoid a lengthy run in which would use up half the record before the concert had even started. The timing had to be extremely accurate.

"Because of this problem of timing I was concealed in the orchestra with a telephone connected to the control room in the van outside. When the producer said they were ready in the van, it was my job to give Malcolm Sargent a signal. He then started the concert. It was imperative I kept well hidden as all this was being done without the audience's knowledge and they would have been very confused to see a chap crawling about amongst the orchestra clutching a telephone."

Unfortunately the Lancia mobile came to an untimely end in Manchester during the Second World War when it caught fire in a garage. It was thought that the fire might have been caused by the waxes being left on overnight but nothing was ever discovered to substantiate the rumours. Very soon afterwards Hands got a replacement mobile, again with the dependable Lancia chassis.

Back at Abbey Road the equipment chosen for the new studio was the WE system from America which, unfortunately, posed a few problems as it was protected by various patents both in America and the UK. Isaac Schoenberg, head

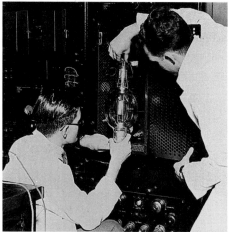

Above: **Two engineers, in the regulation white coats, replace a valve in one of the cutting machine amplifiers way back in 1935.**

Below: **The teenage Yehudi Menuhin and the grand old man, Sir Edward Elgar on the steps of Abbey Road in July 1932 when he first recorded Elgar's Violin Concerto.**

of research and development for the old Columbia company, was asked by Sterling to research and develop a new electrical recording system avoiding the use of any WE patents and consequently halting the large royalties being paid to the Western Electric Company in America.

Shoenberg, who later went on to develop the EMI broadcast system adopted by British television, knew just the man to head this important new research team. Alan Dower Blumlein already had a string of patents to his name and, since 1929, had been working on the moving coil system microphone which was to be used by EMI for over 20 years and was utilised by the BBC at Alexandra Palace in their television broadcasts.

Prior to the merger between The Gramophone Company and Columbia, Blumlein had been using the Petty France studios for his work but the new Abbey Road studios and the improved EMI research and development budgets meant quicker results. Within a few months Blumlein's new microphone system, his unique moving coil recorder and flexible wide range equaliser were all installed in Abbey Road and the WE systems hastily shipped back to America. The resourcefulness of Blumlein and the quality of his new products can be judged by the fact his system of recording remained in full use in the studios until 1948.

Bicknell well remembered Blumlein's inventions. "Right from the very start Studio Three was pretty satisfactory. The old WE system had been pretty good, except for piano recording, but Blumlein's was much smoother altogether and, with this improvement, piano recording in Abbey Road was placed far ahead of any other recording studio in the world. Unfortunately Studio One was far less satisfactory and remained so for many years. The acoustics had been done by some German company who had filled the place with damping material the roof and walls were packed with the stuff and it was dead as could be. Only when this stuff was pulled out after the war, and replaced with resonating material, did it become a good studio."

While all these technical improvements were taking place, the musicians were quickly coming to realise the benefits of this new studio in North London. Yehudi Menuhin can boast of an association with The Gramophone Company which goes back into the late 1920s and a relationship with Abbey Road which began in 1931. A year later Sir Edward Elgar, aged 75 and in failing health, agreed to conduct his own Violin Concerto with the then 15-year-old Menuhin. They got on so well during that July recording session that they agreed to repeat the performance; only this time in front of audiences in London and Paris.

Menuhin recalls his first visit to Abbey Road and Studio One in particular. "Studio One has seen more transformations than any other. At one time they felt that sound had to be just pure sound with no reverberation whatsoever, that was a false conception. Then they went the other way and the room was dotted with loudspeakers all the way round so they would create echo effects [known as ambiophony] that could be heard for miles around. Now I think it has very fine acoustics."

His love of Abbey Road, where he recorded nearly 250 works, is best summed up in his own words. "Every time I go past Abbey Road studios I blow it a kiss I feel so strongly about the place." But he can still recall the early days when perhaps it wasn't quite so lovable. 'I remember the green room – it was the artists' room – and it had the most horrible sofa I've ever seen. I've had more uncomfortable rests on that awful sofa than I care to remember. I think of all the famous people who have sat on that same awful piece of furniture; people like Gigli, McCormack, Sir Thomas Beecham and a whole lot more."

Above: **33 years later in December 1965 Yehudi Menuhin re-recorded the Elgar Violin Concerto with another grand master, Sir Adrian Boult.**

Perhaps it is for this reason that in recent years Menuhin has taken to eating picnics in the studio between sessions and practising yoga exercises which include balancing on his head on a piano. "Personally I never like to eat much between sessions it's not the best use of that hour-or-so break. I often rest on a piano, it is ideal for having a complete rest and it doesn't matter whether it is a good piano or a bad piano so long as it is solid and has a good flat surface."

Changes in the studio were not the only changes taking place in St John's Wood. The late Gus Cook, general manager of the studios between 1969 and 1974, worked at Abbey Road from the day it opened and remembered some of the sights which could be seen in the better parts of London in the Thirties. "I used to walk to Abbey Road in those days from the old Marlborough Station and quite often would see the butlers in full regalia – the high stiff collars and long morning coats – first thing in the morning, collecting the papers from the doorstep. Then gradually the ladies moved in; quite a lot of the aristocracy and members of Parliament used to keep their pretty little ladies in St John's Wood. I remember that when this first started someone said to me, 'The only people in St John's Wood these days are whores and artists'."

But Cook's memories were not confined to butlers and pretty ladies. He well remembered the introduction of electrical recording in 1925 and the develop-

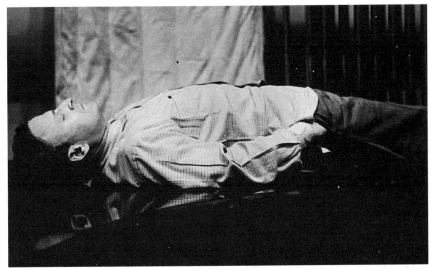

Left: **'It doesn't matter whether it's a good piano or a bad piano so long as it has a good flat surface.' Yehudi Menuhin takes his regular lunch break –relaxing on top of a piano in the studio.**

Gus Cook, before he became studio manager, checks out the early amplifier racks.

ments of Blumlein for the Abbey Road studios. "Electrical recording transformed what the balance engineers could contribute; the change over from the old horn to two mikes meant being able to spread people out. One of the strangest things was to hear Blumlein's early stereo demonstrations which he began work on in Abbey Road in 1931. He used to have a record where he talked about stereo which had the sound of someone walking backwards and forwards across the stage recorded in the background!"

As recording grew in importance and improved in quality, so the artists were faced with the question of whether to involve themselves in these new sophisticated methods of record making. Arturo Toscanini was not easily convinced of the merits of Abbey Road in particular or recording in general. A bad experience in an American studio in 1929 had left him cautious to say the least but, finally, in the mid-Thirties, he agreed to record a Brahms Symphony in Abbey Road with the BBC Symphony Orchestra. David Bicknell takes up the story. "He got as far as climbing on to the podium, taking up his baton and looking around the studio which had been newly decorated for him. Then he dropped his hands to his head and said, 'I couldn't possibly record in a dreadful hall like this', and with that he ran out of the studio into a waiting car and drove off. We had suspected there might be a bit of trouble so we had Sir Adrian Boult standing by and were able to continue. Personally I think the whole thing was manufactured by Toscanini because he just didn't want to record in Abbey Road, he really wanted to do it in the Queen's Hall and that was where we eventually did it. He was a very difficult man."

Artur Schnabel, the world famous pianist, was virtually a resident at Abbey Road during the Thirties when he recorded all 32 Beethoven piano sonatas and five concertos. But it was apparent when he first walked into the studio to find the orchestra set up and his piano in place that his stay was not to be a happy one. He paced around the studio, stopping in the middle of the room and declaring, "I play here". Hastily his piano was moved and work began. But still the recording did not go smoothly and on one occasion 29 waxes were required for a single record because Schnabel continually slammed down his piano lid or kicked his stool and muttered, "Impossible, impossible", as things went from bad to worse. Recording the 15 volumes, made up of 100 records, took more than a decade to complete.

It was the classical artists who dominated Abbey Road during those early years and fortunately not all of them were as difficult as Schnabel. Pablo Casals, the world famous cellist, had a much calmer approach. During the recording of a concerto the D string on his cello snapped and he calmly tied it together with a sailor's knot and continued playing. Fritz Kreisler took no chances when he recorded with his violin in Abbey Road. He changed into carpet slippers (to avoid any inadvertent squeak from his shoes) when he arrived at the studio, always a good hour or so before anyone else. Armed with a small meter for reading the humidity of the studio, he would decide which violin to use – his Stradivarius or the Guarnerius. Once decided, he would toss the other violin away casually and it would be left lying about in a corner during the recording.

David Bicknell recalled another great violinist who had problems coming to terms with recording. "Jascha Heifetz, who probably had the greatest technique of any violinist since Paganini, was a terrible bundle of nerves in the studio. He would arrive rigid with fright and we soon learned that the only way to record him was to have absolutely everything set up before he entered the studio so that when he did arrive we could start immediately and get him totally absorbed in the music before he had time to get nervous."

But it wasn't just violinists who had problems with recording and the new technical advances. "The problems both in Abbey Road and with the mobile, in those early days, were immense. Singers, when hearing their voices played back, would categorically deny that it was their voice coming through the speakers. They were tremendously concerned that their records were going to be around an awful long time with their name on them," said Bicknell.

Sir Thomas Beecham (left) with violinist, Jascha Heifetz.

One man who had no such problems in Abbey Road was Sir Thomas Beecham who, throughout his long and distinguished career, was a regular visitor to the EMI studios, as his widow, Lady Beecham, recalls. "He liked Abbey Road – not only because it was close to home – but because it had an intimate atmosphere compared with Kingsway Hall which he always thought was a great barn of a place. There was more of a family atmosphere and he had probably been going there very nearly since it opened. Abbey Road was for him *the* place to work and he made a tremendous amount of records there over the years."

Bicknell remembers fondly the work he did with Sir Thomas Beecham over the years. "He was a much easier man than most to work with but still very unpredictable. He was one of the pioneers of recording and his enthusiasm had a positive effect on a lot of other people who were somewhat dubious about recording. He added much to the already considerable prestige that existed throughout the world for the HMV recordings... we were the elite. At one time it was impossible for first grade classical artists to make a career for themselves unless they recorded for HMV. I worked closely with Tommy Beecham for many years and without doubt he was a very great man, although he said a lot of foolish things and a lot of very profound things. Many times he would change the things he was supposed to record, dashing off into a cupboard at Abbey Road and producing a totally different piece for the orchestra."

Lady Beecham well remembers the antics her husband got up to throughout his career. "He would persistently arrive late for sessions and when he did arrive everybody would be out on the steps of Abbey Road waiting for him. When he finally got there, as if nothing was wrong, he would casually discuss the weather or politics before walking slowly into the studio. When he was told what was to be recorded he would say, 'No I've changed my mind. I think we'll do so and so. The parts are all ready, I called last night and arranged it all.' Everybody was thrown into chaos – he was sometimes very much a law unto himself. He did all

this in good humour and with an impish look on his face; like a naughty boy who'd got his own way."

Bicknell was more concerned with the technical problems this attitude caused. "Often he would do different parts from different works and the balance engineers had a terrible job getting the balance right for each different piece but in the end it all worked out fine. Tommy's recordings still sound absolutely different from anybody else's. He most definitely made orchestras sound different under his baton; he was a truly great conductor."

While classical recordings dominated the work done at Abbey Road during those early years, there were some popular artists who, if not pop stars by today's standards, did have broad public appeal. Joe Loss with his dance orchestra made his début at the studios in 1934 and was still recording there in the Eighties. The big bands of the Thirties were every bit as popular as the classical artists and in fact one dance band which recorded regularly in Abbey Road remains a mystery to this day. The New Mayfair Dance Orchestra was a band which was made up of famous musicians of the day who 'moonlighted' from their regular bands to record under this name and the material they used was made up entirely of numbers rejected by EMI's star big bands led by Jack Payne and Henry Hall.

Other regular visitors to Abbey Road at that time were Geraldo, Flanagan and Allen, Al Bowlly and Ray Noble, while Fred Astaire, Paul Robeson, Gertrude Lawrence and Noel Coward made the by now familiar journey to St John's Wood. As Germany prepared for war, work went on as normal at Abbey Road with music hall favourites such as Gracie Fields, Max Miller and George Formby recording the songs which made them household names.

Royalty, too, was involved in Abbey Road even if they never actually stepped inside the building. Christmas broadcasts by reigning monarchs were for many years recorded at Abbey Road (via land-lines from the BBC's studios) and released as records by EMI. The coronations of George VI and Queen Elizabeth II were recorded in the same fashion, this time via land-lines from Westminster Abbey via the BBC and on to Abbey Road, thus enabling EMI to issue recordings of the two services.

One unique piece of equipment which was used in Abbey Road throughout the Thirties was a huge Compton organ, installed in Studio One in order that the popular cinema and theatre organ recitals, which were a feature of the day, could be recorded more precisely and more comfortably. Reginald Dixon, who celebrated 50 years of recording, remembered the great Abbey Road organ. "I was a corporal in the RAF when I first went there and recorded on this huge instrument. I remember that when we finished a session I would often stay on and play until the early hours of the morning, fortified only by a bottle or two of Bass beer. To be totally honest, though I never said anything at the time, I

Left: **Carroll Gibbons** (at the piano) celebrated his birthday with a party in Abbey Road and was joined by a host of pre-war celebrities including **Bud Flanagan and Chesney Allen** (centre, leaning on piano) and **Stanley Holloway** (second from right). Above: **Chesney Allen** made a return visit to the studios nearly 40 years later in March 1982.

Below: **Fats Waller**, on one of his rare visits to England, enjoys himself at the organ in Studio One.

never really liked the Compton but, because of the problems of recording in cinemas, theatres or even at Blackpool, I had no choice but to use it."

A visitor from America who used to play the Compton organ regularly, but again always after hours, was Fats Waller. In 1938 he recorded an album entitled *Fats Waller in London* and, as an admirer of pipe organs, he couldn't resist the temptation to play around in the wee small hours. With the aid of a bottle of whisky, Waller put the staid old instrument through its paces and extracted sounds which had never been heard before.

Sadly, with the coming of stereo and improved facilities for working on location, the Compton organ was removed from Studio One as the need for more space increased. Unable to find a cinema prepared to house the old master, it was shunted off to the West Country and apparently to this day it stands unused in a tithe barn near Liskeard.

Towards the end of the thirties two men went to Abbey Road one to stay for just a day and the other to spend many years there establishing himself as one of the great classical music producers of all time. Walter Legge was employed by HMV as a writer, primarily to edit the company newspaper, and he came with the highest possible credentials. On many occasions he stood in for the late Sir Neville Cardus and wrote

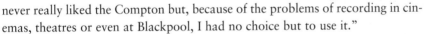

Above: **Engineer Douglas Larter prepares to record the coronation of His Majesty King George V1 on May 12, 1937.**

Above right: **Reginald Foort, popular organist of the Thirties and Forties at the Compton organ in Studio One.**

articles for *The Times* but, more importantly, he used his visits to Abbey Road to get to know the artists and involve himself in their musical activities. In the early thirties, when the Great Depression caused record sales to slump, he was able, with a great deal of perception, to launch the various record societies which made available all the best recordings on advance subscription to people throughout the United Kingdom. But that was just the beginning of his career in classical music.

Sir Winston Churchill made a brief one-day visit to Abbey Road before the war. On entering the building, he noticed that all the studio staff were wearing the regulation white coats. Pausing for breath at the top of the steps he commented, "My God, I thought I'd come to the wrong place. It looks like a hospital." In many ways it was as institutionalised as a hospital with the strict rules of dress – collars and ties with white coats at all times – and the strict three-hour recording schedules of 10 am to 1 pm, 2 pm until 5 pm and 7 pm through to 10 pm, with no exceptions.

3
Listen, Do You Want to Know a Secret?

The Second World War didn't bring Abbey Road to a complete standstill but the amount of recording done there between 1939 and 1945 was, not surprisingly, greatly reduced. About one third of the staff were recruited for radio work in the armed forces or for government work at EMI's factory at Hayes, while a good few more were called into the armed forces. This left a skeleton staff at the studios who were principally engaged on ENSA work for forces entertainment. These programmes, which were made up as records, were never released as they were claimed as the property of the government and tagged 'propaganda'. They were either recorded in Abbey Road itself or via land-lines from the BBC head-quarters where some of the shows were broadcast on radio.

Glenn Miller conducts the orchestra in Studio One shortly before his ill-fated aeroplane journey to Paris in 1944.

Under the leadership of studio manager W.S. Barrell, Abbey Road, by the time war broke out, had assembled a fine team of producers, primarily in the classical field. David Bicknell had established himself as one of the leading pro-ducers in the world and Legge was intent on following him into the ranks of the producers. Leonard Smith was doing sterling work as was Lawrance Collingwood who joined The Gramophone Company in 1925.

Bicknell fondly remembered Collingwood. "Lawrance was chosen to sing the solo on the steps of St Paul's Cathedral at Queen Victoria's Diamond Jubilee. He went on to win an organ scholarship to Oxford where he was a contemporary of another man who was to be closely involved with Abbey Road in the years to come – Sir Adrian Boult. While Boult went on to Leipzig, Collingwood chose to go to Russia and entered the *conservatoire* at St Petersburg where he gained a degree in Russian Music studies. He met and married a Russian girl and for a while they shared a house with the great watch makers and court jewellers, the Fabergés. I have no doubt he would have spent the rest of his life in Russia but for the revolution and he came back and joined the Gramophone Company as part-time head of the musical staff, which he remained until his retirement in 1971." Collingwood, who became conductor and artistic director of Sadler's Wells, joined Bicknell and Fred Gaisberg in producing the bulk of the records to come out of Abbey Road between 1931 and the war years.

The merger which took place in 1931 between The Gramophone Company and Columbia, had, not surprisingly, left a number of people with divided loyalties,

Engineer Laurie Bamber peers through the tiny control room window of Studio Two. This was a typical, bare control room of the Thirties and Forties with the disc recorder in the background.

despite the fact they all fell under the corporate EMI umbrella. There was intense rivalry between the old Columbia men and the Gramophone people who, in the main, worked on the HMV label. The late Bob Dockerill spent his life with EMI since joining as a teenager in 1920 and he was acutely aware of this problem. "The rivalry between the two labels was so intense it resulted in a lot of people actually not speaking to each other. They certainly wouldn't consider discussing projects with each other as each label was looking to outdo the other. The whole subject of recording was still a mystery when the war began; I think it was deliberately kept that way by the people involved, in order to keep everything to themselves."

Despite the fact that the majority of people at Abbey Road had been recruited into the armed forces or to do war work of some sort, the studios were still employing people during the war years and, in 1941, a young lady named Vera Samwell began a career at Abbey Road which was to last nearly 30 years. She well remembers the time she first visited Abbey Road studios. "It was just like a house from the outside and although there wasn't a real car park I think the lawns had been turned into a gravelled front. I was surprised to find it was a recording studio inside and even more surprised when I discovered that most of the offices still had coalfires in them which the secretaries had to make up each morning."

Vera Samwell's job was to take the studio bookings at a time when there were very few, although in later years her job became an integral part of the studio's smooth running. "In those days I did the bookings at the same time as working the switchboard and the bookings were really only a small part of my job. The studios were loosely described to me as Number One being primarily for orchestral use; Number Two for the big bands which were the pop acts of the day or solo artists and Studio Three for mainly piano recitals. There was very little evening work, mainly because most of the artists were working in the evenings, either in shows or giving concerts." She, too, was quick to notice the rivalry which existed between the Columbia and HMV labels. "We didn't make any effort to 'sell' the studios in those days, the whole thing was most secret. We didn't want rivals like Decca to find out what we were recording and I was told not to tell HMV people what Columbia were doing and vice versa. Funnily enough there was only one secretary between the two main artists' managers – one from Columbia and one from HMV – and she had the most difficult job in the building, she was sworn to secrecy by both of them."

As the war neared its end, Abbey Road was treated to a visit by one of the most successful band-leaders of all time. Glenn Miller, with an Allied forces band, recorded a number of titles with Dinah Shore in Studio One on September 16 1944 and they remained unreleased and unheard by the millions of Glenn Miller fans around the world until the expiry of their copyright in 1994. Two explanations for this extraordinary situation have been put forward. Firstly, that the recordings, as with the British ENSA recordings, were the property of the American Government, coming under the heading of propaganda, and, secondly, that both Miller and Shore had recording contracts which specified top billing for each of them on all albums released; this contractual wrangle was never sorted out and so the last recordings ever made by Glenn Miller remained unheard for fifty years. It was a few weeks after this session that Miller's plane, on a trip to France, was reported lost over the English channel with no survivors.

The end of the war coincided with the appointment of Walter Legge to the International Artistes Department where he and David Bicknell were given a particular and most important task which Bicknell remembered vividly. "We were given the job of re-building the company's roster of artists along with Leonard Smith. Legge was sent to Vienna and there he signed nearly all the German singers who had made a reputation for themselves before and during the war. I went to Italy and the first person I tracked down was the conductor, Carlo Maria Giulini, who had great talent and was most anxious to join the company. Then I met up with Tito Gobbi and he, too, had no hesitation joining us, such was the reputation of EMI and the quality of its recordings. Mobile equipment was dispatched to Vienna for Walter and some was sent to Rome for my use."

Although the war with Germany was at an end the problems of recording German musicians were only just beginning. Many of the musicians who had stayed in Germany, and even played in front of Hitler, were questioned at length and often accused of being Nazis. Bicknell recalled one such incident. "Artur Rubinstein, one of my greatest friends, whose whole family was killed by the Nazis during the war, wanted to know what we were doing working with German musicians. We finally took the line of only working with and signing those people cleared by the de-Nazification courts that were set up to investigate these sort of things. As the years went by things began to sort themselves out although many German musicians were unable to get out of Germany let alone to Abbey Road because of travel restrictions placed upon them by the Allies. The Italians had similar problems but they were not hit quite so badly."

While these sort of problems were a direct result of the war there were other problems to be solved. Legge had found the conductor, Wilhelm Furtwängler, in Vienna and soon after he came across an up and coming conductor named Herbert von Karajan. Soon after signing them both, he realised that they disliked each other intensely. Furtwängler threatened to leave and take the important Berlin Philharmonic Orchestra with him but finally Legge came up with the solution; he appointed von Karajan principal conductor of the newly formed Philharmonia Orchestra in London.

While all this was going on in Europe, back in London another problem had risen from the ashes of the Second World War. In 1927 The Gramophone Company had purchased from a German named Lindström the Parlophone label. (The logo thought for many years to be a £ sign was in fact a German L.) At a post-war planning meeting it was decided that EMI should continue to operate only three labels – the HMV, Columbia and Regal trademarks – and that the German Parlophone label should be dropped. There was a hint of anti-German feeling about this decision and certainly it followed requests by artists (who had regularly appeared on the Parlophone label) to be moved to other labels. When it was discovered that contractually EMI could not simply refuse to use the Parlophone trademark, they switched UK acts such as Victor Silvester and Harry Roy to other labels, leaving only the German singer, Richard Tauber, on the German label. For many years, within EMI, the label was referred to as "Tauberphone".

As the world got used to peace once again, so a whole new era in recording began. Work was begun to extend the range of Blumlein's moving coil system and, in both England and America, experiments were taking place to extend the recording range in the upper frequencies. There was also one interesting development which proved that out of adversity there sometimes comes the odd bit of good. In 1946, a team of audio engineers from America and England, including Abbey Road's Berth Jones, visited Berlin to study the developments in magnetic recording which had taken place in Germany during the war. They found

Walter Legge's protege, Herbert von Karajan, seen here at work in Abbey Road's Studio One.

Tea time for (from left to right) pianist, Gerald Moore; producers, Walter Legge and Suvi Raj Grubb and soprano, Elisabeth Schwarzkopf.

amongst the military equipment that had been captured, a system of monitoring using magnetic tape which the German command had used in an effort to break codes. The information gathered from this equipment enabled EMI to manufacture tape and tape recorders, resulting in the production of the famous BTR series which remained in use at Abbey Road for over 25 years.

While all these technical advances were taking place, Legge and Bicknell were still chasing around Europe trying to outdo each other. Certainly Legge, whose recordings were issued on Columbia, was not opposed to pulling a fast one on his colleague from HMV. They were both intent on completing the most prestigious recording programmes possible for their respective labels and so intense was the rivalry, that they continued with a policy of glorious isolation. This attitude meant that quite often Bicknell would be recording in Italy the identical works that Legge was busy working on in Vienna.

Whatever their professional differences both men found one thing in Europe over which there was no disagreement... a wife. Legge had met, and signed in Vienna, the great soprano, Elisabeth Schwarzkopf, who was to become Mrs Legge and, over the next couple of decades, she and her husband were to produce some of the finest operatic recordings ever made. Bicknell, a man who, despite Legge's reputation for being difficult, had a long and close working relationship with him, recalled his unique talent. "He was without doubt the supreme classical producer of his or any other era. His work with Elisabeth Schwarzkopf, Herbert von Karajan and Sir Thomas Beecham remains today some of the finest ever done. He was a difficult perfectionist and despite being mainly a Columbia producer he somehow managed to work with artists who were HMV artists, such as Beecham."

Bicknell's wife to be was, as he recalled, one of the first Italian artists to be

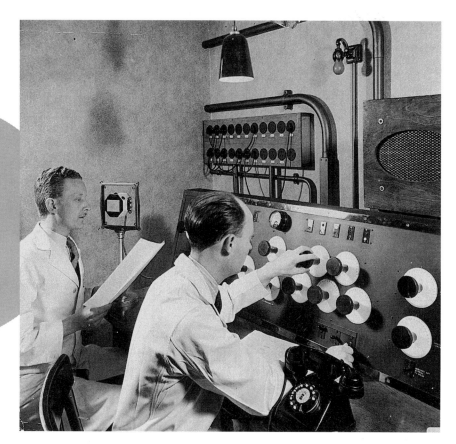

In the 1940s Abbey Road took delivery of the most advanced mixing desk in the world which cost a staggering £1,000. Chick Fowler (left), later to become studio manager, and Laurie Bamber inspect the new addition.

allowed to visit England after the war but they had first met during one of his scouting missions to Italy. "All the people I met in Italy spoke about this young violinist. Unfortunately her mother had just died and she was not appearing in public at the time. A few months later I brought an Italian soprano over to Abbey Road to work and she brought with her a young travelling companion who turned out to be this young violinist, Gioconda de Vito. She was still not performing in public but she did agree to record a session with me at Abbey Road on the understanding that if it didn't work out, it would be destroyed. Fred Gaisberg was in the studio at the time and afterwards he wanted to know all about her and said she was one of the finest violinists he had ever heard and we signed her on the spot. I recorded many times with her after that, both before and after we were married but in all honesty I would have preferred someone else to have produced her and then I would have been able to listen to her recordings in a totally detached manner."

Following the introduction of magnetic tape (as a result of the discoveries made in Berlin after the war) recording became much more flexible. Gus Cook explained the main advantages: "Tape allowed high quality programmes to be recorded, edited and replayed without any processing and these advances fitted in nicely with the development of the microgroove record by Dr Peter Goldmark in America."

In 1948, Goldmark (who worked for the CBS company) announced the arrival of the "long playing record", a microgroove disc which revolved at 33 1/3 rpm and lasted 23 minutes per side and RCA quickly responded with the smaller 45 rpm record. These new developments brought about a most significant change in record manufacture – the disappearance of the old wax masters. Until this time masters had been cut on either a thick wax blank or on a wax-coated glass plate known as a "flow coat". But processing for the new microgroove records presented problems and it became necessary to change to a lacquer disc for mastering purposes. Cook recalls this latest advance. "Although still under development, and not without its teething troubles, the new process of producing lacquer masters heralded the end of an era in recording. The advantages of the new system were, however, very quickly apparent; the lacquer could be played back with minimal degradation and, unlike the wax, was not rendered unusable after one playing. The way had become clear for the development of automatic groove spacing on records."

However, despite all the technical advances, Abbey Road kept to its rigid three hour recording sessions although, as Vera Samwell recalls, the demand for evening work was very limited. "We did very little work after 5 pm. I think Walter Legge was the only one who worked odd hours and he mainly used the weekends. One of the problems with working in the evening was that the sound from the echo chamber in Studio Two leaked and the residents were not too happy about having Wagner or whatever disturbing them in the evening. It was not too bad during the day because with the traffic and all the other noise it wasn't quite so noticeable."

During the Forties, along with Legge and Bicknell, the main producers at Abbey Road were Joe Batten, Oscar Preuss and Wally Moody, who did most of the pop work, but plans were afoot to add to this team of producers, particularly in the emerging area of pop music. Two men came to Abbey Road within a few months of each other; Norman Newell and Wally Ridley both had distinguished careers in the music business as song writers, arrangers and, in the case of Ridley, running two of the most popular radio shows of the time.

Ridley still remembers his first visits to Abbey Road as a music publisher. "I used to go to meetings there when the artists' managers would decide which songs would be recorded and by whom. I was working for a publisher then and it was my job to take songs along for selection. Very soon after, in about 1946, I made my first record at Abbey Road. I played a song called 'Penny Serenade', by a singer named Gil, to the head of Parlophone, Oscar Preuss, who agreed to give him a test. I played piano on the session and Preuss was so impressed that he released the record. My next visits were to do arrangements for orchestra leaders such as Harry Roy and Joe Loss and I used to stay around while they made their records."

In 1948 practically no British pop records were being released at all, the HMV catalogue consisting mainly of RCA Victor recordings from America, and Ridley recollects that there was only a handful of British pop acts under contract, people like Joe Loss, Harry Roy, George Melachrino, a French Canadian named

Paul Cavalle and Harry Hayes, a saxophone player who never actually released a record. "About that time I got a call from Cecil Guloff, who was then working at the BBC but had previously worked for HMV. He told me that David Bicknell, then head of HMV, wanted to talk to me about the possibility of me joining HMV to create a roster of popular acts for the label. So I went to Abbey Road to see David and he told me that he wanted somebody to build up the popular music side of HMV and did I want the job. I told him that I was heavily committed with two of my own radio shows running at that time– *Educating Archie* and *The Donald Peers Show* – and I could only give two or maybe two and a half days a week."

Bicknell accepted the situation and hired Ridley on a part-time basis. "I had become more involved in administration by the end of the Forties and was given control of the pop area of HMV as well as the classical side. I knew little or nothing about that side of the business so I employed Wally and, even though he could only work part-time, I was happy to shift the responsibility to someone else; someone who was obviously very talented and very aware of the pop business."

So Ridley joined HMV working two and a half days for an annual wage of £750 but within a few weeks he was working virtually full-time at Abbey Road and somehow managing to fit in his other work at odd times. "My first job was to decide which of the American releases to put out in this country. RCA Victor had many of the biggest names around then, people like Perry Como, Vaughn Monroe, Phil Harris and Dinah Shore, and it was up to me to work out which of these records had a chance of succeeding in this country." But Ridley's aim was to build up a roster of British acts to rival the American superstars and, along with Norman Newell, co-writer of hit songs such as 'More' and 'Never, Never, Never', he looked forward to establishing the next decade as the era of the British pop star.

4
The Discovery of Fred Flange and Ray Cathode

One of the first decisions taken at Abbey Road studios as they moved into a new decade was the abolition of the "white coats" rule. Over a decade after Sir Winston Churchill's casual remark, the studios were slowly beginning to realise that the determination to establish a thriving British pop scene required a less formal attitude from the country's leading recording house. It also required new blood; people who understood the making and marketing of three-minute pop singles. Following the retirement of studio general manager, W.S. Barrell, Chick Fowler took over the reins and inherited the cream of classical producers and engineers. In addition to Bicknell and Legge, Gaisberg and Collingwood there were Bob Beckett, Teddy Holmes, who recounted his tales of taking the Lancia mobile to Russia to record in the palace of the Russian Tsars, Douggie Larter and Harold Davidson and new faces such as Chris Parker, Bob Gooch and Neville Boyling who joined Francis Dillnutt in spearheading the use of new techniques in classical recording.

However, it was in the pop area where the greatest changes took place. Norman Newell and Wally Ridley had been joined by Leonard Smith who took more and more interest in pop recording but the need to establish a sizeable pop repertoire area was blatantly obvious to the people in control. Norrie Paramor and Ray Martin were employed, principally as conductor/arrangers, and George Martin joined the relatively unimportant Parlophone department run by the veteran, Oscar Preuss, who, many years earlier, had made the original Charles Penrose version of 'The Laughing Policeman'. Paramor and Ray Martin joined the Columbia division, Ridley was running HMV and Newell was given the same kind of freedom offered to Legge in the classical field.

When George Martin joined the Parlophone company he met not just Preuss but also the young lady who was to become Mrs Martin – Judy Lockhart-Smith – who worked as the Parlophone secretary. She remembers the office which Preuss had at the front of the old building. "Originally it had been the drawing room and it had a huge sofa and long heavy curtains. And, of course, there was the big open fire place with the coal fire which I spent most of the time keeping alight. It was a very friendly place and everybody knew everybody else. The chief engineer, Arthur Clarke, wasn't a great one for letting people get to know the

Ruby Murray is the first female artist to have had five records in the 'Top Twenty' at the same time... all of them recorded at Abbey Road.

Singer/songwriter Ivor Novello and Faye Compton listen to records on a studio gramophone during a break in recording.

artists or having unwanted visitors in the studios but I managed to meet Ivor Novello when he came in to record 'King's Rhapsody'. The sessions I got very involved with were when Oscar recorded girls choirs in the evenings; nobody else seemed to want to use the studios in the evenings. There were about 150 girls and the biggest problem was that the building only had two ladies' lavatories; it was a major piece of organisation getting all the girls to the toilet in the recording breaks."

George Martin arrived at the studios in 1950, one year after his wife-to-be, and was totally unaware of the work which had gone on there for three decades. "I didn't even know what EMI stood for. I only took the job as a stop gap, I really wanted to be a pianist – sort of Rachmaninov the third – and I think I was brought in initially to handle the Parlophone classical material." Judy Martin has her own version of why he was employed. "I think it was because Oscar wanted an assistant as somebody else in the building had just got one and he decided that he'd have one as well."

It didn't take Martin long to realise exactly where Parlophone stood in the battle between the labels which took place at Abbey Road. "The rivalry between HMV Columbia and Parlophone was a bit like Austin and Morris within British Leyland. Columbia and HMV were the chief protagonists and Parlophone was on the sidelines, a bit like the Liberal party. It was the weakest of the labels and just after the war its repertoire had been bled and been put on to the other labels. Columbia and HMV had the advantage of having American repertoire while Parlophone was the only one that had to find its own repertoire; it was a very poor relation."

Martin gave up his plans for a career in classical music and knuckled down to the task of building up the Parlophone label to an acceptable commercial level – for the princely sum of £7 4s 3d a week. "Oscar took me round and introduced me to everybody and eased me in with a shoe horn. All the engineers were much older than me and they had a close rapport with the artists which they were intent on retaining. They ran the sessions in those days; a producer wasn't called a producer... he was an artist's manager and it was his job to see that everything ran smoothly, that the artist was happy, that the session ran to time and didn't run over budget."

The continuing technical advances meant a new school of technicians and two young engineers, Stuart Eltham and Peter Bown, moved into the rapidly developing area of pop balancing, taking over from the more experienced engineers who found it difficult to adjust and keep pace with the new methods. Blumlein, who had done so much in the very earliest days of Abbey Road to develop new recording techniques, was tragically killed in June 1942. The Halifax bomber which was being used to test his new radar system, crashed with the loss of all those on board. Meanwhile, his coleagues continued working to perfect his stereo system, which he had first started work on in 1931. His brainchild, now a familiar sight in most households, was originally intended for the film industry but the recording industry, not unnaturally, was excited by the possibilities of stereo. Strangely, despite Blumlein's close association with EMI, it was Decca who were to release the first stereo records, although EMI did claim a world's first with their series of commercial pre-recorded tapes marketed under the Stereosonic trademark.

Above: **Stuart Eltham at an early eight channel mixing desk in Studio Two's original ground floor control room.**

These advances led the way for multi-track recording and a three-track system was developed which, although used in a number of studios both in the UK and America, was not suitable to Abbey Road. Ultimately four-track facilities were developed by the EMI research and development section, with the help of equipment from Siemens Telefunken, and installed in the studios.

These developments captured the interest of the newly appointed chairman of EMI, Sir Joseph Lockwood, who recalled that by the time he joined, the board of EMI had taken a rather strange decision. "The EMI board had, two years before I joined, decided that there was no future in long playing records and although we were then partners with CBS and RCA in America, and had access to all they were doing, it was simply ignored. We helped sort out the problems of 33 1/3 and 45 rpm to satisfy both of them but we ignored it, whereas Decca came out with a stereo album two years before us."

Since its earliest days Abbey Road studios had adopted an EMI only policy, never allowing artists from other companies to darken its doors, but exceptions were made for major American stars who were signed to the two companies – CBS and RCA Victor – whose records were released in the United Kingdom by EMI. This meant that artists such as Paul Robeson, Guy Mitchell, Phil Harris, Fred Astaire, Fats Waller, Johnnie Ray, Paul Anka, Eddie Fisher and the first lady

of German recording, Marlene Dietrich, were able to record in the studios in North London. Not that it was made that easy for all of them to get in. Eddie Fisher arrived one day in the uniform of a member of the American Armed Forces and, because he was not an officer, he was promptly sent around to the side door as only officers were allowed through the front door.

Left: **Geoff Love, Norman Newell and Paul Robeson hold an impromptu studio meeting.**

Early in the Fifties the two major American companies split from EMI and moved to rival British record companies, making the need to unearth home grown talent even more urgent. Wally Ridley, more aware than most of what was required of him, set about the task. "Donald Peers joined me at EMI and then Max Bygraves, the Tanner Sisters and the Hedley Ward Trio all came from the *Educating Archie* show. Max Bygraves' first record was a thing called 'Cowpuncher's Cantata' which was an odd shaped piece of music and we had great difficulty in getting Maxie to come in on the beat because there were long gaps in between the vocal lines. He had trouble finding when to enter and in the end I had to stand next to him and squeeze his arm when he had to come in. It all worked out fine in the end and we had a big success." In fact this record could be the first chart record ever to come out of Abbey Road, entering the then "official" British pop chart, as printed in the *New Musical Express*, in November 1952 and reaching No. 11. Strangely it was to enter three more times between then and March 1953, reaching an all-time high of No. 6 in March 1953.

Harry Secombe was another artist brought from *Educating Archie* to Abbey Road by Ridley. "Harry's first record was done in Number One studio with a full orchestra – the size of orchestra you wouldn't be able to afford these days – and he was very scared. When we finally got through the first take Harry did his famous falling flat on his back routine and collapsed in a heap on the studio floor as we finished the last note. The whole orchestra fell about and that was it for the day."

Although this was the time when wax was being phased out in favour of tape, Ridley did many early recordings using the antiquated system of wax. "Because it was still on wax all the performances had to be done in one complete take, there was no re-making and it was all straightforward recording. There was a delightful man named Arthur Clarke, who was the senior recording man, who had done some beautiful classical work, as had another man named Bob Beckett, who had been in charge of the company's German recordings in Berlin before the war. When he returned, he worked with people like George Melachrino at Abbey Road and did some very fine recordings. As we got into the beginning of echo some of the recording men, including Clarke and Beckett, objected to this new system and refused to use it. Not only that but because they had spent all their lives getting a natural sound they objected to the whole business of echo, making it difficult for other producers and artists to use it on the records they were making."

George Martin was by now getting to grips with Abbey Road and quickly noticed the emphasis put on classical recording at the expense of pop. "There was no sharp division between pop and classical when it came to the people, they were all good mates. However classical was still the most important thing for EMI and pop was to be used to provide money for classical recording. Many of the classical recordings were subsidised by the pop end without the pop people ever knowing about it."

Even then Parlophone was not in the same league as HMV as Martin well remembers. "We provided light orchestral music, popular song music such as Eve Boswell and Lester Young, and Scottish dance music with a certain amount of classical music, mainly baroque and chamber music. The development of new artists was a gradual thing, it didn't come overnight. The comedy records were a thing close to my heart and something Oscar had been interested in. He had recorded Elsie and Doris Waters and the label was steeped in music hall tradition and I took a leaf out of his book."

Another new recruit joined the Abbey Road staff in 1954 and Ken Townsend, managing director at Abbey Road, looks back to his first ever session. "I remember it was my first session and, by coincidence, Peter Dawson's last in Abbey Road before he returned to Australia. He did 'The Road to Mandalay' in Studio One, which, although it wasn't a hit, did become a very popular song."

But while the emphasis among the new breed of producers and engineers was to build up the pop roster for EMI, the classical division of the company was still going strong and Chris Parker, now senior classical engineer, was one of the young men brought into the company to help convince the classical artists of the benefits of the new recording techniques. "I joined just at the end of the wax era when everything was done by direct cut on to wax with a gear driven machine with a rubber belt – a fantastically primitive machine. It was gravity driven with a weight falling slowly from the ceiling to the floor. I only did a couple of wax transfers from tape as we were changing over to tape entirely at that time. As soon as tape had been in use for a couple of years then editing really developed very, very fast. Artists jumped in when editing was possible without even considering the musical pros and cons. Classical recording, for me, became very artificial but it got that way with the connivance of the artists."

With the introduction of stereo in 1955, Parker was the man chosen to play around with the experimental equipment, which at that time consisted of one pair of amplifying channels, flat plain straight channels and one pair of driven microphones. This was about the time that Lady Beecham, then working as Sir Thomas' secretary, paid her first visit to the studios she was to get to know so well in the years to follow. "I walked around with Sir Thomas in the early Fifties and as I had never been in a recording studio before it was a fascinating experience for me. After that I accompanied him on many trips to the studio and I know he enjoyed working in Abbey Road in particular. In the end he did more recording sessions than concerts and I don't remember any really bad disagreements or tantrums. His insults to people were never meant to be malicious and he always said them in his best honeyed tones in order not to upset anybody."

As an autocrat who did exactly as he liked and answered to nobody, it was obvious that any dealings Sir Thomas had with Walter Legge would be memorable. They had worked closely together in the late thirties, and again just after the war but the relationship was not to last as Sir Thomas tended to believe that every decision which went against him was due in some way to Legge. "Tommy could never understand the mysterious power of the EMI people all over the world who decided what would be recorded and by whom, particularly after his Angel contract in America had expired and been picked up by Capitol. He was convinced that Walter Legge decided firstly what the Philharmonia would record and then he was allowed to do what was left."

Lady Beecham has her own view of the situation. "You see Walter was very like Sir Thomas in that if he wanted to do something he was going to do it; this wasn't out of malice, more out of one upmanship. He was a perfectionist and while he wasn't a musician or a conductor he brought something in an administrative level to recording in Abbey Road that neither Tommy nor anybody else had experienced before." If Sir Thomas wasn't a man concerned with administration, he was a man who came into his own in the studio as Lady Beecham remembers. "He was a great man for letting the orchestra play right the way through a piece and then go back and do it again if necessary. He never did understand the thing where you could only record a limited number of minutes of music in a session because of the payment situation. He never understood that – or he professed he didn't understand it – that was another element about him."

Yet another facet of Sir Thomas' character was his great wit, and the stories of his remarks are endless. The one that is well remembered at Abbey Road concerns his visits to McWhirters, the local cafe used by Abbey Road staff and artists before the arrival of a canteen in the studio basement. Dining there one day, so the story goes, Sir Thomas asked for the wine list only to be told by a straight-faced proprietor, "We've only got Tizer, sir".

While all this was going on, Sir Joseph Lockwood was getting to grips with the problems that faced him as chairman of EMI and the first thing he noticed was the poor quality of EMI records. "My early experience was that there was something very bad about our lacquers, when I heard them on the radio I could tell which were our records because of all the crackles and pops. Then I became very worried about the quality of our recordings of classical music; they weren't bad but they seemed dreary with a lack of dynamic range, and the young people I spoke to noticed this as well. The tempo was perfect but the sound was lacking something – you'd hear a violin playing and you'd think the bloody thing was at London Airport. We had the best artists and the performances were marvellous, but we were losing out in the recording quality."

Nor was it long before Sir Joseph came across Walter Legge. "Without doubt he was a great man but he was impossible to control, and the people within EMI were always complaining about him and I came to the conclusion that we had to get him under control. He'd do things like arrive in a taxi at Manchester Square and leave it ticking over all day until he went home in the evening. Nobody would dare say a word to him."

In February 1962 Legge decided to record *Fidelio* in Kingsway Hall with Otto Klemperer and I went to Abbey Road on a Saturday afternoon to see how they were getting along. They had done the opening passage which Walter Legge, who was producing, played back to me. There was something wrong with it so I suggested that they moved the microphones. Legge said that Klemperer wouldn't agree and I told him, 'He won't know, he's deaf in one ear anyway – ignore him'. I still wasn't happy so I got Abbey Road to order a complete set of recording equipment for me – which was awfully cheeky of me because I'm no expert – and I had it put in the Kingsway Hall and recorded the whole thing separately the way I wanted it done."

Not surprisingly Legge got wind of what was going on but Sir Joseph carried on. "We came to the dungeon scene with the echoes and I said, 'This is no bloody good, send it over the telephone lines to Abbey Road, put it down the echo chamber and bring it back again!' They did this and Legge was terrified that I was going to bring out my version. He didn't resign – I was prepared for that – but to this day I don't know which version was released. I do know, however, that Walter Legge altered his a helluva lot."

Experiences like this convinced Sir Joseph that the balance of power at Abbey Road was all wrong. "I found that the whole emphasis was on classical recording so I decided to find out who was responsible for the pop side and I made a point of getting to know Oscar Preuss, Norman Newell, Wally Ridley, Norrie Paramor, Ray Martin and George Martin and I discovered that they were treated as very low grade people – rather like sergeants in an army whereas Walter Legge was a field marshal. I promoted these people to be like generals, made them feel important. I don't think I did anything for them financially but they were terribly important to the future of the company."

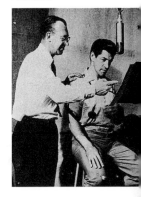

Below: **Hailed as 'Britain's Bing Crosby', Michael Holliday listens attentively to producer, Norrie Paramor.**

Bottom: **The man who started the Abbey Road hit parade. Way back in 1954 Eddie Calvert became the first Abbey Road artist to reach the coveted number one spot.**

How right he was. The people he promoted responded by bringing more and more artists to EMI and into Abbey Road. Norrie Paramor had discovered a sweet young Irish lass named Ruby Murray who with songs like 'Softly Softly', 'Heartbeat' and 'Let Me Go Lover' took the country by storm and established a whole host of records which have stood the test of time. In 1955 she had seven separate chart entries – including one No. 1 single – and five records in the chart at the same time. That same year she totalled 80 weeks in the chart, a figure not even The Beatles or Cliff Richard could beat. And all this was done with records recorded in Abbey Road in the presence of her mother who even then was presumably aware of the temptations of the record business. Paramor also produced the man dubbed as the 'English Bing Crosby', Michael Holliday, who notched up a No. 1 in 1958 with 'The Story of My Life'.

Ray Martin, not to be outdone, came up with a trumpet player supreme and to Eddie Calvert fell the distinction of being the first British artist, maybe the first artist ever, to record a No. 1 hit single in Abbey Road studios. In 1954 his recording of 'Oh Mein Papa' topped the charts for nine weeks and brought Abbey Road, after 23 years in the business of making records, its first chart topping single. Did this mean that at last the studios had arrived on the pop music scene?

Vera Samwell remembers the days of these early pop stars and the time they spent in Abbey Road. "The first real stars were Ruby Murray and Eddie Calvert and then came Max Bygraves, Pearl Carr and Teddy Johnson, Alma Cogan and Ronnie Hilton. We were never really allowed anywhere near them but as I had an office at the front of the building everybody used to crowd in and try to catch a glimpse of them. The sessions were very strict in those days and you could never get in without an invitation. You were not even allowed to ask for autographs."

Nothing, they say, succeeds like success and certainly that was the situation Wally Ridley found himself in. Having brought to the company people like Bygraves and Peers, he found himself on the receiving end of phone calls, letters and personal pleas from people who claimed to have discovered the next big British pop act. But not all the calls were in vain. "I found Alma Cogan during this time, somebody suggested her to me and although I signed her up, it took over two years to get her to the point where she was ready to record. She worked hard but it was a long process and although Alma was very ambitious, God hadn't given her the sort of vocal equipment that we were used to in singers. But we persevered and eventually found a cute song, worked out a different way of doing it and it worked." That "cute song" was entitled 'Bell Bottom Blues' and gave Alma Cogan her first chart record, reaching No. 4 in 1954, and set her off on a career which was to bring her 19 more hit records over the next seven years, including a No. 1 with 'Dreamboat' in 1955.

Another Ridley discovery was Ronnie Hilton who was first brought to the producer's attention when he was sent a song by a contact in the North of England. "I remember that the song was very poor but the singer was extremely good. I found out that his name was Ronnie Hilton and I set off up North to find him. He was working on a machine lathe in a factory, earning about £11 a week and I managed to persuade him to travel down to Abbey Road to record a couple of sides. Those first two sides did nothing at all but with the next two sides we released we had a bit hit with one side and a hit of some sort with the other side. 'Still Believe' was the big hit (No. 3 in November 1954) and 'Veni Vidi Vici' was the other side (this reached No. 12 in December 1954). This was pretty good going for a second record and after that we went on to make many hit records together." In fact Hilton made 18 hit records between 1954 and 1965, his only No. 1 coming in 1956 with 'No Other Love'.

Malcolm Vaughan was another star who was brought to Ridley's attention and this time the tip off came from a well respected disc jockey. "Jack Jackson told me about this boy who was appearing at the Chiswick Empire as half a double act called Earl and Vaughan. I went along to see him and he was so good that I got him into Abbey Road as soon as I could. He made a great many hit records but one I remember in particular came about at the time skiffle and rock'n'roll were beginning to take off. I had been sent this song from Canada which I then got Malcolm to record and that was the start of our problems. The song was 'St Theresa Of The Roses' and at that time we, like all record companies, were heavily dependent on Radio Luxembourg for air play and we spent a lot of money with them. After we released the record I heard that the boss of Luxembourg refused to play it because he thought it might offend their large Irish audience. I went along to see him and did a deal with him. If he could show me two or three genuine letters of complaint then I would withdraw the record. He agreed and of course he never had any letters and the record went on to become an enormous hit." One of Vaughan's 10 hit records between 1955 and 1959, 'St Theresa', reached the No. 3 spot in 1956.

While HMV and Columbia were busy competing with each other in the new all important British pop charts, George Martin was steadily building up the roster of acts on the Parlophone label of which he was now artists' manager, following the retirement of Oscar Preuss. Having caught the comedy bug from his predecessor, Martin went off on his own zany course, ignoring the advice of his elders and betters who forecast only failure and frustration. "Peter Ustinov was my first experiment and he was the prototype for what Peter Sellers actually became. Ustinov was tremendously interested in baroque music and his party trick for many years was to sing mock operas and impersonate all the different characters and instruments. We put these things on record on *Mock Mozart* and *Phoney Folklore* and they were laughed out of court at the monthly supplement meetings we used to have. But I was delighted with them and I do recall that Ustinov had this idea for an album title of *Your Gramophone Isn't USTINOV* but sadly we never actually made the album."

Following the disappearance of Ustinov to the world of films, Martin was left with the problem of finding a follow-up and there was only one likely contender – Peter Sellers. "Peter was the natural follow-up but I've got to tell you that working with him and Spike Milligan was often a hair-raising experience. They both fooled around like mad and their sessions always ended with some kind of bang or explosion... they would pile up all the chairs in the middle of the studio and then kick them all down. In fact on one session Sellers actually had to kick a chair across the studio as part of a fight scene and it went straight into my shins... the shriek I let out can still be heard on the *Best Of Sellers* album."

Aged only 29 and earning, as a head of department at Abbey Road, a salary of £1,100 per annum, Martin stuck to his guns and continued to record anything but the obvious. This included jazz bands such as Humphrey Lyttelton and Johnny Dankworth, and a man who he was to meet again years later, when four young men from Liverpool came into his life. Dick James was an up and coming singer when Martin recorded him singing 'Robin Hood'. It went on to become the theme tune for the famous TV series and earned James a place in the top 20 in 1956. But comedy was Martin's first love, although he busied himself with some baroque and chamber music recordings in Studio Three. Flanders and Swann were a duo close to his heart but always he went back to Sellers and the odd situations which occurred on his sessions. "On one session with Peter I wanted some bugles, so I rang up the Guards and asked for four buglers who could read. When they arrived I sat them down behind their music stands and gave them their music. They looked at me and in a most uncomfortable way said that they couldn't read music. I turned to the sergeant who had come with them and told him that I had particularly asked for musicians who could read and he said, 'Oh they can read sir, they just can't read music'.

"There was also the time when I wanted Peter to sing like Frank Sinatra on his album *Songs For Swingin' Sellers* and I played him a tape of Matt Monro and told him he should try and sing like that. Peter said he could never do it and

Top: **George Martin (left) finds it hard to keep a straight face whilst working with Spike Milligan and Peter Sellers.**
Above: **A then unknown Peter Cook joins Peter Sellers for the recording of 'Bridge On the River Wye'.**

Three of life's unique funny men, clockwise from top, Spike Milligan, Harry Secombe & Peter Sellers.

suggested we use the tape of Monro. I told him we couldn't do that because it was somebody else and as it was a Peter Sellers album then he should be singing on it. But Peter was adamant that we should use Matt's voice and invented the name Fred Flange for him. I had to go and ask Matt if he minded his voice being used and fortunately he didn't. I paid him £25 and we called him Fred Flange."

But working with people like Sellers, Milligan and Ustinov was not just fun, it had its constructive benefits as well. "People like these played a big part in teaching others at Abbey Road how to use tape," says Martin. "It was still in its infancy and a lot of people at the studio regarded tape with a good deal of suspicion but we gradually learnt all about it and working with the likes of Sellers and Milligan was very useful because, as it wasn't music, you could experiment. Our engineer, Stuart Eltham, got very closely involved with the whole thing and became our sound effects person. We made things out of tape loops, slowed things down and banged on piano lids... these were the synthesisers of the day. My first real experience of synthesised music came later when I got from the BBC Radiophonic Workshop a piece of rhythm called 'Time Beat' which I used on a record with a fictitious artist called Ray Cathode. We all spent a lot of time playing around in the studios trying to invent new sounds or new pieces of equipment. This was obviously to our advantage and even today people are still looking for new ways of doing things and creating new sounds. Now of course it's a whole industry but then the studio was a real musical workshop."

Out of all this experimenting and "playing around" came all sorts of weird and wonderful inventions to add to the steady stream of technical advances which were being introduced to Abbey Road. One of the most obvious improvements was a limiter which was used on both Eddie Calvert's trumpet and Ruby Murray's voice – two distinctive sounds in totally different ways. It meant that both artists could record without any restriction on the dynamic peaks and resulted in apparently louder records which permitted the backing to be brought further forward. This equipment was installed in all three Abbey Road studios and the Kingsway Hall.

A steady stream of hits poured out of the studios during those years and frequently four titles would be completed in a three-hour session with no mixing necessary, but still the engineers played around to find new sounds. Peter Bown and Stuart Eltham came up with an idea to reduce the "bathroom" effect created in echo chamber two by placing an assortment of drain pipes and concrete slabs inside. The result was so startling that the echo chamber became one of the studio's most prized possessions.

Another engineer, Gwyn Stock, was busy working on a gimmick box with two delayed echo systems utilising the BTR tape machines which were called STEED (single tape echo and echo delay) and FITE (fader isolated tape echo) and it wasn't until years later, by which time they had become an established part of the studio, that it was discovered that they in fact introduced mismatches in the echo send racks.

Overdubbing was achieved in the Fifties by using two mono tape machines but there were those who preferred more unconventional methods of achieving sound effects. Ray Martin, recording with his orchestra, wanted to add the sound of water lapping against the sea shore. The easy way would to have been to send the output from one machine through the mixer, add the sound effects and record the combined signal on the other but Martin wanted total realism. He installed a bath of warm water in the studio and paddled around in the bath. The studio engineers, fed up with the cries for warm water, decided to get their own back by shutting off the tape machines when the session was over – although Martin wasn't told everything was done – leaving the band-leader paddling about for hours. And that wasn't the end of it because when Martin finally emerged, swearing and cursing, they quickly took the bath and tied it to the back of his car and he drove off, taking with him a real souvenir of the session.

A few years earlier Martin had in fact fallen foul of one of the finest pianists of the day, a man known simply as Solomon. Martin's dachshund was in the studio during a recording session and decided to 'perform' in a big way on one of the piano pedals. When Solomon put his foot down to start playing he soon realised what he had trodden in. He was so upset he stormed out of the studio refusing to work any more that day.

Sir Joseph Lockwood's decision to promote pop producers was paying off handsomely. More and more hit records came out of the studio with the emergence of star names such as Dickie Valentine and Lita Rosa, although one man, who was to record nearly 30 hits, ended his career with EMI after making only two records for HMV. Frankie Vaughan was another Ridley discovery and he well remembers the circumstances of his departure from the company. "We had recorded his second record for HMV – a thing called *Happy Days And Lonely Nights* – and Frankie had gone off to Torquay for some shows. While he was down there he went into a shop to get a copy of his record and found that they didn't have any. He rang up to talk to me and unfortunately, as I was out at lunch, he was put on to the sales manager of HMV who was very off-hand with him and told him it was nothing to do with him. The conversation got a little heated and by the time I came back from lunch Frankie Vaughan had left us to join Philips."

One year later, in 1956, Ridley found himself sitting in his office in Abbey Road when a package arrived from America containing tapes by a new American singer. "Steve Shoals, who I had met on a visit to America, worked for RCA Victor and he sent me six sides with a note saying that I probably wouldn't understand a word and wouldn't know what on earth the records were all about but that I should release them as the singer was going to be an absolute giant. I listened to the tracks and he was right, I couldn't understand more than a couple of words but I decided to release them anyway. We put out 'Heartbreak Hotel' as the A-side with, I think, 'Blue Suede Shoes' on the B side [actually, the B-side was 'I Was The One' – Ed.] – and the singer was Elvis Presley. We got the worst press we had ever got for an HMV release – they said you couldn't understand a word and it was a disgusting record – and we got no broadcasts on Luxembourg. Then nine months later the whole Presley thing suddenly broke

Below: **Bert Weedon, pioneer of the electric guitar in Britain, in the studio with producer, Wally Ridley.**

over here with the *Daily Mirror* doing a double-page spread on him, which was unheard of in those days, and, lo and behold, suddenly Presley was a huge star."

As a result of hearing what Presley could do and seeing the eventual public reaction to his records, Ridley found himself with a problem. "I had to make a conscious decision at that time as to whether to pursue that kind of music or not. I realised that we didn't have guitar players like that and we certainly didn't have singers like Presley. I decided there was still a long way to go before we could make those sort of records in this country so I decided to stick with the things I knew best." One of the things that Ridley did know and understand were West End shows and he went on to make recordings of *The Boy Friend, The Pyjama Game, Cranks* (which featured a young man named Tony Newley), *The Great Waltz, Show Boat, The Good Companions* and *The Good Old Bad Old Days*.

Sir Joseph Lockwood was still very much involved with the studio in those days but one suggestion he made was not taken up by the staff at Abbey Road. "I wanted to see the studios used more fully. I never thought Studio One was used properly and I was certainly in favour of opening the studios to non-EMI acts. I always believed in a bit of competition and although I didn't want to give the opposition any particular advantage, it would have been handy to know what they were doing.

Writer/composer Noel Coward shares a joke with American star Elaine Stritch during the recording of his musical Sail Away.

"In those days the whole place was drab and dreary – you've no idea how awful it was. I played hell when I first got there about the old horse hair sofa in the artists' room and all the corridors were done in an awful dirty green. I was very much in favour of modernising the place and giving the studios what they wanted in the technical line; squeezing them down was not the way to save money. Parlophone was a perfect example of something that was nothing in those days and I encouraged George Martin, even though he only brought in a few odd bits each year. I always wanted to support people who wanted to succeed and there was far too much infighting between HMV and Columbia even up until the early seventies. It was a conscious decision of mine to support pop music and play down the importance of the classical people a bit – not to discourage them but not to let them think they owned the bloody place."

Looking back, after time has proved the wisdom of his decisions to promote the cause of British popular music, Sir Joseph reflected on just what he had in mind. "We would never have been anything in the music business without pop music, we couldn't just go on relying on classical. I have always been dedicated to being No. 1 in what ever I did. There's no point in being second and I was determined that EMI should be the best and that meant that Abbey Road would be the best studios in the world."

Chris Parker, who began working the experimental stereo equipment, and Philip Vanderlyn, from the research and development division, took the stereo recording a stage further by recording the Glyndebourne Festival's presentation of *The Marriage of Figaro* in 1954. A year later two sets of stereo equipment became available, one for Abbey Road and one for the Kingsway Hall. They each comprised six inputs, two crossed pairs and two mono injections and von Karajan used the Kingsway Hall set-up to record *Falstaff* and *Rosenkavalier*.

George Martin, too, was becoming interested in improving the technical side of Abbey Road and a trip to America to see Frank Sinatra recording *Come Fly With Me* made him realise what was lacking at Abbey Road. "I was terribly impressed with the techniques used over there and soon realised we were a long way behind. The mikes we used were very non-directional and the amps we had were crude by comparison. The sad thing was that the people at the top were reluctant to buy better equipment however, we slowly managed to change the studios and make progress."

While this progress was being made, albeit slowly, new acts were pouring into Abbey Road and hit records were coming out. Martin himself had auditioned a young singer and his backing group in 1957 with the result that he turned down the singer but signed the group. The Vipers skiffle group went on to make three hit records while the singer signed to Decca, changed his name to Tommy Steele and collected 13 chart records over the next dozen years. The same year Peter Sellers charted for the first time with his version of 'Any Old Iron', and one year earlier an even more unlikely hit had emerged on the Parlophone label – Eamonn Andrews singing (?) 'Shifting Whispering Sands' which actually reached the top 20.

Wally Ridley had the idea of putting the cumbersome TV star, Bernard Bresslaw, together with an unlikely song entitled 'Mad Passionate Love'. "The combination, of that silly voice and that romantic song appealed to me and, strangely enough, it was a hit." In fact it reached the No. 6 spot in 1958.

In the world of classical music, landmarks were also achieved with the stereo equipment being combined with a new mixing console developed in Cologne by Len Page and Peter Burkowitz. This highly effective piece of equipment was flown, with the Abbey Road mobile, firstly to Paris where Sir Thomas Beecham recorded his famous version of *Carmen* and then on to Vienna where Sir Malcolm Sargent recorded with the Vienna Philharmonic Orchestra.

An aerial shot of Studio One, during an opera recording. Apart from the orchestra in the foreground, there is also a small ensemble on the rear of the stage. The soloists can be seen standing on a clearly numbered floor covering, this facilitated accurate continuity in stereo positioning for any subsequent retakes. Note too, the numerous ambiophony speakers around the walls.

Back at Abbey Road work was starting yet again on the acoustics in Studio One which had caused problems for years. The problem was how to offset the effect of having a large number of people in the studio, such as an orchestra or choir, when the absorbtion dried up the reverberation time at the mid and top ends of the range, leaving an imbalance with the lower frequencies. Dr Gilbert Dutton of the research division came up with the idea of ambiophony in 1958. A series of magnetic delay drums was designed while a total of 100 loudspeakers were fitted symmetrically to all four walls with the intention of artificially tailoring the acoustics to any

individual situation by feeding different banks of speakers with signals delayed at differing intervals. Unfortunately the system enjoyed only limited success, although a recording by the Sadler's Wells Company of *Hansel and Gretel* does show what could be achieved.

The use of stereo recording in its early stages of development was confined to classical recording in order not to affect the "bread and butter" mono product and the first stages of experimental stereo in pop recording involved a complete duplication of microphones which were balanced in a remote stereo control room. This provided valuable experience but resulted in a hectic change-over period between sessions. One of the first 'guinea pigs' was the Victor Silvester Dance Orchestra with a crossed pair of microphones, taking care of the pianos, bass drums and accordion and a second pair in a crossed figure of eight on the front melody line with the saxophone and clarinet at the rear. The solo muted violin of Oscar Grasso was at the front, within 15 cm of the stereo microphone, and, because Grasso had a habit of swaying slightly when he played, the results in the control room were quite startling with rapid movements of the violin in the stereo picture.

Victor Silvester (seated) with (left to right) musical arranger, Helen Frizzel; violinist, Oscar Grasso; producer, John Burgess and engineer, Norman Smith

The next sessions were with Joe Loss, who began recording in Abbey Road back in the Thirties and had experienced the various changes in recording first hand. Because of the problems his orchestra encountered with the extreme level differences between open and muted brass, it became obvious that this system of stereo pairs was inadequate for pop work. Additional, four-way pre-mix boxes were provided on each left, right and centre injections and the problem was solved.

As the pop work increased so the classical people were ousted from Studio Three and left with only the cavernous Studio One and another new young pop engineer was appointed. Soon after he arrived, Malcolm Addey introduced new techniques, one of which was the close miking of individual drums and he justified his developments with the phrase, "If you can't make it good – make it loud".

Peter Andry was another new addition, this time in the classical field, and the man who headed up EMI Music's International Classical Division well remembers his first visit to Studio One. "It was awkward in many ways and there was always an awful lot of stuff in there. The Compton organ was still there until we finally managed to get it moved and there was a huge platform which was never really used. My main concern was to try and get the studio uncluttered but no sooner had we got it empty than somebody would put some more stuff in there. It was known as the biggest and finest studio in Europe in that it was a recording studio for the classics. Kingsway Hall was a specialist church, not a studio and all the rest of the European studios were either concert halls or churches. This made Studio One at Abbey Road the most distinguished of all studios in the world."

Although Andry joined in 1956 many things had not changed from the days of the Thirties. "It was very much like a house from the front and smacked of the Thirties inside with the porters in their brown coats and some of the technicians in the white coats they chose to wear. And the rivalry still existed between the HMV and the Columbia staff; they really didn't talk to each other."

Andry did manage to get back into Studio Three for certain recordings which were not suited to No. 1. "We used Studio Three for solo piano work but I never really wanted to use it because it was too small and gave a rather nasty colouration to the sound of the solo piano. There was a funny little glass window which you could open from the control room in order to shout to the artists."

Before joining EMI, Andry had worked at Decca where he had been involved in the beginning of stereo recording and the one thing he pushed for in his first days at Abbey Road was new loudspeakers, describing the existing ones as "rubbish". He also encountered the research and development people from Hayes whom he remembers as "living in ivory towers rather than using any practical experience as we do now. We had quite a struggle with them for many years".

The power of the producers was also quickly evident to Andry. "When I joined, people like Walter Legge were almighty men and they used to throw out thousands of test pressings and have them re-cut every five seconds. Walter Legge, I recall, got to dash 35* on a *Merry Widow* recording and after rejecting it said, 'somebody's trying to sabotage my recording'. What had happened was that he'd had it transferred so many times that he'd wiped the top off the tape. He was a very autocratic man but I managed eventually to change the system to the one still used nowadays, where the studio people make the final decision on test pressings and not the producer."

As a classical producer, Andry worked with many of the world's finest performers, people like Maria Callas, Victoria de los Angeles and Giuseppe di Stefano but for him, like so many others before him, it was Sir Thomas Beecham who stood out. "He was the greatest character of the lot – a great conductor and a great human being. He loved recording and experimenting with the sound texture which he couldn't do in the concert hall. He always turned up late for his sessions and always wanted to do something other than the agreed piece and his great trick was always, at the end of a session, to start the next piece so you had to record it."

Even in the Fifties many classical artists had to be convinced of the merits of recording and many of them distrusted the technicalities which surrounded them in the studios. "We had recorded many opera singers," recalls Andry, "when we had to put in a dummy mike with wires leading off which were never plugged in. Every singer liked to feel that they had a special microphone and we would push it nearer them if they wanted because they used to like to think it was helping, but in actual fact it didn't make the slightest difference to the recording. And when somebody like a bass singer said there wasn't enough bass voice then we would turn the wick up 4 dBs and immediately they'd say it sounded much better. The secret is to turn it up, turning it up always works. Ignorance in these sort of cases is very much bliss."

Andry also experienced at first hand the early encounters between Legge and the chairman of EMI, Sir Joseph Lockwood. "Legge was the most expansive and the most expensive producer in the whole of Europe and Sir Joseph was probably the first man to try and pull him into line and make him aware that things had to be commercially more acceptable. He was consistently difficult and he had rows with many of the great conductors. The usual pattern was for him to make every effort to sign them and later on to fall out with them; he was a one man band and you certainly wouldn't be able to afford people like him now."

Another character Andry remembers vividly from those days, if for totally different reasons, is the great eccentric Gerard Hoffnung. "I worked on the sessions he did in the Albert Hall on his concert with Hoovers when Ken Townsend was the electrical engineer. Without any doubt Hoffnung was a madman who took himself too seriously. At heart he was a tragic character, like so many of life's funny men. I shall never forget when he and the off-beat composer, Franz Reizenstein, chased each other down the corridors of Abbey Road after a row about their recordings."

But as this exciting and important decade in the life of Abbey Road neared an end it was the pop producers who were once again stealing the headlines. Norman Newell had worked steadily through the years producing the likes of Vera Lynn, Norman Wisdom, Geoff Love, Paul Anka, the Beverley Sisters, Billy Cotton, Marlene Dietrich, Bud Flanagan, Stanley Holloway, Van Johnson, Howard Keel, Eartha Kitt, Laurence Harvey, Paul Robeson and a pianist with such a distinctive style that it brought him 18 hit records in six years. Russ Conway began working with Newell in 1957 and two years later they produced two No. 1 records, 'Side Saddle' and 'Roulette', which made the Conway style of piano playing a part of pop history.

Another young man who was destined to play a major role in British pop music in the years to come made his first visit – albeit totally unofficially – to Abbey Road around that time. Mickie Most, then one half of a singing duo known as the Most Brothers, remembers the time he went there to visit some friends. "I went in there with a skiffle group called Les Hobeaux and it was just like being in heaven. I didn't know anything about the technicalities, but it looked a pretty impressive place except that some of the people wore white coats which I thought was a bit strange. I never saw it but one of my mates told me that there was a sign up on the wall that said, 'Sports jackets and flannels may be worn on Saturday mornings'."

Above: **Dame Vera Lynn,** *the 'sweetheart of the forces', when she was a regular visitor to Abbey Road.*

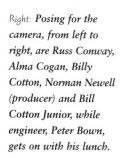

Right: **Posing for the camera, from left to right, are Russ Conway, Alma Cogan, Billy Cotton, Norman Newell (producer) and Bill Cotton Junior, while engineer, Peter Bown, gets on with his lunch.**

While Studio Three was used for both classical and pop recordings and Studio One was almost exclusively the property of the classical people, Studio Two was fast emerging as the major pop studio. Painted in plain white with huge baffle boards which could be brought out when needed and then folded back into the walls, the studio stands today almost exactly as it did 30 years ago with linen bags of seaweed hanging down the walls to help the acoustics.

Five young men walked into this room in 1957 for an audition with producer Norrie Paramor that heralded the birth of a totally new concept in British pop... home grown rock'n'roll. Paramor introduced Cliff Richard to an audience attending a live recording in Abbey Road, as "a young man whom I feel sure you will hear a lot of in the future".

"It was 1957 when I first went there for an audition with Norrie," recalls Cliff. "We recorded some old rock'n'roll songs we all knew and at the end Norrie said we had recorded well. After that, The Drifters (later to become The Shadows) and I left and Norrie went off and found this Bobby Helms song called 'Schoolboy Crush' while Ian Samwell sent us a song he'd written called 'Move It' which we had to sing to Norrie in his office one day. He quite liked it and said we could do it as the B-side."

Cliff and his backing group were called back to Abbey Road in 1958 to make their first record on the Columbia label. Two of the members of that backing group stayed to work with Cliff as The Shadows and to go on to make a string of hits in their own right. Hank Marvin was there and so, too, was Bruce Welch who remembers that first session. "We did three songs in each three-hour session we had, it was written into our contracts and even if they were crap you still had to do three songs. When we first went in there Abbey Road wasn't famous, it was just a studio but it was the biggest one we'd ever been in. We were totally overawed by it all; remember we were only 16 or 17 years old and everything was overseen and organised for us. All we had to do was turn up and get on with it. We were overwhelmed to see an A & R man, an engineer and a tape operator on a session for us and we just did exactly as we were told."

Cliff, too, remembers that they were very much the new boys although Norrie Paramor did a lot to ease the nerves. "He never laid down the law and wasn't the least bit dictatorial in any way which was a great help to us. He used to help me to sing within his arrangements on some of the slower numbers but left me alone on the rock'n'roll stuff which was a lot freer."

Although he never appeared in public with a guitar in those early days,

Above: **Abbey Road's number Two control room, circa 1958, with what can only be described as a highly unsophisticated mixing console with engineer, Malcolm Addey (left); producer, Norman Newell, and engineer, Peter Bown.**

Below: **Bruce Welch, Brian Bennett, Hank Marvin, Brian 'Liquorice' Locking and Cliff Richard with engineer, Malcolm Addey.**

Cliff recalls that he wore one on that first session. "The strange thing was that I couldn't sing without the guitar even though I never played it very well. I started the session without the guitar and it wasn't working out too well and Norrie suggested I put the guitar on. I just held it and it all happened. The whole thing was nerve-racking and we were all just a bundle of nerves which was probably just as well as there was a lot of nervous energy on 'Move It', which, funnily enough, did come out as the A-side after all."

When it was all over the next thing was the playback, another new experience for the youngsters which Bruce will never forget. "Hearing our guitars and voices after those first sessions, we were totally overawed. We could hardly play and everything was so simple and then when we heard it back there seemed to be so much going on. We played everything live and there was no mixing or overdubbing and it was all done in mono."

Goodness knows how many recording sessions in Abbey Road later, Cliff still remembers the part played by Studio Two in those early recordings. "We always used Number Two in those days and it really was a great studio. We loved working there, even though looking back it was probably a bit big for us. We did everything in mono and I think it was the ambience of the studio that helped make everything sound so good."

*Below: **Actor, manager and former Sixties pop star, Adam Faith (right) with musical director, John Barry.***

Hot on the heels of Cliff came another young man destined to carve a career for himself in the music industry and he, as if to maintain the balance of power within EMI labels, carried the Parlophone colours. Adam Faith brought EMI its final No. 1 in 1959 when, in November of that year, he topped the charts with 'What Do You Want'. It had been a good year for the company with Russ Conway twice topping the charts and Cliff Richard and The Shadows reaching the top spot with 'Living Doll' and 'Travellin' Light'. In fact it had been a very good decade and as the Fifties drew to an end, the company which had declared its intention to break the American stranglehold on the British pop charts and replace it with home-grown talent, boasted a dozen No. 1 hit records and countless other chart entries.

5
Snap, Crackle and Pop

The 10 years which became known universally as the "swinging Sixties" started out just like any other new decade with a plethora of political and financial decisions which quite rightly took second place to a handful of events that fully captured the imagination and interest of the nation. While the bank rate went up and down like a fiddler's elbow, the state of emergency in Kenya ended after eight years, only to be succeeded by a similar state being declared in South Africa, and the Bank of England issued new pound notes and withdrew the dear old farthing, Princess Margaret married Tony Armstrong-Jones, Prince Andrew, the Queen's third child, was born, and the Olympic Games opened in Rome.

Above: **Sophia Loren & Peter Sellers sharing an Anglo-Italian joke during a studio playback of 'Goodness Gracious Me' in 1960**

Tenuous though the link may be, the Anglo-Italian connection which began in Rome's Olympic stadium in the summer of 1960 was continued later the same year when our very own Peter Sellers teamed up with the ravishing Italian actress, Sophia Loren, to make a record with George Martin in Abbey Road studios. It wasn't the making of the record which Martin remembers but the financial arrangements. "Because Peter was a rising star I was allowed to offer him five per cent which was the top royalty rate. There was a rumour going around that Walter Legge had paid Laurence Olivier 10 per cent to get him to do something and everybody was up in arms about it. Although we made most of the album at Abbey Road, I had to go to Milan to discuss the details of Sophia Loren's contract to record with Peter. I saw her lawyer who told me that they wanted 12 per cent; this was impossible nobody had ever got 12 per cent. I tried to discuss the matter but her lawyer was adamant and so I decided there was only one way out – to divide Peter's 5 per cent and give half to Sophia. This meant persuading Peter to take a cut, which we did, and excluding Italy from the deal so

Left: **Peter Sellers and Sophia Loren arriving at Abbey Road.**

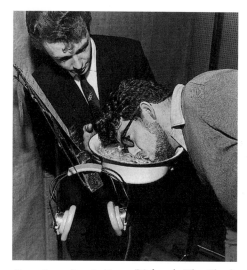

Above: **Australian Rolf Harris went for authenticity during the recording of his song In The Wet** *with engineer, Peter Vince assisting.*

that the lawyer could negotiate a separate 12 per cent deal for Italy. Those were the sort of compromises we had to make in those days. We were given strict instructions to offer artists a penny a record and never agree to a percentage unless we had to, because percentages went up with the price of a record while a penny stayed the same."

While Sellers and Loren earned themselves a chart record with their version of 'Goodness Gracious Me' (it reached No. 4 in November 1960) another unlikely record was released on the Columbia label run by Norrie Paramor. Rolf Harris was an up and coming Australian who introduced the wobble board, an instrument from his native land, on his recording of 'Tie Me Kangaroo Down Sport' and was rewarded with a top 10 record.

After two years' performing and recording with Cliff Richard, The Shadows began the Sixties by recording by themselves as well as working with Cliff, a combination which had resulted in 18 hit records by mid-1960. Bruce Welch remembers that the system of recording was the same with or without Cliff. "We would run through things for about five minutes to give the engineer a chance to get a level and for us to get used to the number. Then, when the red light went on, we just got on with it and put it down in one take. Things like 'Apache' were done in mono and we had no say in how things were recorded; Norrie was the boss and you never argued with him and anyway we really didn't understand what was going on."

Although they never argued with Norrie in the studio, The Shadows did offer up their suggestions when it came to the type of numbers to be recorded, often with surprising results. "Funnily enough Norrie did change his mind over 'Apache'. Jerry Lordan wrote the number and played it to us on his ukelele. We took it along to Norrie and he said he liked it but had this idea of doing a version of 'Quartermaster's Stores' as the A-side. We did both in the studio and we told Norrie that we still preferred 'Apache' for the A-side.

"So Norrie did what he always did with his recordings; he took them

Right: **On the steps of Abbey Road... the original Shadows line-up of (left to right) Tony Meehan, Hank Marvin, Bruce Welch and Jet Harris.**

home to play to his kids and because they liked 'Apache' it came out as the A-side. Norrie was a great help to us, he used to teach me chords even though he couldn't play the guitar; he'd play it on the piano and I'd pick it up from there. But none of us were at all interested in production because there was no reason for us to get involved – Norrie was the boss and what he said went. Although we were among the first pop stars to go into Abbey Road we really just went there at that time to do a job and nothing more. It was very businesslike and very staid and when it came to 10 o'clock you just packed up and went home. The lights went off and that was it, even if you were halfway through a hit record you just packed everything away and left like everybody else."

As more and more success came to Abbey Road so the need grew for more and more staff and 1960 saw two young men beginning careers that are still active today. Bob Barratt began his first work at the studio in 1960 when he got a job working for the producer, Norman Newell. "I got my chance when I was in the lift one day with Norman. He said he'd noticed me around the building and that I was always polite; that was because I always called him sir. He invited me to become his office boy even though I was 22 years of age. I made the tea, ran errands and, most important from my point of view, took records round to the artists for their approval. I remember visiting Peggy Mount, Russ Conway and Mel Torme and this was a way of meeting the artists and getting my foot in the door. On one occasion Mel Torme gave me a shilling tip after taking some records round to him. I came back and asked Norman if I could keep it as I didn't want to be seen to be fiddling the company... he said I could."

Norman Smith joined at about the same time as Barratt after answering an advertisement for a recording assistant. "I got the job and was basically just a 'gofor' for the engineers and producers and remember I was 32 when I got that job. EMI had put a ceiling of 28 on the job and I lied about my age to get in which was fine until I suddenly realised that if I stayed working at Abbey Road until retirement age I'd be seventy-bloody-one... I owned up about it but I had the job by then and nobody seemed particularly bothered."

EMI may have overlooked Smith's age but the one thing they refused to change was the principle of artists' tests. "All the artists had to have a test, even if they had been successful with another company; that was the rule," recalls Smith who like so many others got his chance with Norrie Paramor.

Below: **Disc jockey Pete Murray, seen here during one of his regular Abbey Road visits to tape in-flight programmes for the original British Overseas Airways Corporation (BOAC).**

"Norrie found out that I had worked as a musician and within a few months I was allowed to work on the desk doing the balancing on the artists' tests. But I was never allowed to use any of my own ideas. I had to conform with the ideas of people like Stuart Eltham, Peter Bown and Malcolm Addy until I got my own artists which was the next step because all the engineers, like the producers, had their own list of acts."

Barratt also got his chance at that time and, after working on an old time music hall session with Barbara Windsor and Leonard Sachs, he was approached by Norrie Paramor. "When John Schroeder left as Norrie's assistant he asked me if I wanted the job. A lot of people were after it but I think I got it because I knew EMI and understood all the red tape and the forms. At that time Norrie was on the crest of a wave with Cliff and The Shadows, Michael Holliday and Ruby Murray."

Rival Sixties pop idols Eden Kane (left) and Shane Fenton –perhaps better known as Alvin Stardust– get together in the studio.

Although he had started with Paramor on the artists' tests, Smith had moved to work with Ron Richards who was producing sessions while working as George Martin's assistant. "My first session at Abbey Road was with Ron and an artist named Shane Fenton, who of course went on to become Alvin Stardust. We had a minor hit with 'Moody Guy' which boosted my wages a bit because at that time engineers were paid bonuses if they worked on hit records but strangely enough the producers only got a flat salary. Another early session I remember was with Paul Raven who went on to become Gary Glitter. Although Ron was producing and had a certain amount of freedom he couldn't sign the all-important red forms that were needed to sign artists and book studio time. It was all mono then and to set up stereo in a crude way you had to have a second engineer who set up a second set of microphones."

Continuing his almost obsessive interest in oddball records, George Martin found himself in Cambridge in 1961 recording four undergraduates who had a style of humour which, at the same time as being very funny, had a cutting satirical edge. Peter Cook, Dudley Moore, Alan Bennett and Jonathan Miller presented the *Beyond The Fringe* revue which was recorded both in Cambridge on the mobile unit and later at the Fortune theatre in London's West End.

Martin's trip to Cambridge coincided with the news that he had spent 10 years waiting for... he had achieved his first No. 1 with an act he had discovered, arranged and produced. "I found the Temperance Seven through a near neighbour, Brian Innes, who was a founder member of the group. I went along to see them and liked their sound; it was interesting, mellow and steeped in nostalgia. I tried to record them like the old times to keep the feel. We even put scratches on the record and tried using single mikes and Paul McDowell used the megaphone in the studio to achieve that particular vocal sound." Martin's eye and ear for detail paid off handsomely with a No. 1 record in the shape of 'You're Driving Me Crazy' which was followed by another top 10 record, 'Pasadena', later the same year.

What of his recordings with the *Beyond The Fringe* team? "I didn't really like working with the mobile but it was always nice to get out of London for a day. The facilities weren't very good, it was all very cramped but it was good fun; just as it was when we went up to Scotland to record Scottish dance orches-

Left: **One of George Martin's earliest comedy recordings involved the** Beyond The Fringe *review* **from Cambridge University which starred (from left to right) Peter Cook, Alan Bennett, Dudley Moore & Jonathan Miller.**

tras where we recorded in some funny places like tumble down old village halls."

Slowly but surely Martin was establishing the Parlophone label as a rival to the successful HMV and Columbia trademarks and he met with no opposition to his ideas as he achieved more and more success. "There was no real opposition to the signing of people like the Temperance Seven, the *Beyond The Fringe* people or teaming up Sellers with Sophia Loren. There was just an apathetic attitude and, as Parlophone had always been treated with a sneering tolerance, it was my job to make it viable in whatever way possible when I took over. It was difficult at that time to try and compete with American acts like Guy Mitchell, Doris Day, Johnny Ray, Connie Francis, Elvis Presley, Frank Sinatra, Frankie Laine, Ray Conniff and Rosemary Clooney and a whole host more. I figured the only way we had a chance was to find something that the public had never heard before. The risks, I calculated, weren't very high as the only risk I ran was failure and if I was going to fail anyway by doing nothing I really had nothing to lose. It was a challenge to me to find new things and fortunately there was no real pressure on me, nobody was threatening my job or telling me to buck my ideas up."

As the public became more and more aware of the studios in North London that produced so many fine records, they were saddened to hear of the death of one of its greatest supporters. Sir Thomas Beecham died in 1961 but even in failing health he had one trick to play before leaving Abbey Road for the last time. Lady Beecham recalls the background to his last visit. "Sir Malcolm Sargent had visited him in the flat we had in Marleybone Road and, seeing he was very ill, had gone back to the studios and told the LSO that the great man would never conduct again nor visit Abbey Road again. Someone in the orchestra rang me,

Above: **The Temperance Seven – with vocalist, 'Whispering' Paul McDowell (far left) – gave George Martin his first number one with 'You're Driving Me Crazy' in 1961.**

Above: **Connie Francis** *just one of the many American stars who recorded at Abbey Road.*

told me what Malcolm had said, and wanted to know if it was true. When I told Tommy he immediately asked for a car to be brought round.

"We went up to Abbey Road and waited for Malcolm to get into full swing with the orchestra before going into the control room." Chris Parker takes up the story as he was in the control room when Sir Thomas arrived. "He was in a wheelchair and we hid him while Malcolm and the orchestra recorded a Gilbert and Sullivan opera. When it was all over Sir Thomas spoke on the hand mike for three or four minutes; it was a very moving moment but he was still cracking jokes and Malcolm Sargent's face was an absolute picture."

As Lady Beecham recounts, the trip was well worthwhile. "Seeing Malcolm's expression of sheer horror was better than all the medicine they could give him." She also believes her husband would have had no regrets about missing the arrival of the Mersey boom which was just around the corner. "He was horrified about the whole pop affair even as it was in 1960. Fortunately he never saw The Beatles and he never paid any attention to any music that wasn't classical. He would have made a great scene if he had been alive when classical sessions were moved out of studios and took second place to pop recordings. He wouldn't have felt it was right at all; not even for financial reasons."

Right: **Sir Malcolm Sargent** *enjoys a cup of tea, having come to the end of his* 'Patience'.

Left: **American arranger/conductor Nelson Riddle with Shirley Bassey, during rehearsals in Abbey Road's Studio One.**

However, despite what Sir Thomas Beecham might have said about it, the financial reasons were pretty conclusive. Hit records were produced in the studios with alarming regularity, forcing the classical work into the background. Shirley Bassey arrived from Cardiff's Tiger Bay and began a career that still thrives today while Norman Newell found a young man who, despite totalling eight chart records, is remembered for making one of the classic pop songs of all time. Danny Williams' version of 'Moon River' shot to No. 1 in 1961 and was just one of nine No. 1 records produced in Abbey Road during that year. While it's maybe unfair to tag them as one-hit wonders, it is fair to say that in both 1960 and 1961 there were a good few acts who had chart topping singles for which they are best remembered. Johnny Kidd and The Pirates and Ricky Valance made it and one young lady became a national institution at the age of 14.

Left: **Even 'Rock' singers wore jacket and tie in the Fifties and early Sixties Number One hit maker, Johnny Kidd being no exception.**

Helen Shapiro first visited Abbey Road as a teenage London schoolgirl and she wasn't at all sure what she would find. "I didn't know that part of London at all in those days, it was the posh end and the other end of the world from where I lived in Hackney. I was full of anticipation when I first went there

Fourteen-year-old Helen Shapiro made number one in 1961 with 'You Don't Know'.

but it turned out to be bare and plain with pale green paint and every door looked the same."

She had been visited by Norrie Paramor's assistant, John Schroeder, at the Maurice Berman School of Singing and invited to do an artist's test in Studio Two at Abbey Road. She sang 'Birth Of The Blues' and the reaction took her completely by surprise. "The message came back that when Norrie heard the tape he didn't believe that I was either 14 or a girl. I had to go to his office in Manchester Square and sing for him." When Paramor was convinced of Helen's sex, age and talent, she was booked into Studio One for her first recording session. "We recorded in that enormous studio with the back half curtained off because it was so big. I remember going into the control room and hearing my voice for the first time through loudspeakers; it was a most amazing feeling, a thrill I'll never forget. It sounded like me but better."

In the next three years Helen Shapiro was to record 11 hit records in Abbey

Road and she looks back fondly to her days as the most successful schoolgirl in the history of pop. "I recorded most of my hits, and most of my flops, in Abbey Road. Virtually everything was done in one take – I was known as 'one take Charlie' – and if it didn't come out right they'd do an edit on the tape to make it right. Technically the place wasn't wonderful but it was great fun and there was a lovely atmosphere. The way we worked was to choose a song, somebody would do the arrangement, and I just came in and did it. We could quite easily do four tracks in a three-hour session and it all seemed to work out fine.

'It was definitely a different world to recording nowadays – not necessarily any better – but I just know that I enjoyed it. I was just a kid and it was a whole new big wonderful world. I always loved arriving here. I used to love recording and used to really look forward to all the sessions but the biggest buzz was just walking up the steps into the building. Then I'd come in and stand at the window in control room 2 and look down at the musicians and the arranger waiting for me... it was a great feeling. In those days it was all about people and music rather than sounds and of course it was a village industry compared with the high powered business it is today."

However that "village industry" was growing day by day and soon another new face joined the ranks of the technical staff at Abbey Road. Peter Vince joined when new employees did a complete house apprenticeship, starting as a tape operator, going on to disc cutting and working with the balance engineer before there was even a chance of becoming an engineer. "After all that you might, if you were lucky, be given the chance to take over a session. If that worked out OK then ultimately you might move up and at that time there was

From left to right John Schroeder, Norrie Paramor, and Helen Shapiro during the recording of her number one hit, 'Walking Back To Happiness'.

a regular turn round of staff as more and more new studios opened up."

The role of Abbey Road as a training ground is something that Gus Cook recalls proudly. "It has trained engineers and technicians for the whole industry. The high standards maintained at Abbey Road over the years have made the staff who worked there much sought after. At the same time we received applications daily from engineers all over the world who wanted to work and train at Abbey Road... they even offered to work for nothing."

Vince will never forget the first session when he controlled the desk. "It was with Victor Silvester and it was a terrifying experience even though they were comparatively simple tasks. It was a great relief to know that the engineer, Norman Smith, was sitting there keeping a friendly eye on me. The mixers in those days had no more than treble and bass control for each microphone with a means of adding echo but if you listen to some of the records from the Fifties and Sixties – not the group stuff but the MOR (middle of the road) recordings – you'll hear how good the sound was. This could be because the equipment had valves or maybe it was just the way they played. And we used very few mikes in those days. We would probably have had two mikes on the drums in that first session I ever did and now there will be 15 or 16 mikes on the drums alone.'

Above: **The Abbey Road training in all forms of music is legendary in recording circles and here a young Geoff Emerick (standing), later to engineer many of The Beatles' hits, listens and learns from classical maestros (from left to right) producer, Victor Olof; pianist, John Ogdon; Sir John Barbirolli and assistant producer, Ronald Kinloch Anderson.**

Below: **Juliet Mills and Michael Redgrave just two of the stars of stage and screen who have visited Abbey Road.**

Slowly but surely George Martin's Parlophone label was catching up with the more successful sister labels, HMV and Columbia, so much so in fact that in July 1961 he was asked to write an article for the EMI house newspaper on the work of a recording manager. Under the heading 'You Know, It's Really Quite A Funny Job' Martin explained the numerous talents required in running a department of a major record company, producing records and finding and signing new talent.

His opening paragraph gives some idea of the complexities which occurred in a normal working week. "Where else would you be working with Albert Finney and Shirley Anne Field one day, Jimmy Shand the next, auditioning a rock group between dubbing on sound effects for a 'Toytown' children's record or perhaps supervising the editing of a new revue?" It may sound like a pretty glamorous job but Martin goes to great pains to put the record straight in the next paragraph. "But don't let me give you the impression that it is one long, glorious tour through show business. It embraces also a great deal of tedious work and thought, and sometimes unpleasant actions. I remember a very famous band-leader walking out of our studios once because I had criticised the playing of his bass player." Martin added, I hope with a touch of self satisfaction in a later sentence, that a few weeks later the band-leader got rid of that same bass player.

He went on to write about the weekly supplement meetings held each Tuesday in Manchester Square, the head office of EMI Records where most of the producers had moved, leaving Abbey Road more room for expansion. At that meeting the managers played the records they intended to release and listened to the comments of their counterparts. Martin recounted his part in the chain that ends with a record being released. "I have to choose the artist, choose his material and arrange a suitable accompaniment, take him to our studios and make a hit record." That sounds simple enough but where does the talent come from? "There is no set rule for the uncovering of talent – you just keep your ears to the ground (when you're not recording of course!) and hear as many new people as you can."

Matt Monro was one artist George Martin took under his wing after an unsuccessful début on record. Martin teamed up with arranger, Johnny Spence, and they agreed upon a song written by fellow producer, Norman Newell, and Cyril Ornadel called 'Portrait Of My Love'. After routining the song and getting the arrangements written for each member of the orchestra, they were ready to record and Martin wrote about the day they set about recording Matt Monro's biggest hit single. "Everyone assembles in the

Above: **Matt Monro** *(right) who rose from bus driver to star, is seen here at work with musical director, Johnnie Spence, during the making of 'Portrait Of My Love'.*

studio and there is nervous anticipation in the air. I try to look cool and blasé but I always get a tingle of excitement as the band swings into the music for the first time.

"We spend a good deal of time on setting the balance and getting the sound right to my ears. In the studio the artists' manager works very closely with the balance and control engineer who actually operates the recording controls. When a satisfactory balance has been obtained, an attempt is made at making the record. This is then played back and improvements are made until I am happy with the result. Sometimes we reach a master in one 'take – other times we never get it in one go but we have to edit the tape. This 'musical surgery' involves the splicing together of the best pieces, no matter how small." The end product of all this was a record that reached No. 3 in the charts and was the first of the 13 hit records Monro was to make over the next 13 years.

In the summer of 1962 Martin met four young men from Liverpool who were destined to change his life in the most remarkable fashion but, blissfully unaware of what was just around the corner, Martin continued producing hit records by the most unlikely performers. Bernard Cribbins was a comedy actor with no previous recording experience when he went into Abbey Road and he came out with a top 10 hit entitled 'Hole In The Ground' and made two more chart records before the year was over.

EMI had in fact started the year with a No. 1 from Abbey Road in the shape of Cliff and The Shadows with 'The Young Ones' and The Shadows took the top spot themselves in March with 'Wonderful Land'. Bruce Welch remembers what was happening in the world of recording at that time. "The biggest change we noticed was going two track which meant we could overdub and put another guitar on. I was beginning to understand some of the technical stuff by then but I couldn't understand, and never had the bottle to ask, how people like Buddy Holly, The Everly Brothers and Neil Sedaka could sing with themselves. On 'Breaking Up Is Hard To Do' you could hear Sedaka's voice three times and we never could work out how he could do that with just one voice. Nowadays we don't think twice about it. You have 24 tracks and you can have 24 voices if you like, it's as simple as that.

"Two track was a great invention for us. We had recorded 'Wonderful Land', our second most successful single, and had it in the can for years because we weren't happy with it we didn't know what was wrong but we knew it wasn't right. Norrie went off and put strings on it when two track came in, and just presented it to us without ever telling us what he was going to do. We were knocked out with it and it was probably the first pop song with strings. Norrie did the same thing with 'Guitar Tango' when he added trumpets and with those sort of hit records we were able to progress out of doing everything in three-hour sessions, which was a great relief. In those days artists were never consulted about these sort of recording changes, they were just done. We were just somebody you employed to do a job."

Number one here we come! From left to right producer, Bob Barratt; producer/ arranger, Norrie Paramor; Frank Ifield and engineer, Norman Smith, during the making of 'I Remember You'.

Paramor was still busy with his other two major acts, Helen Shapiro and Frank Ifield, who had been with him for a few years but had never achieved the success expected of him. Bob Barratt remembers the session which changed all that for the ex-policeman from Coventry. "Frank had done a lot of re-cording and had had a bit of a lean time; he was probably close to being dropped altogether. On this particular session Norrie was arranging, Norman Smith was engineering and I was in the control room and at the end of the session Norrie said he had a feeling about one particular track and felt it could be a hit. I said, 'I wish I had your confidence, Norrie', I really didn't see it as a hit record. That was 'I Remember You' and it took Frank to No. 1 and his career took off from there."

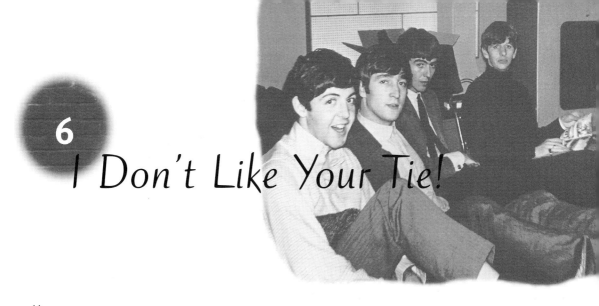

6
I Don't Like Your Tie!

Ken Townsend agreed to stay behind at Abbey Road and work on a commercial test for George Martin one evening that summer – June 6, 1962. Norman Smith was the balance engineer and the button pusher was a young man named Chris Neal. "There was obviously something very different even then about the four young lads from Liverpool who turned up for that test," recalls Townsend.

Norman Smith, too, remembers the night that was to be a turning point in the course of pop music. "I was down to do a test for a group called The Beatles with George Martin and when they arrived, half an hour late, I couldn't believe what louts they looked with their funny hair cuts. They basically played their stage act and it wasn't at all impressive in a studio with their little Vox amps. I had to open up the mike for the bass player and we got more extraneous noise than bass signal so I went and borrowed a Tannoy loudspeaker from an echo chamber to improve the sound and get something on tape but it wasn't very good at all."

After that first audition, the four young men were called into the control room where Smith and George Martin stood waiting for them. "George and I laid into them for about an hour," recalls Smith, "and we were pretty forthright in telling them what they had to give us in the way of sound and we told them how they could embellish the sound.

"At the end of it all George Martin said that we had been talking to them for quite some time, going on at them for most of that time, and was there anything they didn't like. George Harrison looked up and said to George, 'I don't like your tie'. I still maintain that was the turning point. They didn't stop talking for an hour or more after that and I had tears of laughter running down my face; they were so funny and had so much wit, we couldn't stop laughing. When they had gone – Pete

Above: **One of the first ever photographs of The Beatles at Abbey Road**

Below: **Two Georges in Studio Two – Harrison and Martin.**

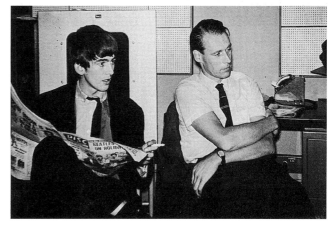

Best was with them then – George Martin turned to me and asked me what I thought. I said, 'We've got to sign them for their wit, that's my opinion', and George said, 'OK, I'll think about it'. I believe to this day that they talked themselves into a contract."

That was not the way George Martin saw it. "I remember The Beatles as very bubbly people, great fun to be with but the fact remains that when I brought them down from Liverpool and worked with them that first time in Abbey Road I was convinced they were star material as live performers. I liked them, fell in love with them. And they liked me, fortunately, because I had done all the Sellers records and Peter was one of their idols. I didn't think they could write music. I didn't sign them because they were great composers because they weren't; they were rotten composers. If I remember correctly there were only one or maybe two of their own songs in the first audition and they weren't very good – 'PS I Love You' and possibly 'Love Me Do' – they hadn't shown any evidence of what was to come in the way of songwriting."

Three months later The Beatles – John Lennon, Paul McCartney, George Harrison and the new drummer, Ringo Starr – were back in Abbey Road and this time it was for real. They had been signed up by Martin and were now ready to make their first record. Norman Smith recalls the confusion that was caused by this new drummer. "The first thing they did was 'Love Me Do' with Ringo but George Martin had a session drummer named Andy White standing by just in case. I think he was on the single version and Ringo played on the album but I'm not quite sure about that."

Whoever was playing, Smith was the man with the problem of trying to do something with the drum sound. "It was a real headache trying to get a drum sound and when you listen to the record now you can hardly hear the drums at all. But they had listened to all the things we told them and they had taken some notice and then they began bringing in the most outrageous gear into the studios, great column amps and things. That was the turning point for me at Abbey Road and the studio itself."

Column amps and other pieces of equipment were not the only things that The Beatles brought into Abbey Road as they made more and more visits during the latter part of 1962. "They brought in loads and loads of records from Liverpool to show us what sounds they wanted. They were so aware of what was going on in America where they most definitely were ahead of us in pop production. They brought in things like Carl Perkins and a lot of Motown stuff and we thought that the Americans must be cheating," recalls Smith.

And if the Americans were cheating then what was wrong with the Abbey Road staff doing a bit of fiddling. Ken Townsend set to work on creating something that would suit, even in these early days, The Beatles' creative demands. "They started off with simple two track, recording with voices on one track and backing on the other but they very soon got into the four track scene and began to revolutionise the very way in which Abbey Road had worked for 30 years. They turned the place into a workshop and used it for rehearsals and songwriting. In 1966, I got the idea of artificially double tracking the vocals in order to cut down the amount of time we spent double tracking. Using various pieces of equipment I was able to create a system whereby we could record two sets of voices at once and then space the second voice at any required time interval either side of the original."

Like all good inventions this new piece of equipment had to have a name and it was christened ADT (Artificial Double Tracking) although John Lennon insisted on calling it Ken's Flanger and such was the influence of The Beatles, that Flanger it has remained, with 'flanging' becoming a technical term in every

day use in studios all over the world. George Martin was quick to appreciate just what Ken Townsend had invented. "ADT came out of a genuine need. We had got so fed up with spending so much time adding voice after voice that Ken and I used to talk about it continually until one day he went off and invented it. We then had to find out the hard way exactly how it worked."

By the end of 1962 The Beatles had begun to believe that they were the best judges of what they should record, although on 4th September (90 days after they first set foot in Abbey Road) at a session for their debut single, they somewhat reluctantly agreed to record a song that George Martin had found for them, Mitch Murray's

Above: **John Lennon in Studio Two control room with Ken Townsend, during a playback.**

'How Do You Do It'. But The Beatles were agreed on one thing... they wanted to record their own material, and the second song chosen for the session was their composition 'Love Me Do'. After carefully appraising both titles, George Martin finally chose 'Love Me Do' for the group's first single. However, Martin could have claimed the last laugh, because Gerry and The Pacemakers, another Liverpool group, recorded 'How Do You Do It' and it reached No. 1 in 1963.

In fact 1963 was a very good year for EMI with 15 of the 19 No. 1's that year, all recorded in Abbey Road; surely an achievement that no other studio could boast. It all started in January, with The Shadows' 'Dance On', followed by Frank Ifield's 'The Wayward Wind' and The Beatles' 'Please Please Me'. From 23 February to 27 July, Abbey Road dominated the charts for 23 consecutive

weeks with further chart toppers for Cliff, The Shadows, Gerry and The Pacemakers, The Beatles, Billy J. Kramer and The Dakotas, Gerry (again) and Frank Ifield. After a brief respite, Billy J. continued the run with 'Bad To Me', followed by The Beatles' 'She Loves You', Gerry and The Pacemakers' 'You'll Never Walk Alone' and finally, The Beatles' 'I Want To Hold Your Hand'.

Billy J. Kramer and The Dakotas were just one of the stable of acts

Left: **Listening to a playback in Number Two studio is a serious business for Gerry and the Pacemakers.**

controlled by Brian Epstein and produced by Martin and he was one of the most difficult singers the producer ever had to deal with. "I treated each of the other artists I had totally differently; it was the only way to work with so many acts at one time. Billy's voice for instance wasn't the strongest or best in the world so I decided to always double track him and I used a wound up piano to cover some of the bad notes."

Martin, who over the years had managed to use each of the studios at Abbey Road, now found himself spending more and more time in Studio Two with its lofty control room at the top of a flight of stairs. "I used all the studios and got to know each of them very well. Studio Three was mainly a rehearsal studio but was perfect for chamber music while Number One was used for big orchestras, not just classical but for pop acts who had full orchestras as well and, as I got used to it, I came to appreciate the fantastic string sound you could achieve in there. Studio Two was mainly used for the pop stuff and it hasn't changed a bit since the Fifties; wisely I think. A lot of people have talked about the magic of Studio Two but I think this is all a bit of a myth; people seem to say things like that just because of all the great records made there."

Billy J Kramer in Studio Two control room

One band who weren't using Studio Two were the Manchester group found by Martin's assistant, Ron Richards. The Hollies still use Abbey Road today and guitarist Tony Hicks looks back fondly to those early days. "We did a two-hour audition in Studio Three when we first came down and recorded two sides, the A and B- sides of our first single which turned out to be a hit, and it's sort of gone on from there.

"Basically the studios haven't changed a helluva lot because they were literally twin track when we first came here. In all honesty all studios were exciting to us at that point because we were still in our teens and going into a studio was unheard of. In those early days you didn't spend an awful lot of time in the studios, we came in to do a single and were out in a matter of hours. Even though the place was full of groups from the North of England we didn't seem to see much of each other. The sessions were still very strict and I remember that the deal we were on with EMI meant that we were paid just like the staff; some guy used to come round the studios with brown envelopes with your weeks wages inside... we got something like a farthing a record in those days."

Hicks and The Hollies were just like so many of the groups that went into Abbey Road in the late Fifties and early Sixties; totally unconcerned with the technicalities of recording. "We were just intent on playing and singing. We left the rest of it to the people who knew about those things. We were not really consulted in those days. We'd get hold of a song, or write one, and then rehearse it on the road and then come into the studios and do it in one go. It was great in those days because you had to have it sounding right between you, both vocally and instrumentally, but later on when you had more tracks you could put something down between you and add instruments later. I think this tended to make people lazy and we find nowadays that the more we go on the worse it gets."

The relationship between The Hollies and Richards was one that grew out of a mutual respect for each other's talent. "He never tried to change our style

*Left: **The original Hollies (from left to right) Tony Hicks, Allan Clarke, Graham Nash, Bobby Elliott and Eric Haydock assemble in Studio Two.***

when we came here because we had a pretty distinctive sound but he did help me to play simpler, I was a complicated guitarist, putting too many notes in, which is something a lot of people do before they have actually recorded in a studio. It may sound fine when you're zooming about impressing yourself but when you hear it played back on tape it sounds an absolute jumble. I used to end up cutting out 50 per cent of my notes to get what we needed on record."

Even with the guitar notes cut out, hearing their music played back over loudspeakers came as a shock to The Hollies. "The first time we ever heard it played back it sounded far better than it ever did when we recorded it, thank God! Some of our early records have a diabolical drum sound when you listen to them now; it sounds as if there are cannons going off. We used all the studios and even though Number Two became known as the pop studio we really didn't have any preference... a studio's just a studio."

Bruce Welch, along with The Shadows and Cliff Richard, had become a firm fan of Studio Two by this time. "It was the pop studio – 'Move It' was done there and so was 'Apache' and then The Beatles went in there. Before Cliff and ourselves went there and began making hits nobody had really established the studio but by the time we'd finished, along with Helen Shapiro and Frank Ifield, then everybody wanted to move in. It's strange to hear people talking about the studio as the place where The Beatles recorded all their hits because before that they used to say, 'This is the place where Cliff and the Shadows recorded all their hit records'."

With four years experience in the business, Bruce was interested to see the latest pop phenomenon which had taken the country by storm. "I remember The Beatles coming in and as the 'old pros' we went to get to know them. It was

My Life' there is an Elizabethan piano solo in it, so he would put things like that in. We would say, 'Play like Bach', or something, so he would put 12 bars in there. He helped us develop a language to talk to musicians."

Norman Smith, too, was affected by the work of The Beatles, and the man who dismissed them as louts when he first saw them and was unimpressed when he heard them was by now a big fan. "As a pop engineer I was always looking for new sounds and we used to get paid ten bob (50p) for any new ideas that were tested and then accepted into the studio. We could apply to use Studio Two when it was empty to experiment and people's dedication to developing the recording industry in this country was quite astounding.

Opposite page: **A music lesson for the 'FabFour' from producer George Martin during The Beatles' early days in Abbey Road.**

"We had done the first Beatles album in one day but by the time we did the third LP we had four track and they were just as interested as the rest of us in creating new sounds. They also changed the discipline of the place. The local council had imposed a midnight ban on recording, this was after EMI had eased their own 10 o'clock curfew, not because of the noise, although the echo chamber still leaked a bit, but mainly because it was a residential area and car doors slamming and people shouting used to annoy the neighbours. But they changed all that as well.

"They worked exactly when they wanted to work and brought absolute chaos to Abbey Road; bringing police with dogs to the studio and causing long traffic jams. To this day I don't know how they did it but girls used to get into the studio. One day I went to a cupboard to get a tambourine or something and found two girls in there. Unfortunately Paul was standing about 10 yards behind me and they immediately made a dash for him. I rugby tackled them and the only way I could control them was by holding them by the hair at arm's length – they were kicking and scratching as I marched them to the front door. They were everywhere in those days, just like bloody ants."

Below: **You couldn't keep it quiet. The fans always seemed to know when The Beatles were at Abbey Road.**

The fact that The Beatles themselves spent so much time in Abbey Road meant that the fans were milling around outside night and day. So what did The Beatles do while this chaos was going on outside? Norman Smith knows exactly why they spent so much time in the studio. "They rehearsed and routined in there and occasionally, though rarely, wrote songs in there. They didn't really know each other's songs as they didn't really write together. Very often Paul would have a song and the first time the others heard it was in the studio and this happened with John as well. They would swop ideas with each other and get the song exactly right before they recorded it."

George Martin has his own views on why they spent so much time in Abbey Road studios. "Coming to the studio

was a refuge for them. It was the time and place when nobody could get at them. The strange hours for their sessions were really necessary because of the frenetic life they were forced into. Just look at what they used to pack into a year; tours here and overseas, TV, radio, press and general promotion. Recording was important but it had to be squeezed in between everything else and they enjoyed recording much more than touring. They got fed up with the vulnerability of it all – the continual pawing – and needed to escape from time to time."

In order to obtain the privacy they craved The Beatles recorded in almost total isolation but there was a reason for this too. "They got more attempts at intrusion than anybody else," says Martin. "Nobody would bother to try and get into some odd classical session but because it was The Beatles everybody wanted to poke their finger in the door. They decided they wouldn't put up with it although we did occasionally have people who the boys allowed in; they had a lot of hangers on whom they liked to have around."

Because of the tremendous success they had achieved, The Beatles were rewarded with the virtual freedom of the studios and they came and went as

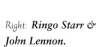

Above: **Paul McCartney**

Right: **Ringo Starr &
John Lennon.**

they pleased, often demanding studios already booked by other artists, which was something that Martin was not in total agreement with. "We were given very much *carte blanche* with Studio Two but we didn't really chuck people out although there were times when pressure was brought to bear and somebody who had the studio booked was told that The Beatles wanted it. I didn't approve of this at all but sometimes the boys would steam-roller people. EMI contributed to this by demanding product and we were often unfairly accused of being arrogant. Personally I always tried to play the game."

The demand for product which came from head office wasn't just for product from The Beatles and Martin found himself, in 1963, trying to supply the company with hit records almost every month. "Brian Epstein helped to make the recording schedule work. 1963 was probably the busiest year of my life; I worked tremendously hard that year and Brian was a good friend. We would meet in the studios and plan the schedules together as he managed most of the people I was dealing with. With The Beatles we aimed for a single every three months and an album twice a year. We would plan a Beatles single for November which meant we could release a Cilla single in October and maybe a Pacemakers single in September.

The results justified all the planning that took place. 'She Loves You' was released in August 1963, reached the No. 1 spot on two separate occasions, going on to become the biggest selling Beatles single of all time. George Martin was setting records too. Out of the 52 weeks in the year, records produced by Martin at Abbey Road were at the top of the charts for 32 weeks, an outstanding achievement which is unlikely to be repeated. Indeed EMI held the No. 1 spot for 43 weeks in that eventful year.

As The Beatles amazing success story continued at full speed, the sedate building in St John's Wood was forced to try and keep up. Peter Vince recalls

The Beatles with engineer Richard Langham, during the recording of their second album, With The Beatles, *in 1963.*

what was happening inside the studios during the mid-Sixties. "People were talking about four track in the most excited way. This enhanced the group sound in particular and at the same time desks were getting bigger and more and more mikes were needed at each session. The Beatles were the great innovators; their music got so complex as they tried to create different sounds. I remember Paul McCartney taking off the front of a bass drum to get a different sound. And their effect on the building was exciting. People couldn't wait for them to come in. People would creep in the control room and try to grab a quick listen to any tapes and try to find out what the next single was going to be. The studios were constantly surrounded by kids and quite often I had to be helped over the railings out the front by the police so that I could go home in the evening."

One man who did visit The Beatles sessions was Tony Hicks of The Hollies. "I used to pop into their sessions if we were in together and Paul used to wander into ours. It would have been most unsociable not to pop your head in if you

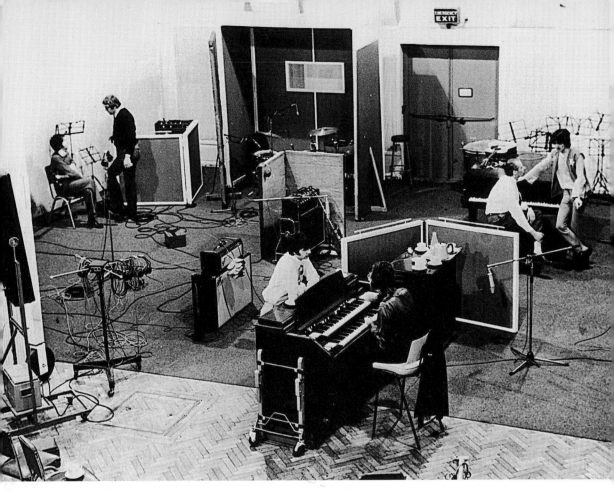

Above: **Deep in conversation (from left to right) in Studio Two are Paul McCartney & Mal Evans; Ringo Starr & John Lennon; George Martin & George Harrison.**

Right: **George and Paul relaxing in their favourite Studio Two, with George Martin.**

Left: **John, Ringo, Mal Evans, Paul & George Martin**

Below: **Rehearsal time in Studio Two for George, Paul, George Martin and John.**

John Lennon &
Ringo Starr

happened to be in the studios at the same time. I don't think they ever got particularly isolated or cut off – we were here when they did their last sessions and they were still very friendly. But a lot of what they did was down to the drugs, I'm sure of that. They were all stoned out of their minds and used to keep on all day and night. Recording all night has never appealed to me but it did become the norm in the studios after The Beatles had changed the rules."

While they may not have been affected by The Beatles' strange working hours, The Hollies were just as interested in creating new sounds and playing around in the studio. "I remember that one day Allan Clarke sang in Studio Two with a bass drum over his head to create some particular sound we wanted. We did a lot of stupid things on reflection to create sounds; once we had everybody banging bottles together, kicking doors and scratching walls to make a sort of manic sound."

Bruce Welch was another who sat and watched the changes taking place at Abbey Road. "The Beatles changed so much. They wrote in the studios which was unheard of and they worked all through the night which was something people had never done before. None of it seemed to matter because they were

The Beatles and they would probably have bought the place if anyone had complained. The silly thing is that I'm sure that for all the time they spent in the studios they really didn't know how things worked. George Martin was perfect for The Beatles because for years he'd been making Sellers' records and all those comedy things with lots of splicing. He was able to create the sounds that The Beatles wanted, particularly when four track came in, because you could overdub two or three times which was a great advantage. If they had come to Norrie it would have been very different because he wasn't into all that. He made dead straight pop stuff."

While Martin was the right man for The Beatles, Paramor was just right for Cliff Richard and The Shadows. "Norrie was a song man and dead right for us and Cliff," says Bruce. "Our things were very melodic and Cliff's were classic pop songs but The Beatles were so inventive. When we did numbers in Studio Two we'd look up at Norrie and he'd say, 'That's OK, next please'. Sometimes we'd never even hear it, Norrie would just say that that was the one to be released and that was it. But gradually we became aware of dropping in notes if a bum note had been played during the take. In those days the trouble was that Hank was a marvellous player but so erratic. You'd get a three and half minute take and he'd screw up the last note which meant doing the whole thing again. Now we could just drop in the last note and everybody accepts that it's just part of trying to make the best record you can."

Helen Shapiro, who had toured with The Beatles during early 1963, maintained her friendship with them and was one of the privileged few to be allowed into sessions. "One day when I'd finished in Studio One, I went into the control room in Number Two to see them when they were doing 'Can't Buy Me Love'. They insisted on playing it back to me and then Ringo had to go down and put on extra cymbal tracks over the top – apparently this was something he did quite often on their records. I had a cousin with me who wanted to meet The Beatles and John Lennon insisted we went into the studio with him while Ringo was recording; we sat on the steps with him. John was always a gentleman to me and he used to look after me on the road because I was the baby. They were the first artists to go into the studio and say, 'I've not quite finished yet', and then rehearse a song and add things to it. This effectively put an end to the old concept of three-hour sessions."

Vera Samwell, who had arrived at the studios 20 years earlier to do the studio bookings as a part-time job, now found herself with the problem of trying to keep everyone happy. "People were quite often asked to move out of the studios for The Beatles and although some of them created a bit of a fuss they always came back to the studios. Things had become much more relaxed by now and some of the artists, Cliff Richard for instance, didn't mind if you sat at the back during their sessions.

"The Beatles just recorded whenever they wanted to. They went into the studios and didn't come out until they'd finished and nobody ever had the nerve to ask them to leave. The scenes outside the building were absolutely fantastic, particularly when they first returned from America. The studio manager, Chick

..

Fowler, had got worried about what might happen and called in a lot of security people and police before anything did happen.

"People naturally got curious about all this security and formed a large crowd and then the school children joined and finally the fans arrived. It was chock-a-bloc for six days but they never saw anything of The Beatles because they always left very late at night if they left at all. This was a regular occurrence when The Beatles were in the studios and we never could work out how the fans found out when The Beatles were here; it was supposed to be a secret."

Sir Joseph Lockwood, even though he was based a couple of miles away from the studio in EMI's Manchester Square offices, was aware of what was going on at Abbey Road. "I met The Beatles very early on and found them very easy going and very amusing. Ultimately they did change the recording schedules of Abbey Road but that wasn't any real problem except for the noise that leaked out the back when they had all-night sessions."

While it's true to say that The Beatles dominated the recording activities of Abbey Road during the mid-Sixties, others making records were as diverse as Cilla Black and a Salvation Army group called the Joy Strings. Cilla had come from Liverpool with Brian Epstein and been offered to George Martin along with the job lot of groups who made up the Mersey Beat package. "I remembered her as a screeching, yelling rock'n'roll singer and it was Brian who decided she could be a ballad singer. Her first record, 'Love Of The Loved', had not done much but Brian found this Burt Bacharach/Hal David song, 'Anyone Who Had A Heart', and I wanted to give it to Shirley Bassey. But Brian insisted that Cilla could do it." She did it in style reaching No. 1 and following it up with another No. 1, 'You're My World', before going on to make sixteen more chart records and create a hugely successful career in television.

Cilla Black tries to persuade producer, George Martin, to pay for the tea.

Cilla Black wasn't the only new artist brought to Martin's attention. "I was brought a large number of people and although I had to turn most of them down I never regretted it as I had more than my fair share already. I always enjoyed recording a tremendous cross section of artists and I was still working with people like Shirley Bassey and Matt Monro. I couldn't be greedy and ask for more."

There had always been something of a rift between the classical and the pop divisions at Abbey Road and the seemingly never-ending stream of hit records that poured out of the building did little to help the situation as Peter Vince well remembers. "There had always been a split between the two areas; the fact that their music differs so much probably serves to create different attitudes and reactions. Basically I think the classical people would have preferred the pop artists and the producers to clear out of Abbey Road altogether although at one time there was talk of the classical people themselves leaving and Abbey Road becoming one large pop and MOR studio with the huge classical studio being converted into three smaller pop studios. The idea didn't get much past the planning stage.

"But on the whole I suppose the two areas do get along reasonably well. In the Sixties, when the canteen had just been opened, the classical people would never frequent it. They would send a second engineer down for tea and cakes; the classical artists never actually went into the canteen. André Previn was one of the first people to break this tradition but, unfortunately, when he first went in and ordered a cup of tea, he was asked abruptly 'Are you a musician?' by the tea lady. Sir Adrian Boult was another who broke with tradition; he used to love the steak and kidney pie they served down there and later you could walk in there and see two Pauls in the same queue – Tortelier and McCartney – and nobody would bat an eye."

'Are you a musician?' Tea lady Dolly Wheeler confronts André Previn.

While both the industry and the media heaped their praises on George Martin as the man who directed The Beatles in the studio, Martin himself is quick to acknowledge the vital part played by their manager, Brian Epstein. "His part in it all has tended to be put down; history has treated him unfairly. He was incredibly honest and a little bit naïve but he entered a world that was totally alien to him. I don't think The Beatles will ever acknowledge how lucky they were to meet up with a man who was devoted to them so completely and an honest man to boot. Similarly they were lucky to meet up with a producer who was honest because there were a lot of sharks in the world, even then."

His own contribution to the music of The Beatles was still immense even as they changed direction with their *Help!* and *Rubber Soul* albums in 1965. "It's probably correct to say that I was as interested as they were in creating new sounds and experimenting in the studios and other producers may have been reluctant to give them the freedom they needed. They were never the sort of people you put in a studio to make three-minute pop songs with a nice arrangement; they needed much more than that and that was the real joy of working with them."

Paul McCartney had written a song called 'Yesterday' – which has since been recorded by over 150 different artists – and Martin in his own autobiography, *All You Need Is Ears*, explained his part in the recording of a song that has become a standard in the truest sense of the word. "There was certainly no genius attached to my role in the early stages. There were probably a number of producers who could have done just as well. The turning point probably came with the song 'Yesterday'. That was when, as I can see in retrospect, I started to leave my hallmark on the music, when a style started to emerge which was partly of my making. It was on 'Yesterday' that I started to score their music. It was on 'Yesterday' that we first used instruments or musicians other than The Beatles and myself (I had often played piano where it was necessary). On

'Yesterday' the added ingredient was no more or less than a string quartet; and that, in the pop world of those days, was quite a step to take. It was with 'Yesterday' that we started breaking out of the phase of using just four instruments and went into something more experimental, though our initial experiments were severely limited by the fairly crude tools at our disposal and had simply to be moulded out of my recording experience."

John Lennon, when asked about the *Rubber Soul* LP, was quoted as follows: "We were just getting better technically and musically that's all. Finally we took over the studio. In the early days we had to take what we were given, we didn't know how you could get more bass. We were learning the technique on *Rubber Soul*. We were more precise about making the album... that's all and we took over the cover and everything."

In 1965 Martin made up his mind to leave Abbey Road and set up his own recording studios. The split had begun a year earlier when his salary had risen to £3,000 a year and Martin started negotiating with EMI for some sort of incentive scheme to reward him for his work with The Beatles, which had earned the company many millions of pounds. "I thought the person doing all the hard work should be entitled to some recompense." EMI didn't agree and so Martin left after fifteen years with the company, many of them spent in the dark recesses of Abbey Road studios. He didn't make the situation any easier by taking with him to his newly formed Associated Independent Recording (AIR for short) Peter Sullivan, John Burgess and Ron Richards, stalwarts of Abbey Road. He didn't ask the advice of The Beatles but just hoped they would still want to use him and they did, which meant that even as a non-EMI man he was to go on producing in Abbey Road. He was the pioneer of the freelance producer now hired by an artist to produce them in whichever studio they choose.

"Even after I left I was still welcomed back at Abbey Road and made to feel at home. There was no resentment at all with the studio people and my only bitterness was over the non-payment of any royalties on any of The Beatles recordings, but that was an argument with EMI, not with the studios. The people in the studios were just as badly off as I was at that time; I was just the one who escaped."

Setting up his own studios gave Martin the opportunity to experience some of the problems which Abbey Road had no doubt encountered over the years. "EMI studios has always been difficult to fathom out. If I had been asked to run the studios profitably I would have found it very difficult and having left to form my own studios, which became Abbey Road's main rivals, I appreciated some of the problems a little better than I did at the time."

The man who benefited most from Martin's decision to leave was Norman Smith who was offered the job as head of the Parlophone label and he started his new career in the most memorable fashion. "The first thing I had to do was get an artists' roster together and I had this idea of sending out a letter to all the agents and managers telling them I was now the producer and that I was looking for new acts. Unfortunately one of the letters went to an executive of a rival record company who was listed as an agent. He wrote to the chairman of EMI alleging that I was attempting to illegally poach artists from other record companies. I got my knuckles severely rapped for that and I'd only been in the job two weeks."

Smith also has the distinction of having a song accepted for a Beatles album at a time when they only recorded their own compositions. "I had written this song for John and although I knew they didn't record anything but their own material I offered it to them during a session in Number Two studio. They were doing an album and John called up to say that they couldn't finish the album because they were a song short and would have to do something over the weekend. I told George Martin that I had this song and he told me to go down to the studio and play it to them. I was too scared to do that and said that I'd prefer to play it to just one of them. George asked Paul to come up to the control room and I told him that I had this song which they might be interested in. We went along to another room where there was a piano and I played it to him. He liked it and suggested we get John in as he thought it would be right for him. Well John liked it as well and they said they'd do it on Monday if I could make some demos for them to listen to over the weekend."

Dick James, The Beatles publisher, was in the studio at the same time and when he heard what was going on he offered Smith £15,000 for the song. Smith was reluctant to do the deal. "I thought that if he was offering £15,000 it must be worth more so I told him I'd think about it. I made the demos for The Beatles and waited for Monday to arrive."

Thinking he had made his fortune overnight, Smith spent an anxious weekend and he was back in the studios bright and early on Monday morning raring to go. "When The Beatles came in they said 'Good morning' and disappeared down into the studio without saying a word about my song. Finally Paul called me down and explained that they had suddenly realised over the weekend that there wasn't a song for Ringo on the album – he always sang on one track on every album – and that John had written something for him over the weekend and that would be the last track on the album. But they said not to worry as they would keep my song for the next album. But they never used it and I never heard another thing about it. The song has never been recorded and I've still got it somewhere."

Even with his production co-operative and available as a freelance producer, Martin was regularly back in the familiar surroundings of Abbey Road with the group which had enabled him to branch out on his own. With a single long overdue, Martin and The Beatles were forced to sacrifice two songs which were packed with creativity and emphasised the differing musical directions that John Lennon and Paul McCartney were intent on following. 'Strawberry Fields Forever' and 'Penny Lane' were songs written individually by the two young men who were rapidly establishing themselves as major songwriters as well as formidable hit makers. Cilla Black, The Fourmost, Billy J. Kramer, Peter and Gordon and Ella Fitzgerald were just a few who had recorded their songs; the great American jazz singer had even chosen Abbey Road as the venue when she recorded 'Can't Buy Me Love' with producer, Ron Richards.

Above: **Peter Asher (right) and Gordon Waller – reached the number one spot in 1964 with 'World Without Love', a song specially written for them by Paul McCartney.**

Below: **The incomparable Ella Fitzgerald, during the recording of her version of The Beatles' 'Can't Buy Me Love' in Abbey Road.**

Paul's idea for the finishing touch to 'Penny Lane' was based firmly on the piccolo trumpet passage in Bach's Brandenburg Concerto No. 2 and George Martin invited David Mason of the New Philharmonia Orchestra into the studios for the extraordinary job of playing the notes which Paul hummed for him. Take one of John's 'Strawberry Fields Forever' is far removed from the released version, which was created by editing together the first minute of take seven with the remainder coming from take twenty six. This was despite the fact that these two takes were in different keys and different tempos, causing quite a headache for George Martin and Geoff Emerick, who after careful manipulation of the speeds of both versions managed to make a perfect match. Paul and John's compositions were released as a double 'A' side and reached No. 2 in the charts.

In 1966 Mickie Most returned to Abbey Road studios for the first time since his brief encounter seven years earlier and noticed the difference immediately. "The place was four track when I went in there to record Donovan's 'Sunshine Superman' and the three-hour sessions were still operating in Studio Three for everybody except The Beatles. We always got a minimum of two tracks done in a session and quite often two A-sides and a B-side when the red light went on you used to get on with it."

Most was soon made aware of The Beatles' importance at Abbey Road and he realised that they could get away with virtually anything. "They began the all-night recording because they had nothing else to do. They used to sleep in there; they had beds installed and all sorts of things. John Lennon once told me that because they couldn't get it right on stage they decided not to play live anymore and just record instead. The old three-hour sessions became a bit silly for what they wanted to do so they started the long sessions. They had a lot of time to fill and they lived in the studios and just experimented. And out of it came all sorts of great things but people shouldn't forget that they had the help of a very good producer in George Martin."

Another act Most took into Abbey Road were Herman's Hermits who were to notch up over a dozen hits in just over six years, and the producer noticed this time the efforts that were going on to improve the look of the place. "I remember they used to have chequered floor tiles and John Lennon and I used to play hop scotch on them. It was very hospitalised, though they tried to tart it up with carpet up the walls. I never had any technical problems in there because they've always re-invested in equipment and they have very high quality technical staff. The amazing thing was that if anything went wrong with a desk, the engineer would just phone for a guy – there'd be a pool of technicians on call there – and one of them would come down and fix it; the engineer would never touch it. Without doubt it was the biggest staffed studio I'd ever seen but it is a big complex; that big studio is big enough to park aeroplanes in."

Mickie Most, head of his own RAK recording company, never actually worked for EMI and his visits to Abbey Road were always as a paying client, but that didn't give him dispensation from the rift which existed between the classical and pop people. "I had murders in there once with one of those classical people. I was doing a playback in Studio Three and he was in the old listening room at the front of the building. During the quiet passages in his classical piece he could hear rock'n'roll coming through the wall from the studio. He came in and started giving me a blasting and I had to remind him it was the pop stars – The Beatles, Animals, Herman and Gerry and The Pacemakers – who were making the profits for EMI not the classical records. I didn't even work for the company, I was a paying client, and I got this guy coming in shouting at me."

Bottom: **A hair-raising experience! Comedian Ken Dodd recorded his number one hit, 'Tears', in Abbey Road in 1965.**
Below: **Play it again Burt! Hit group Manfred Mann (left to right) Mike Vickers; Paul Jones; Manfred Mann; Tom McGuiness; producer John Burgess, and Mike Hugg get together with American composers, Hal David (in front) and Burt Bacharach (at the piano).**

Although he recorded many of his artists there, including The Yardbirds and CCS, Most did not bring all his up and coming pop stars into Abbey Road and there was a very good reason why one group from Newcastle found themselves elsewhere. "In the mid-Sixties the expensive studios were charging between £8 and £10 an hour and Abbey Road was a little more than that. But not only was it more expensive, they were totally inflexible on their times. When I wanted to record The Animals during their UK tour with Chuck Berry we had to start at eight in the morning and Abbey Road refused to open up before 10 am so I had to go to another studio. On that session with The Animals we started at 8 am and by 8.15 am we had done the first track, 'House Of The Rising Sun', and found ourselves with two and three-quarter hours to spare. So we made an album and as the price was £8 an hour, we completed an album for £24 which was a good deal. We also asked Abbey Road about recording at midnight but they wouldn't do that either."

The list of artists who entered Abbey Road during those golden years grew almost daily with Manfred Mann, The Seekers, Ken Dodd, Cliff Bennett and The Rebel Rousers, Simon Dupree, The George Mitchell Minstrels, Morecambe and Wise and Gene Vincent, the American rock'n'roll star signed to EMI's

The Seekers came all the way from Australia to Abbey road and (from left to right) Keith Potger, Bruce Woodley, Judith Durham and Athol Guy, were rewarded with two number one hits in 1965.

American company, Capitol. Bob Barratt remembers Vincent's visit with special affection. "He was one of my favourite artists and it was a great experience for me to work with him. He had decided to base himself in England and I was fortunate enough to write a few songs for him; things like 'King Of Fools'. He was a very talented man and, surprisingly in view of his public image, a very humble man. Right up until the end of his life, although we were the same age, he always called me sir. He was a very mixed up young man and he suffered almost permanent pain from the injuries to his leg that he had suffered in a motor cycle accident. Off stage he was quiet and humble but when he got in front of a microphone he sprang into life."

Working with Norrie Paramor meant that Barratt found himself involved in all sorts of recording, from male voice choirs to organ recitals. "Norrie got me interested in a lot of squarer things and slowly I began to appreciate Welsh choirs, brass band recitals and Reginald Dixon's organ playing. He also allowed me to work with great artists like Stan Tracey and Dakota Staton and instilled in me the benefits of rehearsing before going into the studio. Because most of the sessions were still only three hours long we used to have to work very fast and routining beforehand was the only way you could fit anything in. Even when we could work all through the night I still rehearsed everything before going into the studio."

Barratt also had the job of attempting to revive the flagging careers of early Sixties solo stars like Helen Shapiro. "By this time she had become pretty ancient – she was at least 18 – and I did a few singles with her and an album where she actually recorded four of my songs but, unfortunately, the public were not prepared to accept her as anything but a schoolgirl star and at 18 she was being criticised for being past it."

One man who wasn't past it was Vince Hill who had spent many years as a radio singer before Barratt brought him into EMI. "I met with great opposition when I signed Vince but I believed he had a good voice and could make hit records. It took a little while and a lot of people pressured me to drop him but we persevered and finally he came good with a song that he in fact found. I wanted to do a dramatic French ballad as the next A-side but he insisted we did this song called 'Edelweiss'. I agreed to do it just to humour him but it was so good that we had to release it and it was the record that really launched his career."

At this time Wally Ridley had decided to record The George Mitchell Minstrels whom he had seen on television and thought would be just as successful on record. "It took me 18 months to persuade George Mitchell to come into the studios but in the end it was really worthwhile." Morecambe and Wise were another act from the world of television that Ridley brought into Abbey Road and, even if the results were not successful in terms of record sales, it turned out to be great fun with the pair of them reducing the orchestra to tears with their antics and Eric Morecambe continually slapping people around the face with the famous double-handed slap which was a feature of their television shows.

Ridley, Townsend and Eltham were the trio who sped up to Scotland to record the likes of Jimmy Shand and Andy Stewart and while Ken remembers the long drinking sessions that went on throughout the night, Ridley describes the whole set up as... "very Heath Robinson where I had to arrange the music, play the piano and run the recording session."

The Abbey Road mobile unit was also on duty when Norman Newell recorded the great Judy Garland and her daughter Liza Minnelli at the London Palladium and Townsend will never forget that session. "The whole thing was being done in front of a live audience and was being filmed for television so we had to remain as unobtrusive as possible. This was fine until the plug from the piano microphone came unplugged. I had to creep across the stage, covered in a black cloth, and crawl under the piano to replace the plug and then crawl off again."

To emphasise that it wasn't just hit records that were made in Abbey Road, a Christmas pantomime was recorded there in December 1966 with a galaxy of comedy stars including Tommy Cooper, Dora Bryan, Kenneth Connor, Arthur Haynes and Peggy Mount. While all these slightly offbeat recordings were taking place, Cliff Richard continued making hits in Studio Two. There with him was the evergreen Norrie Paramor but this time Cliff began to see another side of his character. "I'll always remember Norrie as the great gentleman of the business but he was also quite eccentric. Often we'd all arrive at the studio, often there'd be 45 musicians, and Norrie would arrive with his music case. He would lift it onto the desk, open it and then shut it very quickly. Then he got up and went up the stairs to the control room and got someone to go round to his house and get all the arrangements for the orchestra which he'd forgotten. That used to happen quite often but despite the delay we would still get through five songs in a three-hour session."

Peter Vince was the man involved in the sessions with Simon Dupree and Cliff Bennett, and they would often end in complete uproar with the band and the technicians playing practical jokes on each other. "Dupree and his band, The Big Sound, were a crazy crowd. They were great practical jokers with the electric handshakes and exploding fag packets. We used to get our own back by rigging up small explosive devices in the studio which were wired into the control room. As the band moved around the studio we set off these charges which frightened the life out of them. During a session with Cliff Bennett we put a smoke bomb behind one of the guitar amps and set it off during the session. One of the sax players saw the smoke, shouted, 'Christ, the place's on fire', and turned a fire extinguisher on to the amp which didn't do it a lot of good. It was all good fun but sadly those sort of things don't seem to happen anymore."

Peter Andry, from his position as a senior classical producer, was able to view the emerging strength of the pop world and exactly what effect it was having on the classical people. "The classical people have always been too wrapped up in

Above, top: **Karen Dotrice, Harry H Corbett and Frankie Howerd (seated)** *during the recording of* Alice In Wonderland *in 1965.*

Above: **Dirk Bogarde** *recording the narration of* Alice In Wonderland *in 1965*

their own world to take much interest in pop recordings but they certainly knew what was going on with The Beatles if only because of the noise coming from Studio Two which interfered with their own work. There was never too much inter-action between pop and classical; they are two different worlds and I think they always will be. As the shift from Abbey Road being a classically dominated operation took place, we soon realised that, in a commercial environment, it was the pop that was making the bread and we had to accommodate ourselves to that fact." With no inter-action taking place between the two areas, it was no surprise to anyone that George Harrison's visit to a classical session should end in an unsatisfactory manner. "He did come down to a session once and one of my producers, not recognising this scruffy chap, told him to 'bugger off'."

Another new face appeared at Abbey Road in 1966 when a young man named Tim Rice, who had been taken on as management trainee, made the move into EMI's A&R (artists and repertoire) department. "I was seconded to work with Norrie Paramor and Bob Barratt and found myself going to Abbey Road virtually every day. The first session I ever attended was when Bob Barratt produced the GUS Footwear Band and then I went along to some of Norrie's sessions with people like Cliff Richard, The Shadows, Frank Ifield, French artists like Mireille Mathieu and Richard Anthony, and Helen Shapiro."

These visits to Abbey Road and the opportunity to 'sit in' on sessions only served to increase Rice's already consuming passion for pop music. "I learnt about record production from great engineers like Geoff Emerick and Peter Vince who helped me an awful lot. The studio was four track then, which wasn't totally primitive, and I was determined to stick with A&R and fortunately I was able to because I think Norrie had a word with someone on my behalf. I became a fully fledged member of the A&R department and this meant that I had to find acts in my own right. The first solo artist I worked with was Murray Head who was signed to EMI and we were contractually obliged to do a couple of tracks with him, but no one was particularly interested. Murray used to hang around the place until finally Norrie said that, as we had to do the two tracks, I could do them but I wasn't to spend any more than £400. This was my chance to produce records and, in addition to Murray Head, I had a group called Shell. Both the records came out on Columbia at the same time and they both sank like stones... the public were obviously not ready for them."

Putting his humble beginning behind him, Rice ploughed on and found a group called Tales Of Justine whose lead singer, a chap named David Daltrey, happened to be a cousin of The Who's Roger Daltrey. With Rice they made a record entitled 'Albert The Sun Flower' which has a place in pop history even if it never actually earned a place in the pop charts. "It was the last but one pop single released on the HMV label before it went completely classical. The last single was Louis Armstrong's 'What A Wonderful World', which was made in America, so in fact it was the last HMV pop single to come out of Abbey Road. Those were the only three singles I produced myself at Abbey Road and I have to admit that not one of them was a hit."

But Rice did not have to wait long to be involved with a hit record even though he left EMI and went to work for Norrie Paramor, as his personal assistant, when Paramor started his own company. "Even after Norrie left he continued to use Abbey Road, particularly for a Liverpool group called Scaffold which included Paul McCartney's brother, Mike McGear. When we did 'Lily The Pink' Paul McCartney joined in the session and, as Norrie was away a lot of the time, I did a lot of work on that particular record and even sang on it – it was the first No. 1 I ever sang on."

Rice did not work on the next Scaffold hit but was back for the next session, a track called 'Charity Bubbles' and this time he got a joint credit for production with Paramor. "I was convinced that after the previous hits it was bound to chart but it was sod's law and the first record with my name on – produced by Norrie Paramor and Tim Rice – sank without trace. Paul McCartney did a guitar solo on the record and I was left in the control room thinking 'Here's the most successful artist in British popular music and I've got to tell him what to do'. At one point I was convinced he was playing out of tune but I couldn't bring myself to say anything."

However, there was an even more embarrassing moment to come for the young producer. "I had a friend named Martin Wilcox who had been involved in finding Tales Of Justine and vaguely worked in the A&R department. I arrived at Abbey Road for a Scaffold session one day and strolled casually into Number Two control room, half expecting to see Martin in there. There were a couple of people in there and I was asking them if they had seen Martin and did they know where Martin was, when in walked Paul McCartney. I presumed he was working on the Scaffold session and then in walked John Lennon followed by George Harrison and I suddenly realised that this was a Beatles session and I should have been in Studio Three. Not only that but the people in the control room must have thought I was extremely rude going around asking for George Martin by his surname – 'Where's Martin?' I slunk out of the studio and bumped into John Lennon, who I never met on any other occasion, and he said something to me in perfect nonsense Spanish – I felt a right prat.'

There came a time in his career at Abbey Road when Rice believed everything he touched became a disaster area because he was in trouble again when he started to audition an up and coming band of young hopefuls in the studios. "I arrived at the studio at about five to ten for a 10 o'clock start and discovered that the necessary paper work had not arrived. Peter Vince, the engineer, wasn't at all bothered and began setting up the studio for the group who duly arrived for the session. Suddenly Alan Stagge, the studio manager, stormed in and in front of this group, who at the time thought Tim Rice was a big shot at EMI, gave me the all-time bollocking about starting without the proper paperwork. I found the whole thing both upsetting and unnecessary and I took an instant dislike to him there and then. It wasn't a particularly important point and he really shouldn't have bollocked me in front of the group; at worst I was only partly to blame."

Another man who has good reason to remember Scaffold is Herbie Flowers, session musician extraordinaire and for years bass player with the highly

successful group, Sky. "The first session I did at Abbey Road is something I'll never forget. I was up in the loft of the house we then had in Uxbridge, rendering up an old chimney; I'd humped a wheelbarrow up into the loft and poured about 12 buckets of cement into it when my wife told me Laurie Gold, a contractor from EMI, was on the phone and wanted me to go to Abbey Road straight away for a session. This was the break I had been waiting for and I zoomed up to the studios, still covered in cement dust, for the session which was Scaffold with Paul McCartney. When I got home – six quid later – all the cement had solidified in the wheelbarrow up in the loft. I had to leave it up there and so far as I know it's still there."

Norman Smith, who inherited Parlophone from George Martin, had by now not only built up a roster of artists as a result of the letter that got him into hot water, but also had a new label to run. The Harvest label was formed because The Beatles still dominated the Parlophone trademark and a new style of 'underground' music was fast emerging. "As a result of my letter an agent called Bryan Morrison called up and invited me to see a new band he was representing called Pink Floyd," recalls Smith. "So I went along to a club in Tottenham Court Road and what I saw absolutely amazed me. I was still into creating and developing new electronic sounds in the control room and Pink Floyd, I could see, were into exactly the same thing, it was a perfect marriage."

This new relationship blossomed even brighter as new and more advanced equipment was introduced into Abbey Road. "We had four-track equipment but then along came eight-track and very soon afterwards 16-track was installed. The decision to put in 16-track was partly made by accountants and the like, but at the same time the technicians and research people at Hayes were involved. Everything had to be tested and God knows how long they'd been testing it at Hayes before we got our hands on it, but they never realised that the perfect way to have tested it was for us to have worked with it. By the time we got 16-track it was near enough obsolete."

In fact David Gilmour, who joined the original Pink Floyd line-up of Roger Waters, Rick Wright, Nick Mason and Syd Barrett near the end of 1967, remembers attending a meeting at Abbey Road studios to discuss the installation of new equipment. "The studio manager, Alan Stagge, invited me to a meeting with a whole lot of Abbey Road staff to discuss the possibility of introducing eight-track recording equipment to the studio. It was one of the silliest decisions ever made at Abbey Road.

"I said that they should ignore eight-track altogether and switch straight from four-track to 16-track; doing that would save them money and put them in front of most other studios. But the Abbey Road people urged that 16-track would never catch on and the jump to eight-track was a big enough risk. So they changed to eight-track and what happened? A year later they changed it all again... this time to 16-track."

The decision made at that time by EMI meant that Pink Floyd were forced to take part of the recording of their next album, *Meddle*, away from Abbey Road as Gilmour explains. "We went into AIR studios to do most of the work on that album, although a couple of tracks were done at Morgan studios. George Martin had managed to switch his order for eight-track machines to 16-track just in time and we had no choice but to go in there as Abbey Road had decided to stick with eight-track."

The company's reluctance to commit themselves fully to the technical advances of the day was confirmed by the then chairman, Sir Joseph Lockwood. "The Beatles were the big drivers in the development of four, eight and 16-track. Our people were reluctant to follow this idea of more separations as there was no guarantee of it being any better. I always suspected that there was no particular advantage in going over a certain number of tracks. I don't know what the number should be, only that after a while it just gets more complicated."

Before David Gilmour joined Pink Floyd they recorded two chart singles in quick succession – 'Arnold Layne' and the top ten hit, 'See Emily Play', which both came out on the Columbia label prior to the introduction of the new Harvest label. They then went on to make their debut album, *The Piper At The Gates Of Dawn*, produced by Norman Smith, with Syd Barrett, then the crucial figure in the band, rapidly becoming worse for wear throughout the album as a result of his involvement with drugs.

As the hits continued to flow out of Studio Two, the demand for bookings increased as Vera Samwell well remembers. "People were always asking for that studio in particular, especially the American artists. Even if they were using one of the other studios they all wanted to go in and look around Number Two. To us it was just a studio but you couldn't get some people to use any other studio they really believed that just by using the same studio they could make a record as good as The Beatles."

Surprisingly there was a time when Studio Two was under-booked and this opened the way for non-EMI artists to start using Abbey Road. "It was opened up before Alan Stagge arrived in the mid-Sixties but only because Number Two was under-booked. When Stagge arrived he opened the whole building up for use by non-EMI artists and the classical people were furious – they were dead against the idea from the start. That was also when the studios were open day and night even though there was no real refreshment facilities – only a drinks machine at night and a tea service during the day. But we did continue the idea of total secrecy; who was actually recording in Abbey Road was never announced to anyone."

Opposite page:
Pink Floyd (from top)
David Gilmour, Nick Mason, Roger Waters, Rick Wright.

Below: **Producer Norman Newell (left)** *in discussion with Lionel Bart (composer of the international hit musical* Oliver), *during the Abbey Road recording of* Blitz!
Bottom: **From left to right, in Studio Three control room: EMI label manager, Mike Sloman; Georgie Fame; P J Proby and producer, Tony Palmer.**

As more and more artists arrived at Abbey Road one thing became painfully clear to everyone involved with the studios... the car park was far too small. The rule became artists only in the car park while session players, backing singers and other sundry musicians had to park their cars out in the street. Unfortunately not all the artists could get into the car park which resulted in a few complaints. Herbie Flowers and his colleagues in Sky posed a real problem to everybody. "When we had a big session on there was a real scramble for the odd spaces in the car park which the percussionist usually won because he carted about a ton and a half of equipment around with him. That's the only criticism I've got about the place, the car park is really too small for the amount of business that goes on there." That sort of philosophical attitude is not taken by everyone faced with the prospect of parking in the street, as Vera Samwell recalls, "Des O'Connor refused to record here again after finding no parking space reserved for him. He finished off the session he was doing, said he was never coming back to Abbey Road, walked out and has never set foot inside the building since."

Maestro of the sitar – Ravi Shankar – became a close friend of George Harrison during the late Sixties and also a regular visitor to Abbey Road.

As he got to know Abbey Road, Tim Rice found himself visiting all sorts of sessions, including a couple of classical recordings. "I only went to a couple of classical sessions and I was amazed at the amount of editing done in classical recording. I thought the pop people were the only ones who cheated but the classical people did even more of it." He also remembers a very special session with Cliff Richard. "I was working with Norrie Paramor when suddenly Paul McCartney walked in to meet Cliff – I think it was one of the first times they had met – and I remember thinking to myself, 'God, Cliff Richard meets Paul McCartney, this is a scoop for *Disc*'." (A sixties weekly pop music paper)

The Beatles were still causing chaos in Abbey Road, none more so than John Lennon, and Tim Rice arrived at the studio one morning to find a heated discussion going on in Studio Two. "All these people were huddled together having a huge discussion. Apparently John Lennon had completely dismantled a new piece of equipment which EMI had just developed. One of the backroom chaps had this phaser thing for The Beatles and Lennon, during the session the night before, had taken the thing apart and put all the parts out neatly in a row in the studio, in order of size. The guy came in that morning and found his creation in something like 141 parts."

Creatively, however, 1967 was the year in which The Beatles reached a high point and the album which emerged that year has become all things to all men. The stories of George Martin's involvement in an album which became more bizarre by the minute are documented in his own book *All You Need Is Ears*. He recalls Lennon's idea for the song, 'Being For The Benefit Of Mr Kite!', involving the pair of them playing electric organs to create a hurdy gurdy effect. But that wasn't the end of it. "It still didn't sound right but I found the answer. I got together a lot of recordings of old Victorian steam organs playing traditional tunes, Sousa marches and so on. I couldn't use even a snatch of any one of them that would be identified so I dubbed a few records on to a tape and gave it to the engineer. I told the engineer to take a minute out of one, a minute out of another and half a minute of another and so on and then cut each length of tape into pieces about a foot long and fling them up in the air. We had about 60 pieces of tape and they were collected up in any order and stuck together. Any that sounded too much like the original were turned around and added backwards until finally I arrived at a whole amalgam of carousel noises which we used as a background 'wash' to give the impression of a circus."

As The Beatles worked their way through *Sgt Pepper's Lonely Hearts' Club Band,* Martin became more and more aware of the group's involvement with drugs even though, like naughty schoolboys, they sloped off into the Abbey Road toilets so as not to annoy their producer who took a disapproving view of it all. In his *Rolling Stone* interview with Jann Wenner in 1970, Lennon recounts one of his drug experiences during the making of *Sgt Pepper.* "I never took it [LSD] in the studios. Once I thought I was taking some uppers and I was in the state of handling it. I can't remember what album it was, but I took it and I just noticed... I suddenly got scared on the mike. I thought I felt ill and I thought I was going to crack. I said I must get some air. They all took me upstairs on the roof and George Martin was looking at me funny and then it dawned on me I must have taken acid. I said, 'Well I can't go on, you'll have to do it and I'll just stay and watch'. They had all been very kind and they carried on making the record."

Martin remembers that night well enough. "Because of all the kids out at the front of the building there was no where else to take John except on the roof of Studio Two. Then I suddenly realised that the only protection around the edge of the roof was a parapet about six inches high, with a sheer drop of about 90 feet to the ground below and I had to keep John away from the edge."

The climax of the album was to be a piece entitled 'A Day In The Life' which began life as John's song, inspired by pieces in the newspaper, and then Paul added a dream sequence which fitted nicely into the concept. But they were undecided about the middle section, so knowing that something would eventually be added they had Mal Evans count out the bars 1–24, and to mark the end of this section an alarm clock was sounded. The problem of what to put into those 24 bars was solved when Paul suggested a full symphony orchestra. Martin booked only half an orchestra (39 players) and then Paul asked for them all to come in full evening dress and Martin to come in similar attire. Tim Rice happened to be in the studio that same evening. "After a Scaffold session I went down to the canteen for a coffee. There was nobody else there except the women behind the counter and suddenly all four Beatles walked in. I was speechless; there I was in the canteen on my own with The Beatles. I tried to hide in the corner. I was so overwhelmed, while the girls behind the counter didn't seem the least bit concerned."

Right: *A close up of the EMI mixing desk in 1967, showing clearly how basic it was compared with the consoles of today.*

Opposite page: *Rehearsal time for George Martin, The Beatles and the orchestra, before the live transmission of 'All You Need is Love' to an estimated 350 million viewers worldwide.*

Not content with fitting the orchestra out in full evening dress, The Beatles handed out funny hats and the leader of the orchestra, David McCallum, wore a bright red nose while violinist, Erich Gruenberg, held his bow in a giant gorilla's paw. The final chord of the album involved only the Beatles and Mal Evans playing pianos as hard as possible while engineer Geoff Emerick, in the control room, held the faders (which controlled the volume input from the studio) right down in the moment of impact. As the sound died away he moved the faders right up and held the sound for 45 seconds catching everything, including the studio's air conditioning. But The Beatles were not finished there, they later recorded odd chants which were snipped out and put into the run out groove of the record so that it went round and round for ever.

Imaginative Beatles fans came to the conclusion that if you played it backwards the phrase said something obscene and even Paul's final private joke was discovered; he had put on a note of 15,000 hertz which could only be heard by dogs saying, "We never record anything for animals, let's put on something which only a dog can hear". Paul McCartney told Paul Gambaccini, in a 1974 interview with *Rolling Stone*: "The piece at the end of *Sgt Pepper,* that backward thing. It was some piece of conversation that we recorded and turned backwards. After I'd been told by some fans what it was supposed to say I went

Above: The Beatles during their satellite performance of 'All You Need Is Love'.

inside and played it studiously, turned it backwards with my thumb against the motor and did it backwards. And there it was, sure as anything: 'We'll f— you like Superman'."

McCartney also recalled the part he was playing at that time with his bass guitar. "I was getting into bass playing on *Sgt Pepper*. Bass was coming to the fore in the mixes. We were starting to take over ourselves and bass was coming to the fore, I had to do something with it. George was not very involved in that album; he had just one song really. It was really the only time during the whole album I can remember his turning up."

Harrison, in Hunter Davies' book, *The Beatles*, reflected on the group's decision to abandon touring and concentrate solely on recording, the difference being emphasised by the fact that while their first album was done in one day and cost about £400, *Sgt Pepper* took four months and cost over £25,000. "Now that we only play in the studio, and not anywhere else we haven't got a clue about what we're going to do. We have to start from scratch, thrashing it out in the studio, doing it the hard way. If Paul has written a song, he comes into

the studio with it in his head. It's very hard for him to give it to us and for us to get it. When we suggest something, it might not be what he wants because he hasn't got it in his head. So it takes a long time. Nobody knows what the tunes sound like till we've recorded them and listened to them afterwards."

The *Sgt Pepper* album not only revolutionised the concept of an album in musical terms it also signalled a breakthrough in recording techniques when Ken Townsend, acutely aware of the limitations which four-track imposed on the group's creativity, invented a system whereby two four-track machines could be linked together. "For the very last track on the album, 'A Day In The Life', George Martin asked if I could link four-track machines in sync. I did this by recording a 50 Hz tone on one track of the first machine and using this suitably amplified to drive the second machine. Although the method worked, one problem was to get the second machine to start at the right time at the remix stage. Thus it offered a maximum of seven tracks and the need for even more tracks was blatantly obvious."

Engineer Peter Vince agrees with Townsend's assessment of the situation.

"*Sgt Pepper* was done on four-track but in fact two four-tracks were linked together and that really signalled that four-track wasn't sufficient. At first there were very few gimmicks around – in fact echo was the only thing that could have been called a gimmick – and again The Beatles were the ones who wanted new and different sounds; they achieved them by doing things like phasing and 'flanging'."

While the world heralded the *Sgt Pepper* album as a breakthrough in record-ing techniques, George Martin agrees that the album was a bit of a nightmare to record with the limited resources available, but is not totally convinced that it was the major breakthrough so many people claimed. "The Beatles were a major part of my life for nine years but it is difficult to differentiate between recordings. I mean working on *Sgt Pepper* was very much like working on *Swingin' Sellers* or the *Best of Sellers,* we used the same kind of techniques. It's an equal toss between Sellers, Flanders & Swann, Bernard Cribbins and The Beatles. I wouldn't take any one of them as being something to be more proud of than any other. Technically, *Sgt Pepper* was not particularly innovative – I've heard it described as a watershed but I don't agree. For instance a lot of the work done by Norman Smith paved the way for *Sgt Pepper,* the innovation of *Sgt Pepper* – which began with 'Strawberry Fields' and 'Penny Lane' – was more artistic than technical."

Martin welcomed the artists' interest in the work of recording. "As time went by artists got more interested in the technical side. I welcomed that, particularly with The Beatles. The studio became a workshop, a permanent experi-mental thing. The Beatles were an example of how well artists could adapt to the technical side but not many other people did. It seemed to work with them and tracks became things that everybody got involved with. On something like 'Tomorrow Never Knows', which was before Sgt *Pepper,* it became a combina-tion of tape loops.

"I turned the control desk into an organ by having tapes going continually on the machine, with people – including The Beatles – holding the tape tension by means of a pencil and we had a total of eight machines in different control rooms throughout the building, all linked up. We had this swirling sound, and you can't do that with one pair of fingers, so we were all doing panning and creating a montage of sound."

Sir Joseph Lockwood had come to view The Beatles in a different light. "In many ways they were a bloody nuisance. When they became famous they often came to see me when they were in trouble, particularly over things like the Sgt *Pepper* sleeve." The idea for the sleeve for their epic album involved using the pictures of numerous famous personalities but Lockwood insisted on certain conditions before he agreed to its use. "I told them that they would have to take Ghandi out as he was a holy man and that they would have to get permission from each of the people included in the picture before we would agree to its use. They gave us an indemnity for 10 million dollars royalties in the light of any legal action and set about contacting the people, remarkably we never had a single claim on that record, even though The Beatles didn't bother to approach everybody."

Lockwood took a totally different stance on their recordings. "I didn't attempt to interfere with their recording schedules even though the first records they made cost £4.50 to make and were done in no time while things like *Sgt Pepper* took over three months and cost more than £20,000. They weren't money-grabbing in the early days but after Brian Epstein died they got a lot worse."

One young man working for EMI at their Hayes factory was affected more than most by the *Sgt Pepper* album. Alan Parsons had just joined the company when he heard The Beatles and it convinced him that his future lay in record production at Abbey Road. "When I started at Abbey Road I was just the tea boy and tape operator; the last of the breed who went through the assault course of making tea, working the tape machines and running errands. Getting out of all that and into a studio was just like being released from prison." By the time he did get into a studio, the revolution had already begun. "The Beatles had begun it with their *Sgt Pepper* album and people then started thinking that you could spend a year making an album and they began to consider an album as a sound composition and not just a musical composition. The idea was gradually forming of a record being a performance in its own right and not just a reproduction of a live performance."

But life at Abbey Road did not always run smoothly as Parsons remembers. "There were occasional conflicts when sessions overlapped, being booked for something else before you had finished what you were already working on. You see all engineers were desperate to finish off any album they had started – the idea of sharing the album credit with another engineer who had probably done only three minutes work on one track was something we really resented."

Surprising as it may seem there were those people at Abbey Road, although anxious to establish themselves in their profession, who actually didn't want to work with the most successful group in the history of pop music. "Some engineers at Abbey Road didn't want to work with The Beatles because they felt there was little creativity involved, because most of the work was dominated by the group and George Martin and because of the totally undisciplined way they had of working. People would be called upon at all times of the day and night at the whim of The Beatles and they preferred working on properly booked sessions which, even if they overran, were at least booked in advance."

The Beatles had achieved most things by June 1967 but there was one engagement which somewhat overawed even them – the prospect of performing in front of an estimated 350 million people. They had been invited to contribute the British section of the worldwide satellite television link up called *Our World*. With wives, girlfriends, balloons and sandwich boards, The Beatles gathered in Studio One at Abbey Road to perform their song, 'All You Need Is Love'. The original idea, however, was that the world would see The Beatles at work on their new single, but, modern recording techniques being what they were, it was obvious that they couldn't do the thing for real.

George Martin had the idea of playing the basic rhythm track through a four-track machine while the assembled orchestra played live and The Beatles sang the words to the song which they had created with a little help from Martin who had concocted a beginning and ending that included 'La Marseillaise', a

Bach two-part invention, 'Greensleeves' and a touch of 'In The Mood'.

'All You Need Is Love' was one of The Beatles' two No. 1's in 1967 and they added two more in 1968, 'Lady Madonna' and 'Hey Jude', one of which Tim Rice remembers particularly well. "The one Beatles session I did go to was a wonderful experience just to be there, but I felt ghastly because I was a hanger-on. I'd gone in with Mike McGear and stood by the door trying to keep out of the way. I felt really bad about being a hanger-on but then thought, 'Stuff it, if I'm going to be a hanger-on at least I might as well hang on with the right people', and you couldn't get anybody more impressive to be seen with than The Beatles. It's something I'll be able to tell my grandchildren about."

As The Beatles' grew apart, Pink Floyd were fast emerging as a powerful force in the world of underground music but not without one or two problems along the way. They recorded two singles and an album in 1968, but by this time Syd Barrett had become the subject of internal wrangling between the band and their management. The album *Saucerful Of Secrets* was recorded with both Barrett and Gilmour, but it seems unlikely that Barrett played on more than one track and certainly the five piece line-up never actually recorded anything together that was released. 'Point Me At The Sky' was the group's last single for 11 years and the last they ever made in Abbey Road.

The Beatles prepare for their performance of 'All You Need Is Love' for the first global satellite television broadcast. Commentator Steve Race is on the left of the group standing under the scaffolding.

Hank Marvin, Cliff Richard, Bruce Welch & engineer, Peter Vince, gather round Abbey Road's first eight-track mixing console just after its introduction in 1968.

Before his famous walk out Des O'Connor recorded his only No. 1 – a song called 'I Pretend' – in 1968 and both Cliff Richard (with his Eurovision Song Contest entry 'Congratulations') and Scaffold (with 'Lily The Pink') topped the charts the same year. Meanwhile Bob Barratt took a leaf out of George Martin's book and began recording the type of comedy records which were to become a major part of his life over the next few years. "I recorded the infamous gay drag artist Lee Sutton in a Camberwell pub with the Abbey Road mobile and it turned out to be the first blue recording I had ever done. I was so worried about the content that I brought the tape back to EMI and asked my boss to listen to it to see what he thought. He saw the problem and suggested about half a dozen cuts; but in fact the things we left on were far more obscene, but you had to be part of the gay fraternity to understand them."

Bruce Welch, too, was moving into new areas around that time. "In the late Sixties I first got interested seriously in production when the thought of creating something in the studio really appealed to me. I never considered myself to be a great musician and my writing began to die off at about that time, so the natural thing to do was to record my girlfriend, Olivia Newton-John. Pretty girl singers were doing quite well at the time and, when the group we formed (called Marvin, Welch and Farrar) failed, I began working with Olivia and John Farrar. He was the technical man, a brilliant musician, and I was the song man."

It was three years, however, before this new working relationship paid off. "I found a song called 'If Not For You' which John arranged and worked on and

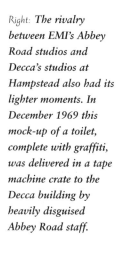

Above: **Olivia Newton-John first found fame via Abbey Road Studios where she recorded with producers Bruce Welch and John Farrar.**

we produced it together, although in the studio John was the clever one. I was learning all the time from engineers like Peter Vince and Tony Clark and on that session we were joined by an up and coming young man named Alan Parsons. People like Peter and Tony gave me so much as engineers; I believe that a good engineer is all the battle. From there I went into production in a big way and we had a lot of hits with Olivia which was a big thrill for all of us.'

By getting involved in production, Welch was able to see exactly what was going on behind the scenes at Abbey Road. "The changes at Abbey Road in those days were controlled by the money men. EMI was run by much older people who didn't understand the technical requirements and put everything down to cost. Finally we got 16-track which was marvellous. All the technology in the world will not make a bad song sound good but, on the other hand, a good song will sound good in a garage. If we had done our recordings with all the technical stuff that was around at the end of the Sixties we would have got a much more complete sound, much fuller so you'd be able to hear everything."

Once the changes had begun at Abbey Road they continued thick and fast. The progression from four-track to eight-track was followed just as quickly by the introduction of 16-track and the even more rapid switch to 24-track, all of which involved the use of EMI consoles which became the backbone of Abbey Road's multi-track recording.

Right: **The rivalry between EMI's Abbey Road studios and Decca's studios at Hampstead also had its lighter moments. In December 1969 this mock-up of a toilet, complete with graffiti, was delivered in a tape machine crate to the Decca building by heavily disguised Abbey Road staff.**

The changes were certainly influenced by The Beatles and they were responsible, once again, for another development at the studio, as Ken Townsend recalls. "The success of The Beatles really opened the floodgates for others to follow and ride on the bandwagon. The demand for studio time far exceeded what was available at Abbey Road, so new independent studios began to mushroom in London and in order to attract custom they began offering facilities in excess of the 'majors' who had been slow to reinvest their profits into the studios. At the same time the days of the 'house producer' also became numbered as producers sought fame and fortune independently. This in turn led to another breed, the engineer/producer who had the advantage of fully understanding the engineering complexities of multi-track."

It was fast becoming obvious to all those involved that the relationship between John Lennon and Paul McCartney could not continue much longer. George Martin sat in the middle, trying to make some sense of it all as they recorded their first and only double album, titled simply *The Beatles,* but known the world over as The White Album because of its simple white packaging. While Lennon and McCartney continued to air their musical differences, George Harrison took the opportunity to establish himself as a major contributor. He had an all-time best of four tracks out of the thirty chosen for the album and invited one of the world's leading guitarists, Eric Clapton, into Abbey Road to play on his classic track 'While My Guitar Gently Weeps'.

It was Ringo who was most affected by the arguments and mid-way through the album he stood up from behind his drum kit in Studio Two and announced he was leaving the group. No one tried to stop him but a week later, when he returned, George and Paul covered his drums with "welcome back" messages. The album that had been recorded as a double package in order to fulfill their recording contract with EMI as soon as possible was finished and Paul McCartney had this to say about it. "It was the big tension album. The rest was pretty untense, not that bad or there'd be a bit of tension. For the White Album, we were all in the middle of the psychedelic thing or just coming out of it. It was weird. Never before had we recorded with people visiting for hours on end and business meetings."

There were no exceptions when it came to signing to take tapes away from the studio... even if your name was John Lennon.

In the book, *The Beatles Apart* (written by Bob Woffinden) the leader of the Electric Light Orchestra, Jeff Lynne, recalled a visit to the studios during the recording of the double album. "There was John Lennon and George Harrison sitting there, and George Martin conducting the orchestra. They were doing this song called 'Glass Onion'. Then I went into this other studio where there was a session going on with Paul McCartney, and he was doing 'Why Don't We Do It In The Road?' I wish he'd been doing something a bit better, but you can't have everything."

Abbey Road, the last Beatles album to be recorded, spawned just one single 'Something' which reached the top five in November 1969. However, while EMI ended the most profitable period in its history without its most successful act ever, they had few fears for the future.

The cast of the Sixties television series, That Was The Week That Was *assemble in the studio – (from left to right, back row) Lance Percival, Ned Sherrin (half hidden), Kenneth Cope, Willie Rushton, (middle row) David Kernan and Roy Kinnear and, crouching, David Frost and Millicent Martin.*

7

Yesterday–
McCartney Remembers

Here's one for all the pop pundits, discophiles and vinyl junkies. What's the connection between equatorial Africa, steamy New Orleans, a boat in the warm waters of the Caribbean, a castle overlooking the English Channel, a farmhouse in a remote part of West Scotland, an office in London's Soho and Abbey Road studios? The answer is quite simply one man – Paul McCartney – who has recorded in all these locations since the demise of The Beatles.

Without doubt the most successful pop musician of all time, McCartney's obsession with recording is well known and with his "other" band, Wings, or just with his wife, Linda, McCartney has recorded wherever the fancy has taken him. *Band On The Run* was done in Nigeria; *Venus And Mars* in New Orleans; *London Town* on a converted boat in the West Indies and *Back To The Egg* in an English castle, a Scottish farmhouse and his London office. 'Mull of Kintyre', among the most successful British singles ever, was first recorded in the same farmhouse, overlooking the landscape immortalised in the song's title.

That single, a British No. 1 for nine consecutive weeks around Christmas 1977, like so many other McCartney records, was finished off in the comparative comfort of EMI's Abbey Road studios, to which McCartney has returned consistently during a career spanning over 30 years.

Brian Epstein, manager of The Beatles during their heyday, was quick to recognise Abbey Road's part in The Beatles' story. In his autobiography, *A Cellarful Of Noise* he captioned a picture of himself and the famous four in the studios with the following words: "The heart of the affair. Where the hits are born – the EMI recording studio in St John's Wood". Since that day in June 1962 when The Beatles paid their first visit to Abbey Road, Paul McCartney has returned time and time again and it was fitting that he should choose it as the venue when it came to an interview about the old building.

"When we first came here in 1962 we'd been trying to get from Liverpool to get a record contract like everyone else in the world," he recalled. "We'd tried a couple of studios up in Liverpool and had also tried Decca – we had a sort of audition there which was a bit seedy and did some tapes which went to Dick Rowe and, to his everlasting bad luck, he turned them down; don't worry I'll let you off, Dick. We had been in a studio before but this was the first real one

Both of these photographs were taken at the same time (in 1980) with Paul (on the left) looking the way he did in the Sixties.

where we were really going to be taken under contract. We came down to record 'Love Me Do' and all I remember is being terrified out of my wits, quaking in my boots, and I can still hear it on the vocal of 'Love Me Do'."

That first major recording session – the first one for real – didn't just pass them by. McCartney recalls some of the things he noticed. "We were in a corner [of Studio Two] looking up at this big window, this big black window where there were people moving around. In those days you just came in, did your bit and they said, 'Thank you very much', and that was it and you kinda went to the pub and waited to hear news of its release. They mixed it, they did everything and told you what was going to be the single.

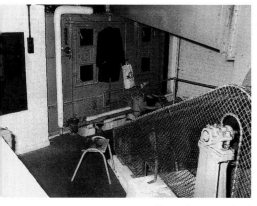

'We'd always look for somewhere to get out of the way of everyone,' and this was one of Paul's hiding places in Abbey Road. The air conditioning chamber was also the place where he chose to do an interview about the studios with the author.

"Coming into Abbey Road for the first time was the old surprise thing – we thought, 'This is a small place', but it just kept going on and on. Over the years we just kept coming back here and eventually got to know about all these sort of places and every other little corner. We'd always look for somewhere to get out of the way of everyone. You got to know the fellas who worked in these corners and in the end I pretty much got to know the whole building."

McCartney remembers the strict formality which was a trademark of Abbey Road until he and his three colleagues changed things in the mid-Sixties. "We were not allowed to touch the desk or anything in the early days. It was all very formal and in our early photos we've all got suits and ties on and so have George [Martin] and Geoff [Emerick]. There were strict three-hour sessions which was great and I've kinda gone back to working that way. It gives you time for life and makes a lot of sense; there's time for lunch and everything else."

During the hectic days of the early Sixties, life for The Beatles became one round of live dates, press and radio interviews, television appearances and recording sessions; and in Abbey Road the most famous group in the history of pop music began to seek some respite from the pressures of the outside world.

"I think to some degree it was a refuge for us," admits Paul, "but to be honest it was the place where we recorded; we had to come here anyway whether it was a refuge or not. It was a nice place to come to; the reason wasn't that it was such a great place to be in that we stayed here through the night, it was actually just the workers taking over the tools of their trade. All that kind of thing was being mooted anyway and we would be working on a thing quite late and we would kinda say, 'What time can we go to tonight?', and we eventually started to sort of stretch it, you know."

The Beatles' ability to work long hours undisturbed is a legend in Abbey Road. Endless cups of tea, fish and chips and Chinese take-aways were ordered as they worked night and day to finish the records that brought them more and more success, increased pressures and, ultimately, greater control of their destiny. "With the touring and everything else we had to do, we got used to kinda rock'n'roll hours whereas now I'm kinda back on a normal kind of schedule.

Now you've gotta get up for the kids and then, of course, we didn't have any kids and we could all lie in till midday and come round here for the two o'clock session and then you'd work until midnight and stuff and it got to be quite nice being here on your own; the only people in the building. You forgot about time and kinda got so much into the music that you just went on and on, but after three or four weeks of that you are finished."

As the success story of The Beatles unfolded, a new chapter was being written with every new release, so their every whim and fancy was catered for and when it came to recording schedules at Abbey Road there was never any question of them being kept waiting for a studio. People, perhaps unkindly, suggested that the wealthy young men from Liverpool would have bought the studios had they been refused a session or a particular studio. "Our thoughts were never in those directions," says Paul in answer to those comments, "but it is true if you look at an index of EMI's earnings and our arrival on the scene, it goes very much hand in hand. It makes sense, you start off wanting to be very much dictated to and after a while – around the 'We Can Work It Out' time (but I can't remember exact dates too well, I think of it by the song or the release) – but around about that time we started to take over things."

As they "started to take over things", The Beatles found that Abbey Road was the perfect place to be in when it came to experimenting with new instruments and new sounds. "One of the good things about EMI was that it was, and still is, the only studio I've ever known in the world where you have one grand piano, one super grand piano, a medium grand, one upright with tinkly things as used by Russ Conway, one upright sorta sounding like a Jerry Lee Lewis, a celeste, a harmonium, vibraphones, glockenspiel – everything was just there in the studio for normal use. This was one thing and because we started to take over, it became a bit more of you just going over and grabbing something that you fancied rather than the producer telling you and organising it all. Rather than preconceived ideas, you'd just pick on the harmonium and say, 'Let's try this on here', because it happened to be there. It was like having a great town house of your own with all these things in."

As the ideas grew so the music developed, as did the relationship between each of

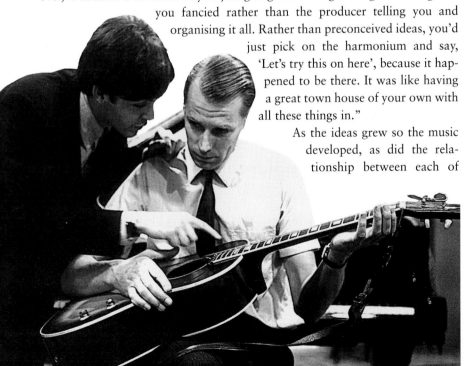

These are the strings George! Paul gives George Martin a guitar lesson.

the four Beatles and producer George Martin. His expertise as an arranger, musician and producer gave life to the oddball ideas that emanated from each recording session. In his interview with *Rolling Stone's* Paul Gambaccini, in 1974, Paul McCartney recalled the creating of one of his masterpieces. "Something like 'Yesterday', I did the tune first and wrote the words for that later. I called that 'Scrambled Eggs' for a long time. I didn't have any words to it. First of all I was just playing it through for everyone – saying, 'How do you like this song?' So George Martin and I got together and sort of cooked up this idea. I wanted just a small string arrangement and he said, 'Well, how about your actual string quartet?' I said, 'Great, it sounds great'. We sat down at a piano and cooked that one up."

The availability of numerous and varied instruments at Abbey Road made a lasting impression on McCartney. "EMI's policy of being generous and providing the things was one of the things I used to think was great. The technical staff were always the great boffins in the background who'd come in, remove a couple of faders, take 'em off to the operating theatre and mend 'em – that's fabulous." McCartney, too, gives particular credit to Ken Townsend. "He invented ADT and all that stuff which he hasn't really got too much credit for. In fact I was in Los Angeles doing the *Ram* album and had to ring up Ken and say, 'How did we do that ADT again?' and get him to tell the guy from the American studio, over the phone, how to do it."

The time The Beatles spent at the studio brought chaos to the streets of St John's Wood. Although all their recording sessions were supposed to be a well kept secret, somehow the news always leaked out and the fans came in their hundreds, some of them spending days and nights on the pavement or huddled in the car park. The braver ones even made it into the building as McCartney

Paul and Linda McCartney pose in the Abbey Road studios' reception area...in front of a picture of themselves with Denny Laine.

well remembers. "One or two used to get in the rafters – there were false ceilings for the lighting and air ducts and we used to find one or two up there every now and then. You'd hear a little scuffle and somebody would come in and get 'em out. They were everywhere; in the woodwork and places like that."

As the era of The Beatles came to end, the four of them made what was to be their last working visits as a group to the studio for the album that, in addition to becoming their best selling work, was to put the name Abbey Road on the map once and for all. But, as McCartney points out, the album wasn't always going to be called *Abbey Road*.

"It was almost called 'Mount Everest'. We were working a lot in there at the time, always wondering what we were going to call it and Geoff Emerick, the engineer, always used to smoke Everest cigarettes, so we were thinking of things like Ever Rest. It was kinda working out to be a biggish album – the big deal – and it was going quite well and then everybody started saying that it wasn't a very good title really. As I remember it, but it's very vague really, but my recollection for what it's worth was that we were in Studio Three, the little one at the front which used to have record covers on the ceiling in those days and looked like a record shop, and kinda said, 'Why don't we call it *Abbey Road* and why don't we have a picture of us on that crossing outside?' – it was the simplest thing to do. It is Abbey Road and for everyone who didn't know the name of the studio, that would imply something kinda mystical – Monastery Avenue sorta thing."

With the title finally fixed and the cover photograph decided upon, all that was left was to actually take the picture. The repercussions of that simple shot spread round the world and McCartney once again explains why he appears without shoes on the album cover. "It was a very hot day when we took the thing and I'd come in sandals which I whacked off for some of the shots."

If that album marked the end of The Beatles association with Abbey Road, it began a new relationship between McCartney and his favourite studio. He embarked on a solo career which blossomed into a new group called Wings and finally swung back to the man working in the old tried and tested arena with George Martin, who had worked so closely with him during his formative years.

His love of Abbey Road, and Studio Two in particular, resulted in problems when other artists were booked in when McCartney wanted studio time. Finding Bruce Welch booked in at the end of 1977, McCartney solved the problem once and for all by building his own studio. "That came about because I couldn't get in here and for me, having been used to the control room in Number Two all these years, I wanted to mix an album and have all that equipment. I was putting a mobile in my basement, so I actually rang up the feller who designed control room Two and said, 'Could you design a movable control room with exactly the same features?' The great thing was that we had a picture of the studio on the wall with a clock that worked."

*Above and below: **When Thames Television chose former World Boxing champion John Conteh as the subject for their** This Is Your Life **programme, the venue was Abbey Road studios during one of Paul McCartney's recording sessions. Eamonn Andrews is pictured plotting the surprise with Paul and Linda, before confronting a shocked Conteh with the famous book. Paul (far right of lower photograph) offers his congratulations.***

Above: **What do the above have in common?** *The answer is the long running British TV series* Crossroads. *Paul McCartney recorded a cover version of the theme, composed by Tony Hatch (pictured here with, from left to right, engineers Peter Mew and Mike Sheady). While Noele Gordon seen here with Geoff Love, starred in the series.*

The likeness between the two is uncanny. The same varnished wooden walls in a room about the same size with alcoves identically placed. Even though you enter McCartney's replica at the opposite end to the original, he has built a false door in the same metallic grey colour as one that opens on to the stairs leading down into the studio itself. And there on the wall is a huge photograph of the view of the studio floor from the control room with the clock positioned perfectly with its working hands.

One thing that McCartney didn't include in his replica studio, or to be more accurate, control room, was the "psychedelic" lighting installed in the studio at The Beatles' request many years earlier. "At one time we said that they'd gotta get lighting in the studio because some of the good new studios have got lighting in and so they sent us three fluorescent bars of red and three of green; that was the light show and they're still there somewhere to this day."

Changing Abbey Road was something that The Beatles made a habit of and on occasions they encountered difficulties, probably because of the way EMI was structured in those days. "People either like or hate EMI and if they hate it," suggests Paul, "they hate it because it's too like a Government building or like the BBC; it has its name on the toilet paper and there's something sorta horrible and huge or impersonal about it. I love it because of all those things. When we were the far out young group wanting changes it was never that hard to get

The Beatles in 1967 working on a track for the "Sgt Pepper" album.

On 8th August 1969 Iain Macmillan took six photographs. This is just one of the five that didn't make it for the cover of the "Abbey Road" album. Since that date it has arguably become the most photographed 'Rock' location in Britain.

When Klaus Voorman conceived the idea for the "Anthology" album covers, it was his intention that all three albums when layed side by side would result in the above. It is incredible to note that the sales of "Anthology 1 and 2" and Beatles' back catalogue exceeded that of any other year in The Beatles' history.

"Going back to that original location was "spooky"...Older and slightly different maybe, but nevertheless it was still three of The Beatles sitting there, and with who?...George Martin..." (Paul McCartney)

To promote a TV documentary on the history of Abbey Road, Senior Executive Producer Scotty Meade (of EPL Pictures) subjected the Studios to the Hollywood treatment, whilst filming the whole event from a low flying helicopter.

Mstislav Rostropovich surrounded by the equipment of Andy Walter's remastering room.

Sir Cliff Richard used the Penthouse studio for the first vocal overdubs on his "Heathcliff" album. The musical was written by composer John Farrar and lyricist Sir Tim Rice. (Left to right: Cliff, Tim, John, engineer Darren Godwin and in the background David Bryce, Cliff's long standing manager).

Mel Gibson during the recording of the music score for his award winning film "Braveheart".

them actually; we used to have to struggle occasionally and at times it would have been better if they had been able to see what we wanted. There was a kinda Forties attitude and they could have been more forward looking. Now, on reflection, I don't take the angry young man approach anymore."

They say that success breeds success and certainly McCartney, after a slow start as a solo performer, received the critical acclaim that had eluded him (since The Beatles' split) with the album *Band On The Run*. Recorded in Lagos, Scotland and Abbey Road, the album sold over three-quarters of a million copies in the UK alone and became EMI's biggest selling album of the Seventies.

McCartney's success, both with and without The Beatles, was honoured a few years back when the *Guinness Book of Records* presented him with a rhodium* disc to commemorate becoming the most successful composer of all time; the holder of the largest number of gold discs and the world's most successful recording artist. While it's difficult to prove all of these claims beyond any doubt, there can be no denying that Paul McCartney can lay greater claim to these awards than any other pop performer.

Abbey Road has played its part in that astounding success story with the majority of McCartney's records being either recorded, mixed, arranged or cut in the studio. And, contrary to the popular myth, it has not just been Studio Two that has seen the man at work. As he himself says, over the years he has got to know the whole building. "I've used them all, including the Penthouse which is very nice, but Studio Two is the great studio. It was always a good studio and in this place, if you think of it sensibly, there's one giant studio which you couldn't possibly put The Shadows or any other groups in, so that's ruled out. Studio Three was a little bit small in those days, so Two was the only studio really."

The fact that both The Beatles and McCartney used Studio Two with such great regularity gave rise to the stories of its "magical" power. "We were very aware of the myth thing," says McCartney, "and about six years ago an American studio guy came here and, just because I wanted to change the look of the place, we had an umbrella, a little cafe table and a few potted plants and things just to break the mood. This American guy came round here and said, 'So this is the famous studio then. Hey, I didn't know you had palm trees and umbrellas', and I told him it helped the sound. I always imagined after that, this string of little West Coast studios with palm trees and things and this guy saying, 'This is how The Beatles did it, guys'. You've gotta play with that kinda thing."

*The metal, rhodium, is estimated to be twice as valuable as platinum.

"That kinda thing", as McCartney so astutely put it, was the reverence shown by some artists and producers towards Abbey Road's Studio Two. Because of The Beatles, and the extraordinary success they achieved, the talk was of vibes and feelings, myths and magic and, while he understands why all those rumours began, he refuses to treat the place as anything more than it is... a large room in a converted dwelling house in North London. "It got a reputation as being the great one in town. It just became The Beatles' studio and ultimately got world fame through that but obviously it wasn't us that made the studio; the acoustics and stuff were done by whoever planned it. Wherever we made those records would have become famous."

8
It's My Party!

Over a century ago Henry Ward Beecher made the astute observation that "clothes and manners do not make the man". While nobody has ever questioned the manners of Abbey Road's staff, Beecher's comments regarding clothing could well have applied to the first 38 years of the studio's life and one decade in particular. The Sixties had been a decade when fashion put on its most bizarre front, accommodating the 'Beatles' look, mods and rockers, hippies and beatniks in all their assorted finery or, in some cases, the lack of it. Throughout all this, the people who were so closely involved in making the music which reflected the ever changing fads and fashions were forced to appear in a style that, in retrospect, seems both surprising and pointless.

The Abbey Road rules of dress insisted on trousers, jacket, shirt and tie for the staff at a time when the artists were appearing with shoulder length hair, wearing colourful and often outrageous outfits. For a bunch of people who spent most of their time locked in the studios with casually dressed musicians, and rarely met anybody but the people they worked with, to operate under such restrictions seemed most extraordinary. Gus Cook, when he took over as studio manager in 1969, thought along the same lines because he finally lifted the restrictions on staff dress, realising that suits and ties had little to do with creating popular or classical music.

Peter Vince (still a suit and occasional tie man incidentally) recalls the moment. "When Gus Cook relaxed the strict rules everybody came in wearing jeans and T-shirts and wore their hair a bit longer. It really made no difference to the quality of the work; they just felt a lot more comfortable. Before then it had been very strict and people were in fact sent home to put a tie on or get their hair cut. The previous manager, Alan Stagge, once ordered a tape operator to get his hair cut, his reply was that when Stagge sent Sir John Barbirolli home to get his hair cut before working in Abbey Road then he would go with him."

While Cook was able to do something about the rules of dress, he was in no position to solve one of Abbey Road's perpetual problems... its car park. The complaints kept coming in and even Bruce Welch had reason to complain. "In the early Seventies, after I'd been going to Abbey Road for about 15 years, I drove up one day in the 'Roller' and found an empty parking space. As I drove

Steve Harley & Cockney Rebel made their No.1 hit 'Make Me Smile' (Come Up and See Me), in Abbey Road with Producer Alan Parsons. The line-up was (left to right) Duncan Mackay, (who later joined 10cc), Stuart Elliot, Steve Harley, Jim Cregan (who went on to join Rod Stewart's band) and George Ford.

into it, the guy on the door came running out and told me I couldn't park there because it was reserved... for John Farrar."

Bob Barratt also suffered from the studio's most persistent problem. "We were doing a session with the Scottish singer, Stuart Gillies, and already running late when he suddenly rushed in full of apologies. He had driven into the car park, told the fellow in charge that he was a singer doing a session in the studio and been promptly told, 'Sorry no room in here for singers'. The rule was that only the main artist on the session could park at the front and session singers had to park in the street. Nobody had recognised Stuart and they presumed he was a backing singer."

Barratt also found himself in a session, that he best describes as bizarre. "I did a session with Basil Brush, and the man behind the puppet, Ivan Owen, would come into the studio and do the session in Basil's voice. Unfortunately on quite a lot of the recordings you could hear a marked difference between Ivan's own voice and the one he used for Basil. In the end Ivan had to bring Basil into the studio and sit in an empty studio with the puppet on his hand in order to get the voice right."

In the early years it had been the Parlophone label, under the guidance of both Oscar Preuss and George Martin, which pioneered the making of records with unlikely artists but, as time passed, it became obvious that there was a market for novelty records. Christmas became the accepted time to release these unusual couplings and, in January 1971, Clive Dunn shot to No. 1 with his rendering of Herbie Flowers' song, 'Grandad'. That was on the Columbia label and they completed a significant double in December that year when Benny Hill reached the top spot with 'Ernie'.

Even though they had split and gone their separate ways, The Beatles were still regular visitors to the studios they had made so famous. In 1970 George Harrison went into Studio Three to record his chart topping single 'My Sweet Lord' and his triple album set, *All Things Must Pass,* with another fine Abbey Road engineer, Phil McDonald. Ringo Starr returned to his old stomping ground that same year to record tracks for his *Sentimental Journey* album. This was a decision that took some people by surprise since it was rumoured that Ringo was the Beatle least enamoured with Abbey Road because, so the story went, he was treated as the poor relation in the group with little or no attention paid to his requests for bet-

Above: **A Glamorous Diana Dors on the steps of Abbey Road Studios.**

Right: **A star for a day! Abbey Road studio technician, Eddie Klein (seated centre), was signed up by producer, Phil Spector, as a joke, to make a tap dancing record with this star-studded line-up, (from left to right) George Harrison, Billy Preston, Klaus Voormann, Phil Spector, Ringo Starr & Gary Wright.**

ter equipment. Paul McCartney, who was to become a most regular visitor to the studio, was making use of Studio Two around that time for his *McCartney* and *Wildllfe* albums.

As the era of The Beatles came to an end, a new and equally determined young band took over the mantle of the Abbey Road "house band", spending hour upon hour in the studio making albums which were technically every bit as adventurous as those of their famous predecessors. Right from the start Pink Floyd were determined to do things their way and, as guitarist David Gilmour points out, they met with some opposition along the way. "When we started off we were pushing right from the beginning. The early pressures came from Norman Smith and EMI who wanted us to make nice pop songs. Maybe they thought they had another Beatles with us. People thought we should cut out all the funny weird nonsense and get on with it. There was definitely pressure there at the beginning with EMI but, after having some success doing it our way, when they said do this or do that, we'd say, 'No, we want to do it this way', and there was nothing they could do about it."

Floyd producer Norman Smith had other things on his mind, however. He was busy establishing a new career for himself. "I'd always wanted to be a pop star and had written this song called 'Don't Let It Die', which I intended to send to John Lennon, even though at that time it didn't have a title or any lyrics. I was working with Floyd at the time and we'd had a particularly bad day. I was so browned off that I didn't go to lunch with them but stayed in the studio and started playing this song on the piano, humming along to it and this phrase, 'Don't Let It Die', kept coming back to me. Suddenly the engineer, who I thought was at lunch, switched on the intercom and asked me what I was playing."

The two of them decided to put the song down on tape and that was where it stayed until Smith ran into Mickie Most. "Mickie was in the studio and I played him the demo without telling him who it was. He liked it and said he would certainly release it himself and thought it was a top three record. When I told him it was me, he swore and told me to forget John Lennon and give it to EMI as it was, with me singing." Unfortunately, EMI didn't like it and decided not to release the record, leaving Smith with only one alternative. "I asked if I could buy the tapes and give them to Mickie to release. They had a re-think and decided it would be embarrassing if a senior EMI producer had a record released on another label so they reluctantly agreed to put it out. I only agreed on the condition that the publishing went to Mickie as a reward for his faith in me." And Mickie Most's forecast of a top three record was proved correct when the song reached No. 2 in June 1971, the first of three hit records for Hurricane Smith.

Success, however, brought new problems for Smith. "At the same time as all this was happening I was still working with underground and progressive bands like Pink Floyd and The Pretty Things and I used to take a lot of stick from them about being a pop star." However much stick he had to take for being a pop star, Smith's role in the development of Pink Floyd is not overlooked or forgotten by David Gilmour. "Norman was the producer on all our albums until he became listed as executive producer, which was a neat way of saying that he didn't

Shoulder length hair and colourful clothes were the order of the day for pop stars during the late Sixties and The Pretty Things were no exception when they visited Abbey Road. (From left to right) 'Twink' John Adler, Wally Allen (later to become an EMI producer), Phil May, John Povey and Dick Taylor (founder bass player with The Rolling Stones).

actually do anything – but that was only on one album. He was wonderful and taught all of us a lot about producing records but it just came to a point when we had learnt enough from him, where he became redundant I suppose. He made suggestions that we disagreed with and life got a little more difficult."

The Seventies also brought back to Abbey Road a man who originally auditioned there 10 years earlier in a group called the Nightriders. Roy Wood had gone on to make a dozen or more hit singles with The Move and Electric Light Orchestra, many of them for EMI but none of them recorded in Abbey Road. "I went back into Abbey Road to do my solo album, *Boulders*, because the studio I wanted to use was fully booked. Someone said that as I was signed to EMI, why not try their studios. They'd re-done Studio Three while I'd been away and it had just gone 24-track but it still felt like being back at school – a little bit straight, like a Government building with the commissionaire on the door. I don't think I ever did feel totally relaxed in there. I found it a bit difficult mixing there because the desk was spread out quite a bit – you had to have a set of roller skates to mix anything in there."

Even though he felt uncomfortable in the studio, Wood persevered and even played a few tricks in the studio. "I had two buckets of water in there for the track, *Wake Up*, which needed this water effect. I sat in there wearing a full fisherman's outfit, with one of them yellow hats on, splashing about in this water. The saving grace for me was the engineer, Alan Parsons, who was excellent. I probably wouldn't have stayed there but for him. In the end I was happy with what I came out with but I found the place a bit unfriendly – you were sort of scared to shout or do anything like that."

Wood, however, was back in Abbey Road within a year with his new band, Wizzard. "The first gig we ever did was a big rock'n'roll concert at Wembley Stadium and we decided that, after the gig, while the group was really 'up', we'd go straight into the studios. It was the first time we'd ever recorded at all with Wizzard and the first time I'd ever recorded two double drum kits together in the same room. We were more or less experimenting to get good drum sounds. That was in Studio Two – the signal box – with the flight of steps leading up to the high control room which looked down on the studio."

Even with all this activity in the studios, there were discussions taking place which would have shocked the world of recorded music had they leaked out. Imagine the headlines: "Abbey Road To Shut" and "Home Of The Beatles' Hits to Close Down". This could well have been the case if the plans, drawn up by the board of EMI, had gone through. Sir Joseph Lockwood recounted the meetings that took place. "The plan was to close Abbey Road and two reasons were put forward. Firstly, that EMI must have a new studio because the other one must be getting old and secondly, because they had this idea to centralise the whole of EMI in one huge office block in London's Tottenham Court Road, including the building of a studio.

"To build a studio there would have been ridiculous and the whole thing seemed totally stupid to me – building a new studio at a cost of about £12 million and with no guarantee that a new one would be any better than the old one. I am glad to report that neither of these plans got any further than the planning stage and Abbey Road was allowed to continue life as one of the major recording houses in the world."

Ironically, while plans were being drawn up for the closure of Abbey Road, one of the world's most durable and successful albums was being recorded there. Pink Floyd began work on the innovative and inventive *Dark Side Of The Moon* album in June 1972 but it was March 1973 before it was released. Alan Parsons, who had previously worked as assistant engineer on *Atom Heart Mother* assumed the role of engineer for that memorable album and remembers it well. "It was the first album I ever felt in a way responsible for. It was a real challenge, particularly as Floyd, in my opinion, were the first band to stretch a studio to its limits. In those days studios were a lot less reliable than they are today. Although it was 16-track, it would be much easier to record now but probably a lot less exciting. The album was total spontaneity – they put the whole thing together virtually in the studio and changed it drastically from the version they played live."

David Gilmour, co-writer, creator and producer of the album, however, sees it differently. "Actually I think it's the least spontaneous of our albums, certainly less than any other of the ones we had done up until then, although there were changes from the stage show which came about in the studio. The recording time was probably no more than six weeks out of the six month period between when we started recording and when the album was released. It never struck me as being a particularly difficult album, but there was a lot of hard work put into it – rehearsing and writing it, formulating it and taking it out on the road. I love to use the studio as a medium but I wouldn't agree that *Dark Side Of The Moon* stretched the studio to its limits."

By November 1981 this album had become the longest running contemporary album in the American *Billboard* charts, having been in the top 200 for 391 consecutive weeks – nearly eight years – and having amassed total worldwide sales of close to 15 million. However, Floyd's next project did not go quite so smoothly and this time Gilmour and Parsons are in total agreement about why the album was never released. Parsons outlines the background: "It was intended to be an album of sound effects, tentatively called *Household Objects* with no musical instruments but, unfortunately, it never got finished. We had egg slicers, rubber bands, cigarette lighters and match boxes plus a load more odds and ends. We did things like stretching the rubber bands across the table

Above: **Roy Wood** *played all the instruments on his solo album* Boulders, *and produced it himself in Studio Three.*

Roy Harper in Studio One control room.

Pink Floyd's David Gilmour turns roadie when the organ speaker has to be moved to another studio.

between a G clamp and a match placed on a cigarette box, then we put matches along the rubber band at different intervals to create various notes. What we created with that was a sound like a bass guitar but it took ages for us to get it right and we could have got the same sound from a bass within a second or two but everybody was obsessed with the idea of not using any musical instruments."

As Gilmour explains, it was the time it took to record things that caused the whole scheme to be abandoned. "It was too much hard work; it was driving us mad. It was a great idea and we could have made a good album out of it if we'd had the strength to continue. We used all sorts of silly things and I suppose we should have made a seven-minute track out of it and stuck it on an album."

Ten years after their initial recordings in Studio Three, The Hollies were still regular visitors to Abbey Road but the sounds created by The Beatles and Pink Floyd did not influence them in the studio. Tony Hicks, one of the three remaining original members of the group is adamant about what the group did not want to do in Abbey Road. "We never really wanted to create a technical album like *Sgt Pepper.* We preferred to work with as few overdubs as possible and there was no doubt in our minds that if we could go into the studios and get a thing sounding great just as we were, then it must be good."

Even though they weren't creating highly technical albums, the Hollies still preferred an air of privacy when they recorded and with 25 hits under their belt they were obviously the best judges of their recording technique. "We never take too kindly to strangers being in the studio when we record; it can be slightly inhibiting although there are those people you are happy to see and have in the studio. We used to see Paul McCartney quite a lot in Abbey Road and Linda's great. She sort of barges in – she's lovely, nothing subtle about it – comes in with the kids and the lot. There's nothing rude about it, she's just interested to know what you're doing and listen to what you've recorded."

Gus Cook's long and close association with Abbey Road came to an end in 1974 when he retired as general manager after a lifetime's work in the business of recorded music. His answer to the critics who claimed that Abbey Road was too institutionalised was quite simple. "A lot of people do believe that Abbey Road has an old fashioned attitude but it's difficult to run a big operation in a small way. It has a reputation as the greatest training centre in the world. No matter where you go in the world and in every aspect of the sound business – TV, radio, films, stage musicals – they all know and respect Abbey Road."

Another of Abbey Road's many operations came into its own in the Seventies when Hot Chocolate, Mud, Smokie and Suzi Quatro, and a number of other acts signed to Mickie Most's RAK label, made a highly successful assault on the charts. While none of their records were recorded in Abbey Road, they were all cut in one of the studio's four cutting rooms which are in constant demand by acts signed to EMI and to its rival record companies.

Chris Blair, in the footsteps of people like George Peckham and Malcolm Davies, is a cutter much sought after by both EMI acts and independent artists and in 1975 he reached a peak in his career when he cut 12 No. 1 records including acts such as Pilot, Steve Harley, Telly Savalas, Mud, Suzi Quatro, Windsor Davies and Don Estelle, and Queen. He, like so many modern cutters, liked to see as much level as possible on a single: "I want the record to leap out, which is why I try out everything on a cheap gramophone. If it works on there it'll work anywhere."

Blair's cuts, so much in demand, are easily recognisable because he signed 'Blair's' on the lacquers – but only if he liked them. "If I don't like them I sign them Porky or Pecko", which was the credit used by Peckham on his cuts. Blair believes the man who has done most to pioneer the amount of level put on a record is Mickie Most. "He was obsessed with level," said Blair.

Most returned the compliment by refusing to cut his records anywhere but at Abbey Road. "I cut there for years because, like a studio, you get used to a cutting room and at Abbey Road the cutting facilities are first class, plus the fact that the people are in general nice. I don't mean that in a condescending way but throughout the whole place there are nice people."

Another of Abbey Road's backrooms is the transcription room where, following a suggestion from Gus Cook, old 78 rpm discs were transcribed on to tape for possible re-issue using equipment, designed by Bernard Speight, which can deal with records from 63 to 90 rpm in order to cope with the lack of standardised speed which existed in the early days of recording.

The Abbey Road mobile units, while far from backroom operations, regularly trek around the world and one of the most unusual journeys was to Oman in the Middle East when one was booked to record the celebrations for an anniversary of the ruler of Oman. The Sultan's personal DC10 was used to fly the equipment out and then it was transported across the desert to his palace in a customised horse box. A far more comfortable journey was to John Lennon's house in Ascot

Mickie Most, producer, businessman and television personality, at work in his favourite cutting room in Abbey Road's Penthouse suite.

During the power cuts and three-day working week in the early Seventies, Abbey Road constructed this heavily sound-proofed home for the generator which enabled them to operate business as usual. Since then the studios have invested £1,000 per year to guarantee delivery of a generator in similar times of crisis.

where mobile equipment was set up to record his classic *Imagine* album, including the title track which was to become a No. 1 single over Christmas 1980 following Lennon's tragic killing in New York.

Bob Barratt took over the mantle from George Martin of comedy producer extraordinaire when he was able to translate his interest in regional humour on to record. "There were four comedians, from different corners of the country really interested me and whom I got involved with, Bob Williamson, from Lancashire, Jimmy Nairn from Scotland, Johnny Handel from Tyneside and Max Boyce from Wales. I met Max through the Morriston Orpheus Choir, whom I had worked with for many years and, despite having no Welsh blood and a distinct hatred of rugby, I decided to record him. We took the mobile to a rugby club in Treorchy which was in fact a tin hut in the Rhonda Valley."

Max remembers the day well. "When you consider the first album was recorded in a rugby club with a piano with a broken leg, propped up with bricks, and my second album was recorded during a live concert, coming to Abbey Road was something totally new to me. The third album had been done partly in concert and then we went to Abbey Road to add a couple of straight songs and I was absolutely terrified at the thought of going into a studio to sing. I've never thought of myself as a great singer."

But the day came and Max arrived at Abbey Road to find an even bigger surprise. "There was an orchestra booked and I was really worried about how disciplined I would have to be working with real musicians. I made a point of going around the studio and talking to all the musicians to make sure they had some respect for me, at least as a bloke if not as a singer. I was terrified at the thought of all those professional musicians wondering what they were doing working with the likes of me but I suppose at the end of the day it was still just another session; another day's work for them. The whole thing about coming into Abbey Road and working in the same building as The Beatles excited me."

Bob Barratt was quick to realise that his plan to record Max with a string section was possibly not the best idea in the world. "I think that was probably the unhappiest day in Max's life. He had real problems singing with the musicians and I learned an important lesson; with Max you add strings, or whatever else is going on the record, after Max has done his singing." That first Abbey Road session brings back other memories for the Welsh comedian with a weakness for unusual instruments. "On one of my early Abbey Road sessions we used an appalachian dulcimer – a three-stringed instrument on a block of wood – and my manager, a man not interested in folk music walked in. I asked him what he thought it was and he said, 'I don't know, but whatever it is it's broken'. Another instrument we had was a melodion that some guy brought in when he auditioned for us. It looked as though it was about 100 years old and, when I picked it up to look at it, the whole thing fell apart in my hands. We had to pay the guy an extra day's session fee to cover the time it took him to put it back together."

Having taken Max Boyce to No. 1 in the album charts with 'We All Had Doctor's Papers', Bob Barratt returned to a project which had begun some years earlier via one of his oldest contacts in the music business. "The man who managed The Cougars back in the Sixties had always kept in touch with me, sending me odd tapes and songs, and one day he sent me a letter with a photograph of a bunch of people dressed up in full Somerset yokels' garb. I couldn't resist them and invited them to Abbey Road for a test."

'Liquor, liquor everywhere but not a drop to drink.' Engineer Tony Clark on location in a beer cellar in the West Country during a Wurzels' recording session.

When The Wurzels, with Adge Cutler, turned up at the famous studios they were dressed in the same costumes with Reg Quantrill, the original Wurzels' guitar and banjo player, wearing a yoke across his shoulders with the two instruments hanging from either side. They passed the test and Barratt's next decision was an easy one. "The obvious thing to do was to take the mobile down to Somerset and record them on their home ground. The first session we did was in a pub and we had to install the equipment in the beer cellar and work from there which was a great hardship! After that we decided to do a second album in the same pub but by this time they had built up a large local following and about 500 people turned up to get into a pub that held about 100 at a push. Some of the people couldn't get in, got a bit rowdy and a brick was thrown through the window and if you listen to the record carefully you can hear it crashing through the glass."

The success of those first two albums meant a third recording session and then a fourth but then tragedy struck when Adge Cutler was killed in a car crash, leaving The Wurzels and Barratt with a problem. "They decided to carry on. I was a bit reluctant about the whole thing but my boss, Vic Lanza, urged me to do it and his persistence paid off in the end. We brought the lads up to Abbey Road and they recorded a version of Melanie's hit, 'Brand New Key', with new lyrics which I had found in Ireland. I got a few shivers down my spine when we were recording it and when I brought it back to the office everyone thought it was a hit. The strange thing, as much as I liked it, I wasn't altogether sure it was going to be a hit." But a hit it was and 'Combine Harvester' went to No. 1 in May 1976 with 'I Am A Cider Drinker' climbing to No. 3 in September the same year.

Although she has never had a hit record, Julie Anthony's recording session in Abbey Road in the mid-Seventies did mean that she was involved in a world's first. Because she was working in London's West End, Miss Anthony was obviously unable to go into the studio in Australia to add the vocals to the soundtrack of an Australian film entitled *Barney* and so Abbey Road's Studio Three was used for the vocal overdubs. Backing tracks were sent from Australia and Miss Anthony added a vocal track which was sent via a

Above: **Julie Anthony chats to her producer in Australia during the unique satellite link between EMI Sydney and Abbey Road, London, which involved (from left to right) engineer, Allan Rouse; Miss Anthony's husband, Eddie Natt, studio manager, Ken Townsend and engineer, Peter Vince.**

satellite link to EMI's studio in Australia where the producer listened to the finished product and made his comments via a second satellite link. This was also used by the Abbey Road staff to swap stories with the studio staff in Sydney, many of whom had worked at Abbey Road. This was the first ever satellite recording link and it resulted in a recording which was made in London and produced simultaneously 10,000 miles away in Australia.

Alan Parsons, by now a fully fledged producer, was fast joining the ranks of the Abbey Road hit makers and in 1975 he produced two successive No. 1's.

Right: **David Paton, session musician and former member of Pilot, relaxes in the Abbey Road bar.**

The Scottish four-piece, Pilot, posed Parsons some problems on their first recording session. "We had a real problem with David Paton's voice on 'Magic' because the original demo was over two years old. When we came to record it he couldn't reach the notes any more and session after session we took his voice a little higher each time until we finally reached the right note." While 'Magic' almost reached the top ten, Pilot's next single, 'January', took them to the No. 1 spot and Parsons remembers his part in the production. "They were looking for direction from me and I became more and more involved in the structuring of their songs."

While Pilot looked to Parsons for direction, Steve Harley with his group, Cockney Rebel, required no such help. "Steve was a totally different situation. He had everything worked out exactly as he wanted it," recalls Parsons who produced Steve's first four top 20 singles including the chart topping 'Make Me Smile (Come Up And See Me)' where he did make an alteration. "I remember I

Recording the latest Alan Parsons Project album in Studio Two are (left to right) Christopher Rainbow, Eric Woolfson, Chris Blair, Tony Richards (son of producer Ron Richards), Ian Bairnson (seated), Lenny Zakatek and Alan Parsons. Without ever performing in public, the group sold over three million albums.

did change the chorus on that but virtually everything was recorded just as Steve wanted it. He knew exactly what he was doing and how he wanted the records to sound."

Pink Floyd opened 1975 by going into Abbey Road to cut their album, *Wish You Were Here,* which was interrupted by a short American tour and when recording resumed in the summer of that year, a most bizarre event took place. Syd Barrett, overweight and shaven headed, wandered into the studio unrecognised while the band continued recording an album, part of which was based on the crazy antics of Barrett over the years. David Gilmour, however, was not particularly surprised at Barrett's arrival in the studio. "He turned up in the middle of the album, but it was not that surprising as he had often popped in over the years."

With total honesty Gilmour assesses the album which had the difficult job of following their multi-million selling *Dark Side Of The Moon:* "Before *Dark Side Of The Moon* the albums tended to be largely musical and not so much lyrics, but *Dark Side Of The Moon* was an opposite where the lyrics meant everything and, for me, it is weak in parts. We tried to fit the songs around the lyrics so sometimes the vehicle for a song was a little weak. What I certainly recognised and hustled the rest of the band to do, was to try and achieve a better balance on the next one where we went back in terms of achieving some of the musical heights achieved on *Echoes* and combine that with the lyrical strength we got on *Dark Side Of The Moon.* It works pretty well for me although it is not quite such a brilliant concept as *Dark Side Of The Moon* but the highlights musically are higher than the musical highlights on *Dark Side Of The Moon.*"

With the album, *Wish You Were Here,* a No. 1 in most territories around the world, Pink Floyd ended their recording career at Abbey Road, although string arrangements and overdubbing for subsequent releases have been done there. Gilmour remembers with affection the eight years he and the rest of Pink Floyd

Pink Floyd's David Gilmour (left) and Roger Waters listen attentively during the recording of the sound-track for the film The Wall.

spent in Abbey Road: "Abbey Road was always fine with me but you can get great things out of any studio. The basic quality of what you are trying to do is all important but I never had any grumbles about the place. The studios at Abbey Road for the most part have been up with the state of the art of the moment more or less. They tend to slip behind a bit sometimes because they are a bit bureaucratic."

One aspect of Abbey Road that never occurred to Gilmour during the long sessions in Studio Two was the magic of The Beatles, so often mentioned by artists and producers who have worked there. "The myth about The Beatles and Studio Two didn't affect me – it was just a studio. It never really occurred to me that The Beatles had used it. The magic of The Beatles to me wasn't that they used Abbey Road, although they certainly put it on the map. It's a good studio but The Beatles would have been The Beatles whatever studio they started off in. You get to do what you want to depending on the success you have. The Beatles, after three or four hit singles, could say, 'We want to do this', and they would be allowed to do it and nobody was going to stop them."

Yet another unlikely No. 1 came out of Abbey Road in 1975 when the stars of the BBC TV series, *It Ain't Half Hot Mum* – Windsor Davies and Don Estelle – got together to record the classic Ink Spots song, 'Whispering Grass'. Strangely the No. 1 position was still something which eluded Paul McCartney, the most active of the former Beatles. During the mid-Seventies he produced three albums in Abbey Road – *Red Rose Speedway, Band On The Run* and *Venus And Mars* – and notched up five top 10 singles during that period.

The technical advances were still coming thick and fast and, in 1976, a change occurred in Studio Three that, while being a definite necessity, signalled the end of an era. The desk in that studio was replaced that year and a Neve with 36 channels was installed, which meant that for the first time a non-EMI console had found its way into Abbey Road.

If Studio Three had the new desk, then Studio Two retained the affection of both artists and producers, and Bruce Welch recalls the moment which gave him his biggest thrill ever in a recording studio. "Producing is a creative thing to me and having the chance to work with Cliff Richard, as producer, was a challenge but exciting at the same time. Cliff had been drifting for a while and had become very much a middle of the road artist. I went out and found three songs for him after his manager had said that whoever found the right songs could produce the next album. The songs were 'Miss You Nights', 'Devil Woman' and 'I Can't Ask For Anything More Than You' and they were the first songs we did. From there it developed into the *I'm Nearly Famous* album."

The first thing that Bruce had to do was convince Cliff that recording had changed since the old days but the singer didn't need much convincing. "As soon as we started the album Cliff really got into it; he was there all the time and became totally involved in the whole thing. Without doubt it's the most satisfying thing I've ever done, mainly because of what it did for Cliff's career. Being in Studio Two with him was real joy, he's such a professional to work with."

In fact each of those three songs, found and produced by Bruce Welch, was released as a single by Cliff and each of them climbed into the top 20 but, more importantly, they re-established Cliff as a contemporary singer of the highest calibre and helped unfold a new career for him. Cliff, too, recalls his encounter with the new world of record production: "The technical advances were a bit frightening at times when you realised that if you sang a bum note they could straighten it out without getting the artist back into the studio. But it is reassuring to know

Nearly 25 years in the business of making hit singles, Cliff Richard remains a fan of Abbey Road. Seen in Studio Three Cliff is suitably attired in an Abbey Road sweatshirt.

that they cannot replace you completely with technical equipment; they need you there to sing the bum note in the first place. I personally prefer to go in and do the note again because that way you maintain the feel which can sometimes be lost by doctoring the thing."

With his new-found enthusiasm for the technical side of recording, Cliff involved himself in new projects which meant he was behind the control desk. "Production is something I really enjoy although at first it terrified me. I soon realised that you need a good engineer because I used to tell people like Peter Vince or Tony Clark what I wanted and they would fiddle around with the

Right: **Two veterans of Abbey Road got together in 1981 to record a new album. Producer, Bruce Welch, and Cilla Black at the mixing desk in Studio Three.**

knobs until I'd say, 'That's it, that's the sound I want'. You find yourself talking in sounds; singing the sounds you want to create to the engineers. But the thing I really liked about being a producer in Studio Two was that you didn't have to run up and down the stairs all the time. Now the artists came up to me which was a nice change after all the time I spent leaping up and down those stairs."

After producing Cliff and helping re-establish his career, Bruce Welch was involved in an interesting project-which brought the memories flooding back. "In early '77 I had to go into Abbey Road and put mock stereo on all the old Shadows' tracks for the TV album, *20 Golden Greats*. It meant I heard all those tracks on tape for the first time in nearly 20 years; they sounded very old but that was to do with the fact that they were original tapes coming out of modern sophisticated equipment. I kept having to remind myself that they were 20 years old and I shouldn't be too critical. Despite all that the album sold well over a million copies and began the whole Shadows' revival."

While his association with Abbey Road does not stretch back 20 years, Herbie Flowers calculates that he must have done over 2,000 sessions in the studio since that first visit for Scaffold in the late Sixties. "Scaffold were the start of it but every time I've gone there, whether it's for a Geoff Love session or to do a Sky album, I've been treated like a gentleman. But after all those sessions

Right: **Sky (left to right) Kevin Peek, Tristan Fry, Steve Gray, Herbie Flowers and John Williams, are regular visitors to Abbey Road.**

I've got to own up about the scrounging I've done there. I've had mike stands and stuff, which I've always taken back, and the odd pair of drum sticks for my son. Whenever I drove past, if I was short of something I'd nip in and borrow it."

Over the years records produced in Abbey Road have been the subject of numerous plaudits and awards but there is one honour that both the studio and, more importantly, the artist concerned, were reluctant to accept. In 1976 the British Market Research Bureau issued a chart for the week of February 21 showing *Rodrigo's Guitar Concerto D'Aranjuez* by Manuel and His Music Of The Mountains at No. 1. However, within three hours, they had discovered a fault in the computer and the chart was duly amended and the correct chart placed the Four Seasons with *December 63* at No. 1 and relegated Manuel (alias Geoff Love) to number four, thus denying Love his first ever No. 1 record. Three hours remains the shortest stay at No. 1 by any artist!

A far more enviable record came Paul McCartney's way in December 1977 when his recording of 'Mull Of Kintyre' held the No. 1 position for nine weeks and became the first pop single to sell over 2 million copies in the United Kingdom; it also gave Paul his first No. 1 since leaving The Beatles. Recorded on the Abbey Road mobile on location at the Mull of Kintyre in Scotland, the record was completed in Abbey Road and held the top spot until the end of January 1978, becoming the best selling single in Britain.

*Below: **At his farm in Scotland, Paul McCartney and Wings are joined by the Campbeltown Pipe Band before recording the multi-million-selling single, 'Mull of Kintyre'.***

Until that year a friendly 'battle' had gone on between Cliff Richard and Paul McCartney over the booking of Studio Two which Cliff remembers vividly: "There's got to be something special about Studio Two – why do you think Paul and I have been fighting each other for years to get in there. When I rang up they always said, 'Sorry, Paul's got it', and it wasn't until years later that I discovered that when Paul rang they told him, 'Sorry Cliff's in there'. We spent the whole time battling for that studio until Paul finally went off and had an exact replica of Studio Two built in the basement of his London office."

'No, I booked Studio Two before you'. Cliff Richard and Paul McCartney have a chat during Vera Samwell's farewell party.

Bruce Welch has cause to remember the occasion, as he was in Studio Two at the time Paul made his decision. "I was working in there doing some things with the live recording of Cliff and The Shadows' reunion concerts. It was December, and the thing was due to go on television in January so I had a pretty tight deadline to meet, when they told me Paul had rung and asked for the studio. They came in to see me and asked me to move out so Paul could come in but as I was already working a 15 hour day to get the thing finished I couldn't even think about moving out. I think Paul got the needle about it and went off and built the replica studio in his basement. It was an amazing thing to do; he put in land-lines and built an exact replica of the place with the same black stuff on the ceiling and even took a photograph from the control room looking down into the studio and put it up on one of the walls."

While Abbey Road was used for McCartney's Wings album, *London Town*, the replica studios were used to record part of the same band's *Back To The Egg* album in 1979, which included the famous *Rockestra Theme* which won the 1979 Grammy Award for the best instrumental recording. Paul McCartney assembled in Abbey Road, for a session that was filmed for posterity, a band comprising of some of the finest rock musicians around. The list reads as follows: Pete Townshend, David Gilmour, Hank Marvin, Denny Laine and Lawrence Juber (guitars); John Bonham, Kenny Jones and Steve Holly (drums); Ray Cooper, Tony Carr, Speedy Acquaye and Maurice Pert (percussion); Paul McCartney, Bruce Thomas and Ronnie Lane (bass); John Paul Jones, Gary Booker, Tony Ashton and Linda McCartney (keyboards) and Howie Casey, Thaddeus Richard, Tony Dorsey and Steve Howard (horns) .

In his interview with *Rolling Stone's* Paul Gambaccini in 1979, Paul outlined the background of the session: "A lot of people in music had been thinking about using a rock'n'roll line-up instead of an orchestra. So I wrote a tune and finally just asked people if they would like to be in Rockestra. Keith Moon was going to turn up but unfortunately he died a week before. But Jeff Beck was gonna come and Eric Clapton and they actually didn't turn up. Beck was worried about what would happen if he didn't like the track. Eric didn't feel like it, there was some kind of reason, he had flu or something, but most of the people did turn up."

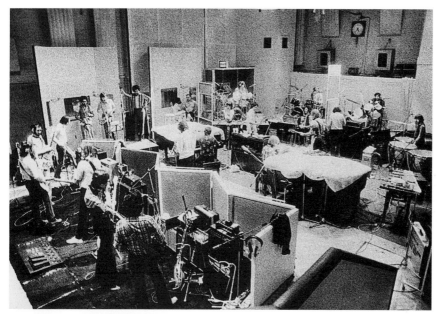

Left: **Linda McCartney was on hand with her camera during her husband's famous Rockestra session in 1979 and captured the greatest 'supergroup' ever formed in action.** Middle left: **(left to right) Ronnie Lane (ex Small Faces), Bruce Thomas (from Elvis Costello's group) and the late John Bonham (Led Zeppelin) exchanging ideas.** Middle right: **She caught Pete Townshend (right) giving percussionist Ray Cooper a few tips.**

Right: **A guitar line-up featuring (from left to right) Laurence Juber (Wings), Hank Marvin (Shadows), David Gilmour (Pink Floyd), Denny Laine (Wings) and Pete Townshend (The Who).**

Co-engineer, Mark Vigars, remembers the preparation involved for that memorable session. "Initially it seemed that it was going to involve a lot of work and a lot of planning and then about a week before we were told that the whole thing was going to be filmed. We thought it would be just a couple of cameras and a few lights but it turned out to be much more than that. Paul had sensibly asked that none of the cameras should be visible but, in the end, we couldn't arrange that. But the film company got in set designers and in Studio Two they built a whole false wall at one end with various levels and windows for the cameras. This added to the problems we already had and it took three days to build all this. In addition we had to use extra lines and about 60 mikes in all and we had two mixers in the control room and two 24-track machines going, one for the record and one for the film sound-track.

"We had four mikes on each drum kit, that was all we had space for, and because of filming we couldn't put screens up. The number of musicians, funnily enough, wasn't really a problem, it was just different. But because of the time problem we only had one day to do it all in, we couldn't spend as much time as we would have liked to create the ideal sound; we just had to get the best we could and in the end I think we did quite well."

The relationship between Paul and Linda McCartney and Abbey Road is more than just business; a fact that is well illustrated by the strange request which came when Wings went off on tour. In an effort to ensure that their goldfish were well cared for during their absence, Linda discovered an engineer at the studio who had a way with goldfish and once a week he dashed round to Paul's nearby house to feed and clean them!

Cliff Richard leads Vera Samwell into Studio Two for her surprise retirement party. They are joined by Welsh Soprano Beti-Mary Owen, and in the background producer Bob Barratt.

Vera Samwell (who began her career with Abbey Road in 1941 and over the years developed a close relationship with many of the artists who relied on her to book studio time for them) retired in 1979 and the studio was the only place considered when it came to organising a leaving party. Herbie Flowers was one of the guests that night: "Everybody was there and Cliff, Paul and I were asked to say a few words and present Vera with various gifts. It's funny but before we had to get up and do it, we were all saying how nervous we felt about going on stage in front of all the Abbey Road people. It's different to put on a stage act in front of those people; you can't bullshit anybody there."

Receptions and parties have, in fact, become a regular feature of life at Abbey Road with Paul McCartney launching his *Back To The Egg* album there (when tables with umbrellas were designed to look like fried eggs) and Stevie Wonder was welcomed to Britain in 1980 with a party in Abbey Road. Those fortunate enough to be around when the fun had died down were treated to an impromptu performance by the great man at the piano in Studio Two.

Above: **Paul McCartney admits to 'not being very good at speeches'** *during Vera Samwell's retirement party. The interested spectators are Linda McCartney, Vera Samwell and studio manager, Ken Townsend.*

Left: **Stevie Wonder gives an impromptu performance at the piano in Studio Two** *after a reception to launch his album Hotter Than July.*

Live albums, too, became a feature of life at Abbey Road with both Chas and Dave and Little and Large performing there in front of invited audiences. But the day to day work at Abbey Road continues to be the producing of high quality recordings for artists from all areas of the music business. The trend which began some years earlier of artists using several different studios during the making of one album continues today and it's unlikely that one studio will ever dominate the recording world as Abbey Road did during the Sixties and early Seventies.

The list of artists who recorded some part of a record in Abbey Road during the seventies is almost endless and includes names such as Spandau Ballet, Simple Minds, Boney M, Kiki Dee, XTC, Mike Oldfield, Jeff Beck, Gillan, Dexy's Midnight Runners, Greg Lake – who, in fact, recorded his Christmas hit of 1975, 'I Believe In Father Christmas', in Abbey Road and there are tales of

Above: **Surrounded by session musicians, conductor Michael Nyman, former Police members Sting (right) and Andy Summers (seated centre) can be seen here in Studio Two, during the recording of the soundtrack for the film Brimstone and Treacle.**

Right: **Sting performing into an RCA 44BX ribbon microphone c.1940's.**

strippers being brought in to entertain the musicians and add to the festive spirit – Magazine, Tom Robinson, Kirsty McColl, Gang of Four and The Vapors.

Early in 1982 two members of the supergroup Police spent a week in Abbey Road's Studio Two. Andy Summers and Sting were there working on the sound track for Sting's latest film, *Brimstone and Treacle*. Another star visitor to Abbey Road during the early part of the year was Adam Ant. He chose the famous old Studio One for one track that required a particular drum sound and the result was his No. 1 hit single, 'Goody Two Shoes'.

Elton John spent many hours in Abbey Road (before establishing himself as a super star) as a session piano player and later returned to record orchestral parts for his albums. Ian Dury hired the Abbey Road mobile unit to record a series of concerts at London's Hammersmith Odeon. But it isn't just the artists recording there who pass through the doors of Abbey Road. Many American acts, when they visit Britain, ask for a trip to Abbey Road to be added to their itinerary.

Andy Summers

Martyn Cox, for many years head of EMI's Capitol Records' operation in London remembers some of the calls he got. "The Knack came over in 1979 to meet the people at EMI in London and the one thing they really wanted to do was visit Abbey Road and when we took them up there they just stood in Studio Two in total amazement. The Shadows were in there at the time and let the guys in to have a look round and for them it was like being on hallowed ground. They even achieved their ambition of recording in Studio Two when they came back later in the year to promote their hit single, 'My Sharona'. They had to do some backing tracks for a TV show and no other studio was even considered – it had to be Studio Two at Abbey Road."

Cox recalls two other men who wanted to visit Abbey Road: "Sammy Hagar was desperate to record there and in fact did two albums there simply because it was the place The Beatles recorded. Afterwards he said that he got a sound that couldn't have been captured anywhere in the world. Miami Steve Van Zant, guitarist with Bruce Springsteen's band, turned out to be another Beatles freak who wanted to pay homage to Studio Two."

While Studio Two ran the risk of being regarded as a shrine to The Beatles and all that had gone on before, a new modern studio was being finished on the top floor of the building. Walls were knocked down and rubbish was removed to make way for the Penthouse studio with its 48-track-plus Neve console and windows which looked on the outside world; a rare feature for any recording studio. Bob Barratt, a producer whose experiences over the years had taken him through each and every one of Abbey Road studios, was an early arrival in the Penthouse, possibly a little too early. "I went in there in 1980 with the King's Singers and we were in some ways guinea pigs for the new studio. There were a

lot of teething problems but now that they've been ironed out it's my favourite studio – even though it's a long way from the bar."

The Penthouse, since its official opening in 1980, when all the technical teething troubles had been sorted out, has become a firm favourite with most of the artists who have recorded there but there have been exceptions. Roy Wood, who hadn't really enjoyed any of his three previous visits to Abbey Road, tried the Penthouse soon after the re-building and the installation of equipment had been completed. "They'd put the new Neve desk in but unfortunately I couldn't give an opinion on that because it didn't work. It took nearly three hours to get any sound out of it at all; the technical blokes were all in there and by that time I was getting a bit cheesed. I'd been round to the pub a couple of times while they were trying to get the thing to work and got a few drinks down me and consequently the session didn't go too well after that. The equipment looked very impressive but I can't say I was impressed with the sound!"

Cliff Richard became, after only a few visits, a great fan of the new studio perched high on top of the building. "It's very much the sort of studio I like to work in. It's far more intimate and really useful because most of the things we've done there have been overdubs as opposed to actual recording." Max Boyce, too, felt very strongly about Abbey Road's fourth studio. "I much prefer the smaller studio because I sing better in a smaller room, large studios make me think of a live hall and having to reach all four corners. I discovered there is a definite technique in studio singing – I can sell a song live with all the atmosphere but in the studio I tend to try too hard and there is a danger of overselling the song. I remember that at first the thought of making a mistake in the studio really worried me until I came to terms with the idea that sometimes the mistakes can be corrected technically."

Although Abbey Road no longer dominated the recording world, and the idea of using more than one studio became common practice, there were still artists who were anxious to use Abbey Road and experience the much publicised magic of Studio Two. Kate Bush, who had risen to instant stardom when her debut single, 'Wuthering Heights', shot to No. 1, used Abbey Road and that particular studio for her third album, 'Never For Ever'. "It was a very magical experience. Being on your own in Studio Two is a fascinating experience and I felt there were at least 10 other people with me; the place had tremendous presence. I don't think it's just the fact that The Beatles recorded there but a combination of all the people who have been there over the years and all their combined creativity. I felt tremendous vibes in there, both positive and negative. You know it's built on ley lines which means there are very powerful forces at work."

However, Kate didn't restrict herself to Studio Two. "Studio One is very warm and despite the enormous size of the studio I never felt scared or lonely when singing in there, which is something I have felt in other studios." But Studio Two became a very special place for Kate. "I found the studio tremendously creative to such an extent that I was writing an awful lot of songs in there. I even thought of coming in in the evenings just to write but it would have

Opposite page: **Kate Bush achieved her ambition to record in Abbey Road in 1980 and enjoys working in her magical Studio Two control room.**

been an enormously expensive way of writing. I did the vocals for 'Breathing' in there and I wanted to get a very special sound – to create a feeling of despair after a nuclear disaster – and it was perfect with the wonderful EMT echo plates. The sound in the whole studio is perfect and I'm sure the place has not been decorated for years; I don't think anybody would dare give it a coat of paint or put wall coverings up for fear of changing the sound."

Although it was the first time she had recorded there, Kate's visit in 1979 was not the first time she had been to Abbey Road. "My first visit was as a 15-year-old schoolgirl when I was invited to a Pink Floyd session for the album *Wish You Were Here*. I was absolutely staggered and I really thought I would never be able to record in a place like Abbey Road. But when I started recording I always wanted to go back and record there; firstly because I'm always anxious to try different studios and secondly because it has always been a special place for me."

Kate Bush chose Studio One as the location to make a promotional video for her single, 'Sat In Your Lap'.

Kate Bush also used Abbey Road to record part of her fourth album which was released in early 1982 and one of the instruments she used on that album was a didgeridoo which was sent over from Australia, but somebody had to be

hired to play it on the sessions, as Kate explains: "I'm not allowed to play it. Under the Aborigine beliefs it is an instrument that only a male is allowed to play and I wouldn't dare play it and insult their laws; I'm just honoured to own it." With Kate on her early sessions was co-producer and engineer, John Kelly, who had wide experience with many studios but had never worked in Abbey Road before. "I was very sceptical about the whole myth thing that had grown up around Studio Two and The Beatles, but after a few days recording there I realised that there is something very special about the place; it's a feeling, an aura if you like, that is particularly unique to Studio Two."

Paul McCartney chose two locations to record his single, 'Coming Up', in 1980. The mobile unit was taken to Glasgow to record one version which was subsequently released in America and reached No. 1 in the US charts, while a studio version was done in Abbey Road, released in the UK and reached No. 2 in the charts.

After nearly 49 years as one of the world's premier recording studios, the cavernous Studio One was turned into an auction room on October 15 and 16, 1980, when a sale of recording equipment and memorabilia took place. Organised by Abbey Road and Jackson Music Limited, the sale included equipment, both old and new, valued at over half a million pounds and gathered from studios all around the world. There were mixing consoles, multi-track recorders, mastering and dubbing machines, monitors, microphones, cutting lathes plus tapes and video cassettes. In addition, two 24-track mobile recording studios were on offer but even they could not be fitted into the huge studio.

The sale resulted from the building of the new Penthouse studio which took over much used storage room in the building. In addition to this EMI stock, equipment was gathered from the studios. Even at knock-down prices the mobile studios were on offer at £70,000 and mixing consoles at £20,000. They stood alongside £15 loudhailers and microphones ranging from £45 to over £500. But the items which created most interest were those which came under the hammer of Phillip's auctioneer, Andrew Hilton, on the afternoon of the second day. A toilet roll rejected by The Beatles as being 'too hard' and stamped the property of EMI Ltd was sold for £85; an ashtray standing 2 foot 6 inches high, and used by Ringo Starr on most of his Abbey Road sessions, fetched £130 and a copy of Brian Epstein's book, *A Cellarful Of Noise*, autographed by The Beatles and producer, George Martin, went for £210.

Studio manager, Ken Townsend, with the Mellotron and four-track tape recorder used by The Beatles on their Sgt Pepper album. These were just two of the items in the auction of memorabilia at Abbey Road's 'Sale Of The Century'.

In addition a Studer J37 four track recorder used by The Beatles on their *Sgt Pepper* album fetched £500 and a Mellotron tape organ (with original tapes) used by The Beatles, brought a bid of £1,000 from rock star Mike Oldfield, who also purchased, for £220, two Belcamen valve limiters used on his own multi-million selling *Tubular Bells* album.

Ken Townsend viewed the sale as a complete success with only minor reservations. "The only disappointment for me was some of the bids for the

In 1981 the original Hollies re-formed for one TV appearance and a photo session outside the studio. Gathered round the famous road sign are (left to right) Graham Nash, Allan Clarke, Bobby Elliott, Tony Hicks and Eric Haydock.

equipment associated with various star names. It goes to show that while autographs and souvenirs have great value, equipment used by stars didn't really increase in value at all." The sale was one way of getting rid of surplus equipment, and raising some money for the studios, but it is not the only way that Abbey Road has of disposing of their stock. For years very little ex-Abbey Road equipment found its way to the second-hand market as it was invariably utilised by one of EMI's many studios around the world; studios as far apart as India and Mexico, Singapore and Paris, Hong Kong and Cologne, and Australia and Lagos (which is where Paul McCartney recorded part of his fine *Band On The Run* album).

While Paul McCartney is a regular visitor to Abbey Road, in 1981 a man paid a return visit after nearly a decade away from the old familiar building in North London. Graham Nash left the Hollies for the warmth of California in the late Sixties and joined the super group Crosby, Stills, Nash and Young but he returned to record with his old buddies in late 1981. Tony Hicks was with Nash when he came back: "It had been so long for him that, strangely enough, he'd forgotten a lot of the people which surprised me. They'd also forgotten him although a good few didn't recognise him because he has changed a lot over the years. He was just in a daze – he couldn't believe it. We went to work in Studio Two and that brought back a whole lot of memories for all of us."

Another return visitor to Abbey Road that year was Tim Rice who brought

Elaine Paige, the star of *Evita* and *Cats* along. "We did just one track in Studio Two and the orchestral sound was absolutely great. Just before that I had been in Studio One for the Music For Pleasure recording of *Joseph And His Amazing Technicolour Dreamcoat* with Norman Newell producing and I actually sang on that recording. It was nice to work in there again."

Abbey Road moved out of its St John's Wood comfort for a couple of weeks in the spring of 1981 when the studio took a stand for the first time at the Ideal Home Exhibition to celebrate 50 years of recording. Complete with displays of recording techniques, the staff from Abbey Road answered questions from interested visitors and hosted special star days when artists such as The Shadows, Geoff Love, Herbie Flowers, Iris Williams and Little and Large made personal appearances and signed copies of the records they had made in the famous studios.

Although he had never visited the studio, His Royal Highness The Prince of Wales did figure closely in a recording session at Abbey Road in 1981. His children's book, *The Old Man Of Lochnagar,* was recorded utilising all four studios. Producer was Norman Newell, engineers Allan Rouse, Peter Vince, Peter Bown and John Kurlander, and Peter Ustinov was narrator. All gave their services for nothing and Abbey Road made no charge for the studio time as all proceeds from the sales of the record went to Prince Charles' Charity Trust.

Ustinov, who was Prince Charles' personal choice as narrator, flew from Europe for the recording sessions and he had to make two extra trips when things went wrong. Firstly, a rock and roll session by Greg Lake in Studio Three disturbed his recording in the Penthouse, causing a cancellation and then he was called back to re-record a couple of words after Prince Charles had commented on the Scottish pronunciation upon hearing the test pressings. Everything had to be sent to Prince Charles for final approval and in the end, word came from Buckingham Palace that he was 'thrilled' with the re-cording.

The end of 1980 brought with it the tragic death of John Lennon in New York and, although it had been

A couple of Abbey Road old boys who've made good! Andrew Lloyd Webber (left) and Tim Rice both began their careers in the EMI studios.

10 years since he had visited Abbey Road, the feeling there was not just of losing a brilliant talent but a friend as well. During his years as a Beatle, Lennon had brought a lot of fun to the studio with his irreverent sense of humour and won friends with his warmth and enthusiasm for his work. The fans too,

One of John Lennon's last Abbey Road sessions involved him recording his own heart beat with Yoko, as ever, in close attendance.

regarded Abbey Road as an important part of Lennon's life and when Yoko Ono asked for 10 minutes' silence to be observed at 2 pm, New York time, on the afternoon of Sunday, December 14, they arrived at the studio at the British equivalent of 7 pm to pay their last respects.

Allan Rouse was one of the half a dozen people working that Sunday evening and what took place had a lasting effect on him. "It all started happening at about six o'clock when the first fan arrived and by seven there were about 150 people sitting on the studio steps, or on cars or just standing around the car park. They had burning candles and stood in absolute silence, one of them even took up a yoga position and meditated in the car park. Some of the people from the studio went out and joined them and at the end of the 10 minutes' silence I went into an office at the front of the building, turned the speakers to face out of the window, and played 'Imagine'. It was a very moving experience." Not knowing where else to send them, fans also sent wreaths and cards to the studio.

Pop had, of course, dominated recording at Abbey Road for two decades but the advent of digital recording gave a new emphasis to the classical world, although the first digital single released in Britain was an EMI pop recording of jazz musicians, Morrissey and Mullen, playing 'Love Don't Live Here Anymore'. The first digitally recorded orchestral album also came out of Abbey Road when Geoff Love recorded *Super Natural* as Manuel and His Music Of The Mountains.

Former head of EMI Records (UK) classical division, John Pattrick, believes that one of the earliest classical digital pieces, André Previn's recording of Debussy's *Images,* was a milestone. "It was considered the best illustration of the art and was a notable recording which received critical acclaim." The Academy of St Martin in the Fields with Neville

A rare combination of talents: Yehudi Menuhin, Nelson Riddle and Stephane Grappelli join forces to record the album Top Hat, *in Studio Two.*

Marriner also received great praise for their record of *The Academy In Concert Volume 2,* recorded digitally at Abbey Road.

According to Pattrick the introduction of digital recording had a very positive effect on the musicians and conductors. "It was an outstanding development and, in the first few months, recording artists showed a great deal of interest. They wanted to know everything about it and now it has become the norm for classical recording; in fact it's difficult to persuade anybody not to record digitally nowadays. The important thing is that it does sell records as there is always real interest in any new technology."

While they may not have recorded digitally, Duran Duran did attempt to record their first single in Abbey Road but unfortunately things didn't work out exactly as planned. Original drummer, Roger Taylor, who was searching for a particular drum sound on the track 'Planet Earth' is the best man to tell

Top left: *Ex-Prime Minister Edward Heath visited Abbey Road in 1977 to record an album of Christmas carols. Mr Heath (left) was assisted by engineer, Allan Rouse; producer, Christopher Bishop and (standing) engineer, Stuart Eltham.*

the story. "It was our first single and EMI suggested we use Abbey Road, we thought, 'Great, Kate Bush, The Beatles... they've used it so it should be good enough for us'. The problem was that we wanted to get a really heavy drum sound and when we started in Studio Two it felt great. But we spent a whole day in there trying for this particular sound and we just couldn't get it.

Left: *Duran Duran spent a day in Abbey Road but drummer, Roger Taylor (second from the right) couldn't get the right drum sound.*

We wanted a heavy sort of disco sound – a bass drum sound – but we could only get a sort of normal Kate Bush/Beatles sound.

"It was sad because it's a great studio with a great atmosphere and some really good people. We used the Penthouse for some vocal mixes (we didn't record in there) and that was really good. I loved the fact that it had windows and was nice and light; it's a really good little studio."

Throughout its first 50 years, Abbey Road established itself not only as a recording studio but as a training ground. Many new and exciting talents were given their first real opportunity after passing through the portals of the white painted house in ritzy St John's Wood. This list makes impressive reading by any standards: Yehudi Menuhin, Elisabeth Schwarzkopf, Gioconda de Vito, Reginald Dixon, Max Bygraves, Ruby Murray, Ronnie Hilton, Michael Holliday, Cliff Richard, The Shadows, Adam Faith, Helen Shapiro, The Beatles,

Above Left: **Chesney Allen (centre) with Christopher Timothy (left) and Roy Hudd during the recording of the album from the West End stage show, Underneath The Arches, starring Hudd and Timothy as Flanagan and Allen.**

Above centre: **Classical producer John Fraser (left), Yehudi Menuhin and (right) studio manager Ken Townsend admire the Abbey Road 50th birthday cake.**
Inset opposite page: **Old pals Wally Ridley (left) and Joe Loss get together at the party.**
Opposite page: **Twenty years of Abbey Road hit-making represented by Helen Shapiro (left) and Kate Bush as they blow out the candles on the Abbey Road 50th birthday cake.**

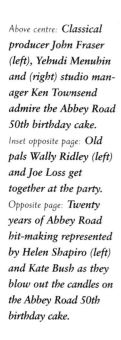

Cilla Black, Manfred Mann, Pilot, Steve Harley, Max Boyce, Iris Williams, Pink Floyd, Alan Parsons and The Hollies.

Among the party-goers on November 12 1981 – 50 years ago to the day since Abbey Road's opening – were former studio manager Gus Cook, producer George Martin, Wally Ridley and Norman Smith, Joe Loss, Malcolm Roberts, Helen Shapiro, Shadows drummers past and present, Tony Meehan and Brian Bennett, disc jockey Mike Read, Kate Bush, Denny Laine, former Pilot men, David Paton and Ian Bairnson, ex-Cockney Rebel members Stuart Elliott and Duncan Mackay, Alan Parsons and champions of the classical cause such as Peter Andry, producer Suvi Raj Grubb, David Bicknell and Yehudi Menuhin who was joined by his pupil, the 12 year-old Chinese violinist, Jin Li, following in the footsteps of his teacher who himself began his career at Abbey Road as a young schoolboy.

There was a giant birthday cake, decorated with strawberries and kiwi fruit and created by Abbey Road's own catering staff which was cut under the bright lights of BBC TV's *Nationwide* by Helen Shapiro and Kate Bush, two young ladies who span two decades of Abbey Road's glorious history.

While the party celebrated the studio's half century, the 50th year ended on a truly historic note when Helmut Schmidt, Chancellor of West Germany, made a brief but hectic visit to the studios just prior to Christmas. Although he

wasn't on official business it was nevertheless a working trip for the politician as he was there to play the piano! The Chancellor, an able pianist and organist, was invited by West German pianists, Christoph Eschenbach and Justus Frantz, to play on a recording of Mozart's Concerto for three pianos in F major K242, along with the London Philharmonic Orchestra in Abbey Road's Studio One. Watched by personal bodyguards and security men, the Chancellor played the third piano part in a session that formed part of EMI's International Classical Division's recording of Mozart's piano concertos. The album featuring Chancellor Schmidt (who donated his fee to Amnesty International) was released in the spring of 1982.

The Chancellor flew from Hamburg on December 22 in his official plane and spent over five hours in the studio before returning home the same evening. Producer John Willan expressed himself well pleased with the session and explained: "We wanted a special player for the concerto because it was not written necessarily for a professional musician. The third piano part isn't the sort of piece you can get a big name pianist to perform."

If Chancellor Schmidt paid his first visit to Abbey Road in 1981, Yehudi Menuhin was on familiar ground when he spoke at the birthday party in November of that year. Watched by his young pupil, Menuhin stood firmly in the middle of his beloved Studio One and looked back over a half century of

recording. "This is a very special occasion not just because it represents 50 years of wonderful work, of some of the best records made in the world, but also because I've been given the chance to introduce a young colleague who himself perhaps – if the world is still in one piece 50 years hence – will be able to tell that he remembers this studio 50 years ago, as I do today. I hope and wish that we will be able to celebrate many more achievements that will be a credit to music, to the artistic and cultural life of this wonderful country and a credit to EMI Music and Abbey Road, the company that has stood behind these works and this progress."

Above: **Pianists Christoph Eschenbach and Justus Frantz, together with West German Chancellor Helmut Schmidt and producer John Willan, appreciate one of classical producer John Fraser's better jokes.**

Right: **In Studio One Chancellor Schmidt (left) and Justus Frantz play the piano while Christoph Eschenbach (right) conducts the London Philharmonic Orchestra**

9

Just for the Record

So how does one go about making a record? Well the first, and probably most important decision, is where rather than how; after all, these days there is almost no limit to the number of studios available for recording. Sadly on occasions, and most usually for tax reasons, many top British acts are forced to record outside the UK. However, and wherever, the choice is very important as it can take anything from a fortnight to six months to make an album. It is essential therefore that the surroundings are comfortable and relaxed, as the pressures on people working closely together for that length of time can be enormous.

Assuming that one of Abbey Road's four studios is the eventual choice, then the procedure would usually be as follows. Before the start of the session, using

Above: **The London sky-line looms up behind the Abbey Road complex. Clearly visible to the rear of the house itself, are the roofs of Studios One, Two and Three, whilst hidden beneath a mass of air conditioning ducts is the new Penthouse studio.**

Left and next page: **Filling in the studio lay-out sheet is a regular practice for the balance engineer at Abbey Road in order that his assistant and the technical engineer know what is required for each session. It is interesting to note that a Beatles session in 1967 required just 11 microphones for four musicians while a Sky recording session in 1981 (for five musicians) has a total of 36 microphones, 17 on the drum kit alone.**

STUDIO 3

Engineers	Artiste	Dates – Times – Etc.	Session Type
AC HB	SKY	SEPT 1987	24TD (30 i.p.s.) *

Input	Line	Purpose	Mic	Boom	Inject	Input	Line	Purpose	Mic	Boom	Inject
1		BASS	D.I.			25		OBX	D.I.		
2		HH	421			26		OB1	D.I.		
3		BASS DRUM	FET 47			27		JOHN AMP	67		
4		SNARE	421			28			D.I.		
5		SNARE	86			29		ACOUSTIC	86		
6		SNARE	84 (mostly breath)			30		KEV AMP	FET 67		
7		TOM	190			31			D.I.		
8		TOM	190			32		ACOUSTIC	86		
9		TOM	190			33		CLAVINET	D.I.		
10		TOM	190			34		DRUM BOX	D.I.		
11		TOM	190			35		PROPH	D.I.		
12		TOM	190			36		TIB	87		
13		TOM	190			Echo Send			Telephone		
14		TOM	190			1		No.3 PLATE	RET REP2 23+24		
15		TOM	190			2		DELAY PLATE 'A'	RET REP2 21+22		
16		CRASH	84			3					
17		OH L	4038			4					
18		OH R	4038			Cue			Extras		
19		PIANO	47			1		CANS	FAIRCHILD		
20		PIANO	47			2					
21		HpSchd	D.I.			3		CANS – KEV + JOHN	AKG DDL.		
22						4					
23		HpSchd	456			Autolocator 1			Autolocator 2		
24			456			24T			STEREO 1		

Scale ⅛" = 1 Foot

REF No 12304 Abbey Rd

* Please line up 16T NON DOLBY 30 IPS as well. thanks

information previously obtained, engineers will have laid out the studio, and set up the microphones, tape machines and any other equipment that may be required so that the business of recording can start as soon as possible. After all, the total costs of making a record can be very high, so any time that can be saved will always be appreciated by the client. Depending on the type of recording, the microphones will be positioned accordingly. For classical situations, the microphones will be placed some distance away from the performers, the idea being to create as close as possible the natural sound and balance of the musicians. Meanwhile, for pop acts the mic's will be much closer, and in certain cases instruments will be connected directly to the mixing desk, a procedure known as direct injection, and one which is regularly adopted with the likes of bass guitars and synthesisers. Also, unlike their classical counterparts, individual musicians or groups of musicians will often be separated from each other by screens in order to keep the sounds from the different instruments as separate as possible, thus enabling greater control over the total balance. The first step will be the 'run-through'; this acts as a rehearsal for the musicians, and also enables the engineer to adjust the levels and sound quality from the microphones.

When the arrangement and the sound balance are to everyone's satisfaction, then the actual process of recording can commence. Abbey Road offers the facility to record directly onto various formats ranging from ¼ inch stereo tape, to 2 inch 24 track. The advantage of the multi-track system is that the different musicians or individual instruments can be recorded simultaneously on to the 24 separate tracks. It is also possible to electronically synchronise two or more multi-track machines together, thus facilitating as many tracks as may be required for the recording. Under these circumstances, the only limiting factor is the number of channels on the desk. If, during the initial recording, some tracks are left empty, then this will permit the addition of further instruments or vocals at a later time. This process is referred to as overdubbing, and forms a regular part of pop recording.

One of the greatest benefits derived from overdubbing, particularly when session musicians have been engaged for the recording, is that, in the event of something not working out properly, only the musician(s) concerned need return to put it right. Previously, if a performance was not totally satisfactory, all the musicians would be needed to re-record the piece completely. The alternative, which did occasionally happen, was that if the mistakes were only minor, then the record would be released as it was... warts and all.

Remixing is the next stage, when the engineer plays back the recorded multi-track tape and adjusts the levels of the individual tracks until a satisfactory balance is attained. It is at this stage that any final adjustments are made to the sound, including the addition of any effects such as echo. Abbey Road has three natural echo chambers, plus a selection of plate echo systems; these are devices capable of simulating the sound of a natural chamber but with variable reverberation times. The resulting 'mix' is then recorded onto the two tracks of a ¼ inch machine, which correspond to the left and right channels of a domestic stereo system.

Of course, this process is not obligatory, and many recordings are still made direct to stereo. And the recent introduction of digital recording has turned the

A worm's eye view of number two echo chamber with its strategically placed sewer pipes, microphone (left) and speaker (right).

Above from left to right:
Multi-track tape
editing – a) the editor
first of all marks, with
a chinagraph pencil,
the point at which he
wants to make a cut b)
the tape is then placed
in a 2 inch editing
block and the cut is
made with a non-mag-
netic razor blade c)
when the cut is
complete the two loose
ends of the tape are
joined with special
adhesive tape to form
a complete section
(note the separate
record and playback
heads with their 24
individual sections d)
any excessive adhesive
tape is trimed with
non-magnetic scissors
before the joined tape
is played.

art of recording, in particular that of classical music, back almost full circle to the principles adopted in the late Fifties.

Another fundamental difference between pop and classical recording is that whereas any corrections and additions required during pop recording are made within the one master take, and then the individual tracks remixed to stereo, classical recordings are treated quite differently. The master tapes containing all the takes of a particular work are passed to one of Abbey Road's editors. He, with the guidance of a music score, carefully marked by the record producer, will join all the best takes together to produce a complete and faultless performance. This intricate process often takes many hours, particularly with musical items such as operas.

The finished stereo master will eventually be sent to one of Abbey Road's four disc cutting rooms, where, using a combination of sophisticated electronics and a specialised lathe, a lacquer-disc version of the recording is made. This first disc is put through a series of stringent tests to check that all technical parameters are correct. Further acetates, as they are known, will also be made and sent to the producer and artist for their approval. When all parties are satisfied with the product, a subsequent master will be sent, unplayed, to the record factory where it will be processed for final manufacture.

At this stage the recording process is almost complete, it remains only for copy tapes of the original masters to be made. These copy masters are sent to the various record companies throughout the world involved in the release of each particular record.

The advent of two track digital recording brought about considerable changes to the recording methods available at Abbey Road. Until 1980, all stereo recordings had been made using analogue machines, which convert the sound waves into electrical impulses and store them on conventional magnetic tape, the process being easily reversed in much the same manner as the grooves on a disc. This system, however, is not without its failings. The main disadvantage is distortion, and background noise in the form of tape hiss, although this problem has been partially solved by electronic equipment such as the Dolby Noise Reduction System.

Digital recording has overcome these problems by converting the sound waves into numbers, which are stored on highly sensitive tape. Industrial video

cassette recorders are used for this process, with the addition of a device known as a pulse code modulator (PCM), the piece of equipment which converts the sound into numbers and back again. When a recording is replayed, it is the numbers only which are converted back into sound waves, which means the total eradication of tape noise and distortion. An additional advantage of the digital system is the fact that however many times you copy a recording, the numbers always remain the same, and consequently the quality of the musical content never deteriorates.

Above two photos: EMI's prototype eight-track digital mixing console; the three racks house the computer equipment needed to operate the desk.

This ability to copy without change is utilised in the digital editing process, as the original principle of cut and join can no longer be employed. Now, special dedicated equipment enables the editor to copy the relevant takes in the sequence in which they are required, electronically joining them together as he goes, eventually ending up with a complete master. Currently this high quality system is limited to professional studios; however, prototypes of digital disc players already exist, and in the not too distant future the public will be able to purchase hardware which will enable them to appreciate the ultimate in sound reproduction.

Ken Townsend, former General Manager of Abbey Road Studios, worked there for over a quarter of a century, and saw many changes in recording techniques over the years. "It was all mono recording on ¼ inch tape when I first began, and we purely and simply reproduced what was being played in the studio with the minimum of editing. When stereo was introduced in 1958, it corresponded with the arrival of the first British pop groups – Cliff Richard and The Shadows and The Vipers – and they were EMI acts who were recorded in EMI studios with EMI producers. As more and more groups emerged in the Sixties, together with the introduction of four track recording, we saw the end of the limited recording sessions. Three hour sessions were no longer sufficient for the groups who, because of the large amount of records they sold, were able to afford more and more time in the studios. This meant that the studios became the centre for innovation. I don't think it will ever be possible for one studio to dominate recording as Abbey Road did during the Sixties. As the number of recording acts grew and grew, so the number of studios available increased; acts were taking weeks and months to record albums, and days to do a single."

The control room of Studio Three with its Neve desk.

The first non-EMI desk was introduced in the mid-Seventies, when the Neve was installed in Studio Three. No longer was a recording studio just a service offered by a record company to its artists. Other companies began making studio equipment and a whole new industry grew up with consoles becoming more sophisticated as these companies battled to create better equipment than their rivals. People also realised that they could make a profit out of studios, so intense rivalry built up between studios who fought to have the latest equipment installed. Developments in 16 track recording and the arrival of 24 track brought computerised mixing desks with the facility to remember and reproduce all fader movements, and also memorise the muting of the tracks during remixing. The ultimate in the rapidly developing technology of recording, was the introduction in the late Seventies of digital recording. "The birth of digital recording means that we have gone full circle, but we are now producing better quality sound digitally than we were able to do with the other methods of recording, and nowadays virtually all classical recordings are done digitally," says Townsend, who views the future as a time when studios will have to change to meet the various demands of the clients.

Townsend also takes a close look at each of the four studios in Abbey Road, and analyses the position they each hold in the recording industry. "The introduction of audio visual work gave the bigger studios the chance to get involved in work that the smaller studios were unable to cope with. When classical recording dropped in Studio One, we had to look for new ways of utilising the studio, and we formed the Anvil Abbey Road Screen Sound operation, following

Anvil's closure of their own studio. This operation has been extended to Studio Two as well, as we still obviously use Studio One for major classical works".

The famous and much vaunted Studio Two comes under the microscope too. "We intend to improve this; we don't want to change the acoustics drastically, but we do need to make it look better. There is no point in living in the past, which is what those people who say we should leave it as a museum to The Beatles are doing. We cannot leave it as a museum, we must look to the future."

Studio Three is, in Townsend's assessment, the best equipped of all the studios in Abbey Road. "The Neve console has been added to considerably, in what is now a very sophisticated control room. This studio is in demand most of the time by groups, and in fact Sky have made all their albums in there."

The final chapter in Abbey Road's development was the building of the new Penthouse Studio, which was built to meet a particular need. "This is a 48-track-plus operation with a £100,000 Neve desk. We wanted to create a new pop studio for bands wanting a smaller and slightly cheaper studio. It is very popular with rock and MOR acts wanting to stay for three or four weeks. The early teething troubles have been sorted out." Those problems were solved by the technical staff at the studios who, in Townsend's opinion, constitute, "the best technical back up of any studio in the world".

Townsend's assessment of the perfect combination for recording is as follows: "The right people, the right equipment, the right acts and the right atmosphere." To this end the studios opened a new restaurant and bar which, in Townsend's words, "Added a lot towards creating the right atmosphere... it's important that people can relax between sessions – it makes for better recording".

Although now based at Elstree, the mobile recording unit is still part of the Abbey Road Operation, travelling throughout Europe and even to the US to record classical works. "The specialist side of the mobile work is to go anywhere in the world and record the finest classical orchestras," says Townsend.

His final view of the studios that for so long were his home is quite simple. "It is a multi-purpose studio offering facilities for every facet of recording under one roof. With digital recording we have the future of the industry and it is certainly a must for all classical recordings, and is also beneficial for certain pop recordings; but as yet we have only just touched on the technology. The intention for the future is to keep a high roster of acts, maintain a high quality of recording and offer a first class service in all areas to the artists who work in Abbey Road."

Composer Howard Blake conducts the orchestra for the score to the film Sophia *starring Sophia Loren*

Whatever Townsend's aims and intentions were for the future, it's fair to say that Abbey Road has a place in recording history, primarily because of the boom period in the Sixties when it was regarded as the home of British pop music. But it would be grossly unfair if the famous studios were dismissed simply as the place where The Beatles recorded; after all classical recording was the backbone of the studio for many years, and many of the world's finest classical recordings are still produced in Abbey Road in addition to an impressive number of contemporary pop recordings.

During his recording of the Debussy Nocturnes, André Previn (seated foreground) is seen here during a playback with producer Suvi Raj Grubb (seated), engineer Christopher Parker (right) with members of the London Symphony Orchestra standing in the background.

Preface to the Second Edition

Whereas when I first joined EMI back in 1950, the number of recording studios could have been counted on one hand, by the late Seventies there were literally hundreds. The vast majority of them had been set up by entrepreneurs and were aimed at making money by attracting pop artists to use their studios. Banks were initially very keen to loan money in this new growth business, and so the number of studios kept increasing. Many of the world's leading artists also decided to build recording studios in their own homes, so that they could use them whenever they wanted, and not be committed to the specific times they had booked at a commercial studio. This also eliminated the inconvenience of moving and leaving all their valuable musical instruments away from base. In the face of this new competition the old original studios owned by record companies, across the globe, had to change their ways or perish, and perish the majority did.

Abbey Road survived, but had to change its whole concept and philosophy. Gone were the days when we were just there to provide a service to the company's own artists; now, like the remaining competition, it had to be operated as a financially viable business. This necessitated a constant close look at every facility we operated to ensure that we were at least as good as, and if possible better than, the opposition. Abbey Road has come out of this transformation as undoubtedly the world's most modern and best known recording studio. The range of facilities offered and the quality of staff are second to none, but the whole nature of recording does mean that although you will find all the top names in classical and film music at Abbey Road, the top names in pop are shared around the various studios more thinly. This change from the "Sixties era" is apparent in these new chapters.

I am delighted that two of Abbey Road's most respected engineers Peter Vince and Allan Rouse have been given the opportunity to write these last chapters. They have evolved over the years as the studio's unofficial historians, and indeed it was they who came to me with the concept for the original book. They deserve the long overdue recognition for their many hours of painstaking research, without which both this update, and the original version could never have been published.

KEN TOWNSEND, MBE
Chairman (Rtd) - EMI / Virgin Group of Studios
July 1996

Dedication

These new chapters are dedicated to those who are sadly no longer with us since the first publication in 1982.

10
Lights, Camera, Action... Music

As the Seventies, and Part One of this book, drew to a close, it was becoming painfully clear that the record business was in the early stages of a recession. Nowhere was this more evident than in Abbey Road's Studio One. Sadly, the classical world was suffering more than most, and this large custom built room was almost permanently empty. Concern was such that contingency plans were being drawn up to resolve the problem, the most ambitious of which was to convert the area into three smaller pop studios, extra storage space, and even an underground car park.

Fortunately fate took a hand in the form of Anvil Films who were about to lose the lease on their large sound stage in Denham, 20 miles west of London. This meant they would no longer be able to record the music scores which had won them so much acclaim from the world's film industry. After meetings between Anvil Director Rich Warren and Abbey Road's Manager Ken Townsend, a deal was struck, and by the end of 1980, the company Anvil-Abbey Road Screen Sound had been formed.

To say that Abbey Road initially erred on the side of caution would be an understatement, as both the technology and operational procedures were vastly different to anything that the studios had been used to, and in the early stages everything was done very much on a shoe-string. Most of the essential equipment had been salvaged from Denham, but apart from knocking a hole through the wall to make a projection window, and having a large roll-down cinema screen fitted, only very basic extra equipment was installed. Ex-Anvil engineers and founder directors of the new company, Eric Tomlinson and Alan Snelling, found things difficult to say the least. No one doubted the quality of sound that Studio One could produce, but the control room left much to be desired. "I'll never forget 19 people in that tiny little room," recalled Eric, "it was like a scene from *Caligula*, with bodies everywhere, all trying to look out of the window to see the screen, and all of them between me and the loudspeakers. And as if that wasn't bad enough, the intercom between the control room and dear old George (projectionist George Williams was the third member of the original team from Anvil) in the projection room was the internal telephone system, so if someone else happened to be on the line at the time, all contact was lost."

This basic method of recording, very much akin to that used for classical recording, is popular with many other film engineers and composers. They include Keith Grant, who works regularly with the likes of George Fenton, Mike Dutton with Michael Nyman, and Shawn Murphy, who regularly visits these shores from the US to work with John Barry and James Horner; all show an initial preference for letting Studio One create its own sound and then using as few microphones as possible to record the result. With most composers writing whenever possible in a classical vein, they agree that no other studio in the world captures that natural sound more successfully than Abbey Road's Studio One. The proof of the pudding be in the eating: the classical record chart success for George Fenton's *Shadowlands*, and James Horner's 'Somewhere Out There' (from *American Tail*), which reached number 8 in the UK pop charts, and number 2 in the USA. There is also a never ending list of Academy Award nominations and winners, including *Amadeus*, James Horner's *Aliens* and *Braveheart*, John Barry's *Chaplin*, Ryuichi Sakamoto and David Byrne's *The Last Emperor*, George Fenton's *The Madness of King George* and Howard Shore's *Philadelphia*.

Trevor Jones was back in Abbey Road to record his score for the Ridley Scott film A Matter of Honour *starring Demi Moore. Here in the newly redesigned number two control room, Trevor (centre) is seen with engineers Simon Rhodes (left) and Peter Cobbin.*

Unfortunately, during 1984, film recording in the UK suffered a brief but damaging blow. The problem initiated in America where a Musician's Union dispute on the West Coast brought a halt to any film music recording out there. The British Musicians Union decided to support their American friends, with the result that film companies were forced to look elsewhere to record. Elsewhere meant continuing eastwards, to Paris, Munich, Rome, Hungary and

Czechoslovakia. Nat Peck, a trombonist for 40 years, and once a member of The Glenn Miller Band (first on the left, in the photograph in chapter 3), was by this time an orchestra contractor for film sessions. He, like many others, was doubly upset, because although the union disputes were eventually resolved, the American producers decided to stay in Europe because the musicians were cheaper. But, as Nat respectfully comments, "The musicians just weren't on a par with those in London, and by the time they'd shipped in all the extra equipment needed, it was taking at least six days, to do what would take only two days over here (London). So, by the time you'd added on all the extra hotel bills, it was a case of swings and roundabouts really."

Gradually, and for the most part, the drift has been back to the UK, much to the relief of all those involved. Trevor Jones, in total agreement with Nat, sums up why there is no better place to work than in this country. "You can take the cream of the top London orchestras, and my word you really are spoilt for choice there, you can put them in THE London studio (a reference to Abbey Road Studio One), and quite frankly from a composer's point of view you've got Heaven on Earth."

During the 1984 lull, Eric and Alan had been forced to follow their clients wherever they went, and as a result reluctantly relinquished their directorship of Anvil-Abbey Road Screen Sound. Although the studios were sad to see them go, enough people were now using the studios, either with freelance, or Abbey Road's engineers, that there was sufficient justification to maintain the film department. Sadly, to rub salt in a slowly healing wound, 1985 was to witness a two-fold irony. Firstly, Studio One's control room, which had never really been suitable for stereo recording let alone the added needs of the film world, was being replaced by a much larger and far better located room, complete with full surround sound monitoring facilities. Secondly, the arrival of the Compact Disc had revitalised record sales, and created a whole new demand for classical recordings. This situation led to untold problems between the two camps, as rivals fought over the availability of Studio One. The film companies were upset when they found that the classical people were already booked in, while the classical contingent weren't taking too kindly to the film people infiltrating their domain.

However, with Abbey Road's Colette Barber acting as peacemaker and manipulating session bookings, the situation has been amicably resolved. Meanwhile, as far as the film side was concerned, Allan Rouse was given the job of co-ordinating the post production facilities, and engineer Dave Forty was seconded to supply permanent technical support to the department. It was this extra reliability, and the fact that Abbey Road had so much back up in both equipment and staff, that appealed to all the customers, especially as new technologies took their hold, and the rapid drift from analogue to digital recording, and from film projection to video took place. In principle the operation was similar to the old methods, except that synchronisation was maintained using a system known as Time-Code. In essence this is like an electronic clock, which is recorded on to one track of the tape or video so that all devices containing this code can be locked together, and controlled from one source. In the case of the video, this code can also be displayed as a clock on the screen (referred to as 'burnt in time-code') which acts as an invaluable aid for the composer. Being able to simply place the odd TV monitor here and there in the studio became much more popular and convenient than full screen film projection. Additionally, video was far quicker operationally than film, and in conjunction with a computer it was possible to add or modify any on screen cues for the conductor.

Although the advantages of this new medium were obvious, the convenience and simplicity of the system itself had a somewhat adverse effect on studios like Abbey Road. It now meant that, other than for large orchestral works, the music could be recorded anywhere, and in the case of synthesiser based scores, anywhere could even mean 'at home'.

However, there are still those die-hards who prefer to work with the big screen. "I think there's something magical for both the producer and the director to see it all happening on the big screen," says Keith Grant, who engineered George Fenton's score for Sir Richard Attenborough's *Shadowlands*. "Some music just does not happen with a small television set; if you've got something like *The Big Country* roaring away, and you're looking at a 14 inch monitor, then quite frankly it looks a bit silly. It's like they say, pictures sound better in colour; if you run a soundtrack with the picture in black and white, and then again in colour, the actual sound quality changes because your perception of it changes too."

John Barry, who also worked here with Sir Richard on the film *Chaplin*, is another who is really only at home with projection. John was persuaded to return to Abbey Road (he was a regular visitor in the Fifties and Sixties, both as an arranger, and with his band, The John Barry Seven) by Shawn Murphy, who through his association with James Horner had become a total convert to Studio One. It was this same duo that also brought Mel Gibson to Abbey Road to record the music for his first film as a director, *Man Without A Face*. Mel was so pleased with the results that he insisted they return to score his next film, *Braveheart*. During one of the sessions, there was a brief but unforgettable interruption. "The activity in the control room was hectic to say the least," recalls engineer Jonathan Allen. "Any space that didn't contain synthesisers or equipment belonging to Ian Underwood (of Frank Zappa and The Mothers Of Invention fame) was taken up by the usual entourage of people from the film company. Suddenly, right in the middle of a take, in walked Paul McCartney, George Harrison and Ringo Starr... apparently they were in Studio Two for a playback, and decided to pop down and say hello to Mel Gibson, although when they arrived, Ringo did jokingly say, 'Oh – I thought we were coming to see Mel

Below: **The score for the 3 Dimensional-IMAX film** Across the Sea of Time *was recorded in Studio One by John Barry (left) with engineer Shawn Murphy.*

Below: *Seen here at a playback, during the recording of the score for* Braveheart, *are from left to right (foreground), Jim Henrikson (film music editor), James Horner (composer/conductor) and Mel Gibson (director).*

Brooks'. Briefly the whole session just fell apart as the four of them chatted together, but then as quickly as they had arrived, they were gone, it was just like a whirlwind passing through."

Michael Kamen was actually one of the first people to use the new video technology, when he was asked to write the music for the cult movie *Brazil*. Michael was already a hardened Abbey Road user, having written arrangements for Pink Floyd and Kate Bush. His familiarity stood him in good stead as he spent an unprecedented 13 weeks recording the score, utilising the services of all four studios at Abbey Road. This has also been the location for many of Michael's other film scores such as *Highlander*, *Shanghai Surprise* (with George Harrison), *Suspect* and *Someone To Watch Over Me*. Whenever the occasion arises, Michael will always opt to use Studio One, and

Above: **When George Martin won the 'Grand Prix' for** The Making of Sgt Pepper, *it was presented to him by film composer Michael Kamen.*

makes an interesting comparison to a famous American landmark. "You know there's a place in New York called Carnegie Hall, which I think was built last century, and totally by accident has a unique acoustic that makes it orchestra friendly. It's one of the nicest places to play music, and the same can be said for Abbey Road. You can be relaxed and happy, play your instrument and hear the sound of it going into the air, and you can hear the guys across the room from you, you can actually enjoy making music, and lo and behold there are microphones and you can get to record it."

Left: **John Williams** *conducts the orchestra at Watford Town Hall, for the recording (by the Abbey Road Mobile) of his composition 'Summon The Heroes'. The music had been specially written for the 1996 Summer Olympics in Atlanta–USA.*

But like his colleagues, Michael's deep rooted dreams are still classically motivated, and working at Abbey Road, in the shadow of the greats like Elgar, the urge to compose in the traditional way becomes greater. Michael fulfilled that dream when he wrote and subsequently recorded his Saxophone Concerto at Abbey Road with fellow American David Sanborn. Coincidentally, John Williams has recently been working in Studio One, recording his 'Concerto for Bassoon', with Abbey Road engineer Simon Rhodes, and on this occasion Shawn Murphy in the role of producer.

Simon's brother Adrian was the editor and sound effects man for the Wallace and Gromit film, *Grand Day Out*, a college project produced by students on a very small budget. As a result of the film's extraordinary international success, Adrian persuaded the writer/animator/director Nick Park and composer Julian Nott to record the music for their follow ups, *The Wrong Trousers* and *A Close Shave*, at Abbey Road. They eventually agreed to do so and, as a result, the Studios are now proud to be associated with what has become a triple award winning success story.

The two media, Stage and Screen, are frequently linked together, and Abbey

Above: **Jonathan Pryce** *(star of the cult film Brazil) seen here in Studio One whilst recording the musical Cabaret.*

Road's association with stage musicals had been prevalent for many years. Legendary characters like Wally Ridley and Norman Newell would regularly produce Original Cast albums of virtually every musical staged in London. But again, by the late Seventies the major record companies, EMI included, were issuing less and less of this particular type of product.

Others felt differently. John Yap was an avid collector of musicals and nostalgia, who around this time advertised his valuable record collection for sale to make way for his new love, opera. The response to just two small adverts was quite incredible. "I had replies from all over the world," recalls John. "People either wanted to buy my records outright, or if they were too expensive, they would ask me to accept a whole lot of other show recordings as part payment." The volume of mail, telephone calls and general international interest convinced John to give up his day job as a graphic designer, take on a partner, and start a small business specialising in this obviously popular field. They opened a small shop in Drury Lane, the first of its kind, and it was an instant success. Their policy was to stock every available cast recording from anywhere in the world. Their fame grew so much that radio stations world-wide would contact them for copies of rare recordings.

John soon realised that demand still existed for new quality material, and so decided to finance the recordings himself, under the name of his new company That's Entertainment Records. He first tested the water with two limited edition, fairly low budget, musicals. To his relief and great satisfaction, they were both complete sell-outs. In 1980, John took the plunge and ventured into Abbey Road, coincidentally the same time that film work started, although John wasn't using Studio One at this time, preferring the acoustics, and the price, of

Right: **Princess Anne** *with performers from the* **Christmas Spectacular** *album, which was recorded to raise money for the 'Save the Children' appeal. They include from left to right Sarah Brightman, Paul Nicholas, Elaine Paige and Anita Harris.*

Studios Two and Three. Being all too aware that he was still green, when it came to record production, he wisely employed the services of Norman Newell, a partnership which blossomed for several years. Among their early successes were *Mr. Cinders* with Dennis Lawson, *Camelot* with Richard Harris and *Underneath The Arches* with Roy Hudd, Christopher Timothy and Chesney Allen. Since then John has gone on to become Abbey Road's most prolific independent client, producing over 250 show albums to date. His most challenging project is to record almost the entire history of musicals, many of them for the first time in their complete form. What has delighted John is that a number of the established stars with whom he has made acquaintance over the years, have agreed to participate in the project without charging exorbitant fees.

Left: Dame Judy Dench receives instructions from John Yap in the control room, during the recording of Cabaret.

Like so many people, John has quickly come to recognise the magic that Studio One can produce, and quite simply will not record anywhere else. It is a situation much applauded by the musicians and singers alike, for they too find performing a more enjoyable experience in such warm acoustics, where the echo is natural, and not added later using electronics. John does occasionally produce the odd 'non show' album, and a recent example revealed fascinating connotations. The artist was the celebrated Elisabeth Welch, who it transpired was no stranger to Abbey Road Studios, as she had made numerous recordings there back in the Thirties.

In an old and recently unearthed issue of the *Radio Times*, dated Friday, 28th January 1938, there is a reference to a television programme, a medium still very much in its infancy at that time, which read: 3.00 p.m. – MAKING A GRAMO-PHONE RECORD. Viewers will see Elisabeth Welch, Robert Ashley, chorus and orchestra recording 'Vocal Gems' of George Gershwin's songs, at His Master's Voice Studios in St. Johns Wood. [A side note bearing reference to the programme states: The HMV Studios are in Abbey Road, St, Johns Wood. In the neighbourhood is Lord's, from where it is hoped a Test match will be televised, and today's broadcast should therefore be an indication of the quality of reception to expect in June. I say 'should', only because in television outside broadcasts, preliminary tests that are marred by all kinds of mysterious interference, are often followed by perfect transmissions on the day, and encouraging tests often lead to disappointment.]

It's a calming thought to read such an item, when one realises how far this particular technology has progressed in such a relatively short time. From Abbey Road's standpoint, it is this very medium that they, and the record industry in general, is looking to for the future of the music business. Interactive Multimedia, and all that is encompassed by those two magic words, is what we are reliably informed will carry us into the next century.

Multimedia refers to the four basic elements of television – Video, Audio, Graphics and Text – and Interactive refers to the control that the viewer has over those four separate parameters. This situation is the reverse of the norm called Passive, which means merely switching on your television set, and watching what the person the other end wants you to see, without you having any control other than the ability to channel hop or simply switch the set off (sometimes referred to as first stage interactive).

Martin Benge, the new Vice President, EMI Music Studios, was very much instrumental in adding a fully operational Multimedia department at Abbey Road. He is also fully aware of the growing place for the computer in the home. "People will now use their computer, not only for the traditional things like word processing, spread-sheets, and all the other boring stuff, but also for entertainment. Perhaps to play games, which often have full motion video in them. But people are now dialling on to the internet, pulling down pretty looking graphics, and using the system to find out bits of information. So the computer really has already become part of home entertainment." Discussions had been going on between EMI and Apple Computers designed to promote a new enhanced CD format called CD-Extra (still sometimes referred to as CD-Plus). The result is that Apple has agreed to supply Macintosh Computers, together with all the necessary latest operating software, and Abbey Road supplies the staff and acquires the customers.

Not only is Martin justly proud that Abbey Road is the first UK music studio to have its own multimedia authoring suite, but he was also delighted with being able to employ a ready made team of operators. "Not only had the three of them worked together before," cites Martin, "but they had also been working on music related multimedia. We also felt they were the right kind of people to fit in with the culture of the building." The team comprises Lynn Carver, graphic designer, Andy Atherton, software engineer and Sam Harvey, audio-visual producer.

The first major product to evolve from this room is the new recording of *La Bohème* featuring EMI's latest discovery, the tenor Roberto Alagna. The CDs, as far as the audio is concerned, are no different from any other, but for anyone with the facility to access CD-ROM using their home computer, then the magic really begins. For it is here that the facility exists, among other things, to view the full libretto (in three languages), pictures and biographies of the artists, and a video of the conductor, Antonio Pappano, relating the story of the opera.

During a break in the recording of La Bohème, *Roberto Alagna and Thomas Hampson share a light hearted moment with fellow soloist Enrico Fissore.*

As well as preparing programs for CD-Extra, this new department, will also be responsible for supplying and updating information for the Abbey Road pages on the Internet. So although this book relates the story of Abbey Road from 1931 to 1996, for those who can access 'The Web' [http://www.AbbeyRoad.co.UK.] the story will continue until the year... ?

11

Never 'Let it Be'

Although The Beatles as a group disbanded in April 1970, it really came as no great surprise that the four individuals would continue to achieve success, each with their own individual style of music. Nevertheless, the continued demand for Beatles recordings is enormous and this comes not only from original fans, but also from a whole new generation of followers, many of whom were not even born in the Sixties, when the phenomenon began.

Since the break-up, EMI Records have carefully monitored, on a world-wide basis, the sales of all Beatles recordings, and have subsequently released either new compilations, or re-released original albums, as and when everyone agreed that the time or occasion was right. Mike Heatley, EMI's General Manager, International Catalogue Development, who for many years has been involved in catalogue initiatives related to many of EMI's major artists, has in recent times found himself almost entirely involved in Beatles related projects.

In the same way that it is the ambition of every Elvis Presley fan to visit Graceland, the Memphis home of their idol, so a visit to the shrine that is Abbey Road equates in much the same way for a true Beatles devotee. There is an almost constant flow of fans who, among other things, risk life and limb being photographed emulating the Fab Four on the equally famous pedestrian crossing. It must be most disheartening to those who make the pilgrimage to St. Johns Wood to find that the commissionaire's desk is the closest they can get to seeing the inside of their Mecca. The simple fact is that Abbey Road is not the museum that some have suggested it should be, but is still operating as a successful and busy recording studio.

There was one occasion however, when this was all to briefly change. In 1983 plans were being made to install a new mixing console in the control room of Studio Two. Abbey Road's Manager at the time, Ken Townsend, all too aware that the studio itself would be empty for four to six weeks, suddenly, to use his words, 'had a mad idea'. He explained, "We were always getting requests from people asking to see inside Studio Two, so I decided to put together a project based on The Beatles at Abbey Road. My main intention was to open it up to the general public. I got the studio's Public Relations Officer, Kathy Varley, involved, together with engineer John Barratt. John had been unwell for some time, but on the days when he felt better, I'd been letting him come in and spend time cataloguing all the information connected with the Beatles recordings at Abbey Road. It was my hope that one day we could eventually produce a book based on John's research. Anyway, the work he had already done would prove a great help towards the project."

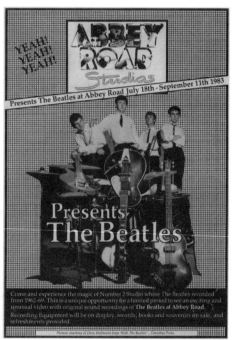

EMI Records was totally supportive of Ken's idea, and gave him virtual *carte blanche* to proceed. Kathy and John co-ordinated the complete package. This involved part of the studio being set up exactly as it always had been for Beatles recordings, complete with all the original microphones. Other exhibits included a display of various studio instruments, tape machines and pieces of ancillary equipment that were used regularly on the sessions. While in another corner was a shop selling a selection of Abbey Road and Beatles souvenirs.

The main attraction though, was a two part video, lasting nearly one and a half hours. This unique presentation, researched and produced by the studios themselves, contained a compilation of rare film clips, still photographs and interviews, together with previously unreleased versions of one or two Beatles' songs. This impressive and often poignant video was narrated by Capital Radio DJ, Roger Scott.

"The whole event was a huge success," recalls Ken. "We had something like 22,000 visitors, from all over the world. There were three shows a day, with 135 seats at each, and it was fully booked for the whole duration. It really created a huge international buzz, and I alone did well in excess of 80 television and radio interviews."

Although the income from ticket sales and memorabilia were mostly outweighed by production and staffing costs, everyone agreed that it had still been a totally worthwhile, and deeply satisfying venture. The vast number of letters of thanks and praise that the studios subsequently received stand as a lasting testimony to the enormous appreciation of those who made the journey from all four corners of the globe.

There is no doubt that the really true fans will find Beatles related anniversaries to celebrate on an almost monthly basis. EMI's celebrations have been somewhat more refined, although since 1982, all The Beatles singles were re-released as part of an ongoing '20th' celebration. Undoubtedly the most exciting contribution to the re-issuing schedule was the arrival of the Compact Disc. This revolutionary new medium heralded a whole new era of listening pleasure, enabling record buyers to hear their favourite recordings in a way never before possible. The restrictions imposed by the cutting and processing of the vinyl disc were no longer a problem, resulting in every little nuance of the recording now being audible. Beatles fans were hearing some sounds for the first time, not always necessarily for the better. "You can actually hear Ringo's bass drum

pedal squeaking," one avid listener was heard to quote.

Unquestionably the most eagerly awaited release on CD was *Sgt. Pepper's Lonely Hearts Club Band*. On June 1, 1987, EMI hosted a huge party in Studio Two as a double celebration, firstly to launch the new CD, and secondly to celebrate the 20th Anniversary of the original release of the record. Guests included Paul and Linda McCartney, Mike McGear, Roy Wood, Tony Hicks, Roy Orbison, George Martin and Norman 'Hurricane' Smith. EMI's Managing Director, Rupert Perry, and Paul McCartney took advantage of the occasion to present a special framed copy of the very first *Sgt. Pepper* CD to artist and designer Peter Blake. Peter, who was responsible for creating the world famous album cover, received his unique award in front of a full size replica of his masterpiece.

Left: Mike McGear (Paul McCartney's brother), George Martin and Roy Wood were just three of the many special guests who joined Paul to celebrate the 20th year of Sgt Pepper, and its release on Compact Disc.

Before cutting the birthday cake, a giant representation of the *Sgt. Pepper* bass drum, Paul took time to make a rather poignant speech. "What has changed in the 20 years since we were working here last? Seems to me the issues are still basically the same, I mean then we wanted to see an end to apartheid in South Africa, we wanted to encourage peace on Earth, and we wanted some love and understanding between people everywhere. So now what have we learned? If anything, change comes slowly. Let's keep our faith and keep pushing, and pray that we have better news to report 20 years from today." [Interesting fact: 20 years from June 1, 1987, Paul McCartney will be 64, and of course 'When I'm Sixty-Four', was one of the tracks on the Sgt. Pepper album.] Paul then joined Linda, Peter and the other guests to face the microphones and cameras of the world's media.

Meanwhile, Ken Townsend's plans for a book documenting the Beatles' career at Abbey Road had come to fruition though, sadly, John Barratt lost the fight against his worsening illness. However, earlier that same year, freelance writer Mark Lewisohn, who wrote a regular column in *The Beatles Monthly* magazine, had been given the opportunity to make John's acquaintance. He had gone to Abbey Road, with EMI's blessing, to observe the production of *The Beatles At Abbey Road* video.

"I came along one Saturday," recalled Mark, "and watched as John took some tape boxes out of the library. The first box he opened contained the original demo of 'While My Guitar Gently Weeps'. It was absolutely mind blowing, the first time that particular tape had been out of its box for fifteen years, I had no idea that such things still existed in the archive." This particular track was subsequently chosen to be included in *The Beatles At Abbey Road* video. "As a fan and record collector," continued Mark, "I knew there were variations of a recording, but I had no idea that there could be one that was so radically different from the final master."

Some time later, Mark was called to a meeting at EMI's head office with Brian Southall, then Head of Public Relations, and Mike Heatley. They explained that they were looking for someone to continue with The Beatles research, incorporating the information into a book, and they wondered if he might be interested. "I think it was one of the most ludicrous questions I've ever been asked," quipped Mark, "about half a second later, after due deliberation, I said yes." In all fairness, Mark had proved his worth on a book he had written earlier. The book had taken seven years to research, and contained the complete details of all The Beatles' stage performances throughout their career. EMI rightly felt that anyone who could turn a list of 1,400 dates and venues into an interesting and readable book must have something a little special to offer.

On January 2, 1987, a trepidacious Mark Lewisohn began work on his new project. Apart from a very tight time schedule, no specific ground rules had been laid down, so he decided to approach the whole thing chronologically. Feeling totally privileged and in awe at being the first outsider to be allowed total access to Beatles information, he was also able to listen to many of their old recordings. This freedom resulted in an accurate documentation of all The Beatles' recordings at Abbey Road from day one.

One detail that fascinated Mark was to discover the previously undisclosed information regarding the names of the engineers involved on the sessions. It had always been EMI company policy not to put engineers' names on record sleeves, and it wasn't until the *Abbey Road* album was released in 1969 that Geoff Emerick first received the credit he deserved. Mark realised that this was an area that would help enormously, as far as the interest factor of the book was concerned. He had already decided to interview a number of people who were involved with The Beatles at the time, and adding engineers to that list suddenly appeared an obvious thing to do. "I interviewed about seventy five people, and almost every one of them was a pleasure. Although I was always said to be the world's leading Beatles expert, the amount I learned was phenomenal. And what I really discovered was that the recordings that The Beatles made at Abbey Road owed a lot to the people that worked there."

"There were all those engineers," Mark continued, "who for 20 years had never been asked officially about their side of the story. I now realised how significant their contribution was. And not just the engineers, but all the other people that work there, including the canteen staff and the security man. It was really great to hear all their stories, and I sincerely believe that it was this that made the Recording Sessions book as interesting as it was."

Although Studio Two was the home of most of the Beatles recordings in Abbey Road, they did use the other two studios. On this occasion it was Studio Three for the recording of Revolver.

Not only was the book interesting, but it was extremely successful too. When it was released in 1988, it went straight into the best sellers. With sales of around 175,000 copies, for what is essentially a reference book, that was no mean achievement. After four years, instead of just simply re-issuing the book, Mark was approached by the publishers to embellish it with extra information. Mark agreed unhesitatingly, and the resulting book, *The Complete Beatles Chronicle*, which contains a complete record of all their professional activities, has become the official reference book for all time.

Mark's proficiency and knowledge, as far as The Beatles is concerned, has led to him being involved in most of the product that has evolved about them since. Whether writing sleeve notes for albums, or as consultant on films or television, Mark is more often than not the man to whom people turn for advice.

George Martin, often referred to as the fifth Beatle, was one man grateful for Mark's help. In 1992 George was given the go ahead to produce a documentary film to celebrate the 25th Anniversary of *Sgt. Pepper*. It was a project that George had wanted to do for some time. "Pepper was such an extraordinary record, and I just knew that people wanted to know how it was made. I had spoken to all of The Beatles in turn, and they all said, 'Sure George, let's do it', including Yoko... I'm calling her a Beatle." Unfortunately, despite their unanimous enthusiasm, neither Apple nor EMI showed any real interest, "Probably because they were already into the gestation period of *The Anthology*, and this may have been taking something away," suggests George. "Anyway, the head of The Disney Corporation got to hear about it, and came over here to see me. He was so impressed, that he decided to put his money where his mouth was, to the tune of around $1/2 million, for us to go ahead and make the film for TV."

© Buena Vista Television

A scene from the award winning TV documentary The Making of Sgt Pepper, *George Martin and Paul McCartney are captured here listening to the four track master of 'Lucy In The Sky With Diamonds'.*

Another man very much involved in this production was Abbey Road engineer, Allan Rouse. Allan, who has been at the studios for over 25 years, got his first involvement with The Beatles back in 1988, when he was given the mammoth task of copying all the Beatles' analogue recordings onto digital tape, primarily as a safety precaution. As a result, he now holds the unique distinction of being the only person to have heard literally everything the Beatles ever committed to tape at Abbey Road. "Even The Beatles and George Martin themselves haven't heard it all of course, because they weren't always recording together," noted Allan.

Together the three of them, George, Mark and Allan, sifted through all the recordings associated with the *Sgt. Pepper* album, and eventually put together a programme for the arts series, *The South Bank Show*. The programme, presented by Melvyn Bragg from Room 22 at Abbey Road (Allan's hideaway), went on to win for George Martin, the prestigious Grand Prix, at the Midem Audio Visual Awards in Cannes.

The dust had hardly had time to settle on the 'Pepper Job', when the team of

Above: **George Harrison and George Martin in Studio Two for the Launch of the re-mastered** Red and Blue **Albums** *in 1993.*

three were back together, although on this particular occasion, because of his specialist inside knowledge, the third member was Senior BBC Radio One producer Kevin Howlett. They had assembled to audition material for a new CD, *The Beatles Live At The BBC*. Hour after hour was spent listening to virtually every BBC radio recording The Beatles ever made. What made the job doubly diffi-cult was that the BBC no longer had the master tapes for a number of the original recordings. Although copies of the missing programs did exist, they had been recorded 'off-air' on domestic tape machines, and the quality, in many cases, was very poor to say the least.

This is where one of Abbey Road's newest tech-nologies was again put to the test. The Sonic Solutions No-Noise computer system, in the adept hands of engineer Peter Mew, was able to make mountains out of molehills. Peter had already proved his and the sys-tem's worth a few months earlier when he had spent some considerable time remastering The Beatles' Red and Blue albums for CD release.

Meanwhile, the double CD set of the BBC Recordings was released on November 30, 1994, and went to number 1 in the album charts (the 13th Beatles album to do so in the UK). At the end of this particular epic, George Martin thanked all those involved, and turning to Allan said, "See you soon!" As Allan was to find out, he wasn't joking.

Just before the release of the BBC set, two very significant Beatles anniver-saries were celebrated in the space of just three months. Firstly, on August 8, 1994, fans gathered from far and wide to walk en-masse across the pedestrian crossing adjacent to the studios. The local police, obliging as ever, were on hand to maintain safety by controlling the traffic, on what is a very busy thorough-fare. This spectacle took place at exactly 11.35 a.m., 25 years to the day that The Beatles made the same journey for the legendary photograph. The event was organised by Richard Porter, the 'Beatles Brain of Britain' and President of the

Right: **Just a small section of the many Beatles fans who turned up on 8th August 1994, to celebrate 25 years to the very minute that The Beatles were photographed for the album** Abbey Road.

London Beatles Fan Club. Richard started bringing fellow fan club members to Abbey Road back in 1988. The trips were very popular, and quickly realising their potential, he did a deal with the company 'London Walks', thereby turning a labour of love into an enjoyable means of employment.

The trips, which encompass numerous other locations of Beatles interest, operate on a daily basis, and bring at least 200 fans to the studios each week. On one occasion, while lecturing to a group of tourists, Richard happened to recognise Paul McCartney's Mercedes car arriving. Continuing his chat as if nothing had happened he said, "And now if you look behind you, here comes Paul's car. You should have seen their faces, I mean how can you top seeing Paul Mac's car on a Beatles tour." In true McCartney tradition, Paul took time to talk to the fans, and then pose for photographs on the studio steps.

"I always feel good if I happen to be going to the studios, and there's a little knot of fans outside, and they're not expecting me to be there," reflects Paul, "the thing is, I used to collect autographs when I was a kid in Liverpool. I used to hang around the stage door at the Liverpool Empire, so I know how good it feels when someone special actually turns up; and anyway it's nice for me too!"

Another activity of these and all other visitors to Abbey Road, is to add their own graffiti to the wall outside the studios. This tradition was first started by Ken Townsend. "I think I made a remark to a journalist once, that we don't mind people writing on the wall. To my mind I think it adds something to the building, there's a buzz about it which says, 'this is where something actually happened, it isn't just a house'. Believe it or not several neighbours actually took the trouble to write to me, saying what a nice idea they thought it was. The only thing I did insist was that every three or four months, before it was repainted, photographs should be taken of it for posterity."

The second 25th Anniversary, on 26th October 1994, just eleven weeks after that for 'the crossing ceremony', was for the *Abbey Road* album itself. This was to be a special occasion, not just for the fans and EMI Records, but equally importantly for the studios themselves. After all, the original album not only gave Abbey Road Studios their new name (until 1969, they had always been known as EMI Recording Studios), but were to affect their whole future, and literally turn them into a household name. The week long celebrations included a marquee in the studio car park, which housed a display based very much along the lines of Ken Townsend's *Beatles at Abbey Road* way back in 1983. The main difference this time was that the video, which played virtually non-stop, contained a potted history of the studios, from day one (November 12, 1931). Once again the event was a great success, with delighted fans and visitors able to leave with various items of memorabilia, including a booklet written and produced specially for the occasion.

Apart from all the fictitious stories that materialised surrounding the picture on the *Abbey Road* sleeve, one piece of genuine mystery had remained unsolved for 25 years. Just who were the other people standing in the background? Well, after all the media publicity surrounding the associated events, two people were prompted to write to the *Daily Mail* newspaper and dispel any rumours that may have grown over the years. It can now, therefore, be officially disclosed that the gentleman standing next to the police van on the right, is Tony Staples, a local resident who was on his way to work at the time. while the three gentlemen standing outside the gates of the studios were Derek Seagrove, Alan Flanagan and Steve Millwood. They were doing a decorating job at the studios, and had just arrived back after an early lunch.

In 1989, Paul, George, Ringo and Yoko Ono sat down together and drew up plans for what they saw to be the definitive television history of the group. The main criteria of the project, was simple: for the series to be authentic it would have to be 'The story of The Beatles, as told by The Beatles'. The principles were agreed, and the hard work began. The result was *The Anthology*, a series of six, one hour, screenings, which received international acclaim in 1995.

The announcement that a set of CDs, also called *The Anthology* was to be released, created unprecedented chaos. As Apple Press Officer, Derek Taylor was quoted as saying, "It's a new strain of Beatlemania. My phone should have stopped ringing in 1970, but I've never been so busy." Quite simply it was as if The Beatles had never been away.

When George Martin had said to Allan Rouse, "See you soon," just after they'd finished the BBC Recordings, it was probably one of the biggest understatements of the year. 1995 had barely begun when George 'moved in with Allan' and work first started on the *Anthology*. It was obvious from the start that it was going to be a monumental task, and several important decisions had to be made at the outset. Firstly, like the TV series, the CDs had to run chronologically. Secondly, it was unanimously agreed that Geoff Emerick, The Beatles engineer from *Revolver* onwards, should be brought over from his home in America to work on all the tracks that were selected. And thirdly, any equipment that had been used for the original recordings, that was still in existence, should be acquired for use on the project. Ancillary equipment such as Fairchild Limiters, Altec Compressors and old EMI equalisers had still been kept in working order, but one of the biggest problems was going to be the mixing desk. Fortunately, Dame Fortune was in a benevolent mood on this occasion, as Geoff Emerick readily admits. "We discovered that Jeff Jarratt, who used to be an engineer at Abbey Road, and actually did some work with The Beatles, had bought one of the old consoles when it was sold off in 1987. It was one of EMI's first transistorised TG Series desks, and although this particular one had been taken out of the studio, and adapted for use by the Mobile Recording Unit, it was basically the same desk that I'd used for the *Abbey Road* album."

Sixties analogue technology replaces the very latest Neve Digital Capricorn mixing console in the Penthouse Studio for 16 weeks in 1995/96. This was to enable the re-remixing of tracks for the Beatles' Anthology.

All the equipment was subsequently installed in the Penthouse Studio. Ironically, this meant the removal of the very latest, computer controlled, Neve Capricorn digital mixing console. Unfortunately, there was still one more hurdle to overcome, and that was echo.

As George Martin confessed, "In the true spirit of the exercise, there was no way I could justify using modern effects processors like digital reverb, they simply didn't exist in the Sixties." Always eager to please, Abbey Road immediately set about re-instating Studio Two's acoustic echo chamber, as close as possible to its original condition.

Above: **Abbey Road's Number Two echo chamber was completely re-furbished to maintain authenticity during the making of** the Beatles' Anthology.

Before Geoff could get to work on the tapes, it was necessary to listen to all the material that might be suitable for inclusion. The very early, pre-Abbey Road, material had to be taken from whatever source was available, including items from Polydor, Decca and the BBC. A fascinating addition to the early years, was the inclusion of two recordings made during 1958 in a make-shift Liverpool studio. The first was of a rendition of the Buddy Holly hit, 'That'll Be The Day'. The second, a song called 'In Spite of All The Danger', which was co-written by Paul McCartney and George Harrison.

Below: **Twenty five years and three months after the four of them last worked together in Abbey Road; George, Ringo and Paul were reunited with George Martin in Studio Two on 31st March 1995 to audition tracks for the Anthology.**

The rules laid down for the CDs, regarding The Beatles involvement, were exactly the same as for the TV programmes. This strict criteria led to one particularly special moment in the proceedings. "It was March 31, a day I shall never forget," recalls Allan Rouse, "I was in Studio Two control room at the time, playing back some more archive recordings to George Martin. At any other time, this would have been par for the course, but on this occasion we were joined by Paul, George and Ringo. This was the first time all four of them had been together in that studio since 1969, and quite honestly the atmosphere can only be described as sheer magic. They were all totally at ease in each others company, taking photographs and videos and obviously enjoying the unique occasion as much as everyone else." Paul McCartney shares Allan's excitement for that special day. "Going back to that original location was spooky as Dame Edna (Everage) would say, because the studio itself is largely unchanged, and there were those same steps up to virtually the same control room. And then just looking at each other, older and slightly different maybe, but neverthe-less it was still three of The Beatles sitting there; and with who?... George Martin; and what boxes were we looking at?.... the actual boxes from the sessions. And although it sounds

The studio canteen March 1963.

silly, I swear to God, as we played the tapes I was praying I wouldn't make a mistake." Further evidence of how at home they felt was seen during the afternoon when they decided to pop down to the restaurant for a snack.

"They just strolled in natural as anything," remembers a stunned Doreen Dunkley, "there were no airs or graces, they just served themselves with salad, tea and coffee, and then apologising for any inconvenience, asked if it were possible for me to get them a large bowl of chips. They then took their meals, sat down at one of the tables and tucked in. I just stood there behind the bar, totally fascinated by the casual presence of these idols from my past. Mind you, I couldn't help thinking how sad it was that John wasn't there with them."

The 'Anthology Team' worked on relentlessly, George Martin, Mark Lewisohn and Allan Rouse (who by this time had been officially recognised as Abbey Road's Beatles' Co-ordinator), searching for material, with Paul, George or Ringo coming in whenever possible, to appraise everything they'd found. Paul is the first to admit to an initial air of doubt with regards to issuing, what were after all is said and done, rejects the first time round. On reflection his views on many of the tracks have changed completely. "In actual fact I think some of them are better than the originals," confesses Paul, "and it has given me the opportunity, for example, to take all the strings and heavenly voices off 'Long And Winding Road', which I never really intended in the first place. And it's interesting to hear George Martin now saying, 'Why did we have to go to take thirty-six?' I know what he means, I can only assume it was part of the creative process, you know, keep on till we get it better. But looking back on it, take two was often better, particularly when you listen to *Anthology 3*, because by the time take twenty-six or thirty had arrived, we'd lost the enthusiasm for the tune. Yes, we were getting slicker and more in tune, but what I like about the early takes is the 'soul' on them. You can really hear us enjoying ourselves on songs like 'Dig A Pony', 'Let It Be', Long And Winding Road' and 'Two Of Us'." (Note: Paul's take references are of course only hypothetical).

As each item was eventually given the OK, it was passed on to Geoff and his assistant Paul Hicks, son of Hollies guitarist Tony Hicks. [Interesting fact: Geoff was the assistant engineer on The Hollies' recording audition back in 1963.] It was then Geoff's job to remix the tapes, recreating, as close as possible, the sounds that he had been achieving some 30 years before.

Clockwise from bottom left, George Martin, Allan Rouse, Paul Hicks and Geoff Emerick - The Beatles Anthology Team - in the Penthouse control room.

Strangely, this wasn't as difficult for Geoff as one might think. It's those very sounds, and the way in which he produces them, that have kept him in constant demand to this day. Geoff had always been pleased with the old analogue sound, and not really been one for change. "I have fought very shy of being pushed into using a lot of the modern devices. So many of today's digital processors are based on the sounds that we used to achieve manually, but quite honestly I don't think they sound as good. We can still get those sounds by the old methods quite easily, and much quicker too. In fact, thinking about it we haven't really progressed that far, if anything it's probably the opposite. The old 4-track masters are on one inch tape, so every track is almost a quarter of an inch wide. As a result, apart from the lack of noise, the quality of the bass is outstanding, you just can't create that now. The same applies to the snare and bass drum, they sound so natural it's uncanny." Whatever the strength of Geoff's feelings towards the technical aspects of the recordings, it was the results that mattered, the enormous enthusiasm and adulation resulting from the release of Anthology 1, would only serve to prove this point.

As if the excitement surrounding these new releases wasn't enough, the total package was heralded by one very special bonus. Early in 1994, news broke that The Beatles were back together, at Paul's studio in Sussex. The reason for this totally unexpected reunion was explained by Ringo, "Yoko came up with a handful of songs that John had made just before he died, and the suggestion was made that the three of us add our own bits to them and finish them off." With ex-ELO leader Jeff Lynne in the producer's chair, and Geoff once again at the controls, they worked on two selected tracks, 'Free As A Bird', and 'Real Love'. The outcome was the first new single from The Beatles for 25 years. As a result of special Anglo-American arrangements regarding the first international broadcast of this unique product, the security arrangements surrounding every aspect of the CD, vinyl and cassette manufacture, were quite extraordinary.

After two years of painstaking work, Anthology Three *completed the trilogy and was given a press launch in Studio Three in October 1996. Neil Aspinall, Head of Apple, was joined on this occasion by Noel Gallagher, who was working with Oasis in Studio Two at the time.*

It was just before eleven o'clock on the evening of November 19, 1995 (New York time), that the world first heard 'Free As A Bird', and this special event was closely followed by the release of *Anthology 1* (which contained the new track). The occasion caused chaos, as the sales on the first day broke all previous records. A statement from The Beatles press office on December 12, 1995, best sums up that incredible year: "The Beatles have hit a new success as Britain's leading rock and roll export this Christmas. Global demand for the greatest British band has reached a new 25-year high, with the album *Anthology 1* winning 24 platinum discs and 8 gold awards worldwide, and the TV series selling to 102 countries.

"Demand around the world has astonished the Beatles' record company EMI, who have now shipped seven million Anthology albums in just two weeks. 'Beatlemania is raging again throughout the world,' says EMI Records Chairman Rupert Perry. 'Once again The Beatles have proved that their songs are among Britain's greatest exports. Our country should be proud of them'."

There is no doubting the pride in the hearts of the British people, for the band that changed the course of musical history throughout the world. However, nowhere is this pride felt more strongly than at Abbey Road Studios. For it was there, in 1962, that The Beatles took their first step to recording stardom. 35 years later, it is that same association that continues to produce success. When asked if this was now the end of The Beatles' story, Paul's prophetic answer was, "In a way you could say let's hope so, but you know 'The Beatles' is an amazing beast, it doesn't always sit down when you tell it to. When John died, we thought 'Well there's no way we'll make a record with John again', and then suddenly I find myself in the studio with John in my headphones.... mysterious indeed. The Beatles have always defied convention, The Beatles have always defied the rules, so who knows? " With no great surprise, *Anthology 2* and *Anthology 3* have continued to illustrate the unprecedented and historic series of events so far, which only goes to prove one thing:

'The Beatles Were, The Beatles Are, and The Beatles Always Shall be...
For Ever and Ever... 4 Men.'

12
'Simply the Best'

"Working in this place raises your game. Its hallowed history, from Elgar to the Fabs, makes you try just that little bit harder. And there's always the plaques on the walls to keep any runaway egos firmly in their place."

Jimmy Nail
July 1995

'Classics is Classics and Pop is Pop, and ne'er the twain shall meet'... how true that was for so many years. Fortunately over the last decade or two, with the arrival of a new generation of performers, producers and listeners, together with a large portion of that indefinable ingredient 'taste', the barriers, like the Berlin Wall have finally been broken down. A wonderful example of this unique equalising factor, and an inspiration to all who visit Abbey Road, was experienced recently by Allan Rouse and Peter Vince. Lunching in a rather crowded restaurant, a small elderly gentleman brought his tray to their table and asked if he might join them. Their somewhat embarrassed visitor was brought a glass of wine by Doreen, a member of the restaurant staff; he gently cuddled her to his side and in his best English said, "A young lady, but a very old friend." This charming and most unassuming guest was none other than the internationally revered Russian maestro of the cello Mstislav Rostropovich, who was on a special visit to England.

It would be futile to even attempt to list all the artists who have worked at Abbey Road since 1982, but thanks largely to the arrival of the Compact Disc, classical recording has continued to flourish after its brief decline during the early Eighties. Changes in the very nature of pop recording has considerably affected Abbey Road's involvement, as Ken Townsend aptly points out in his preface.

Ex-Abbey Road engineer Haydn Bendall, now a successful freelancer, places much emphasis on cost effective use of studios which best serve the various elements at each particular stage of the

Above: **In November 1984, the great talents of Yehudi Menuhin and Paul Tortelier came together, in Studio One, to record the 'Brahms Concerto for Violin and Cello'. The orchestra on this occasion was under the baton of Paavo Berglund.**

Below: **Seen during the recording of his album Big River, is Jimmy Nail (right) with his producer Danny Shoggar.**

recording. Taking the 'pop' recordings he did with Kiri Te Kanawa (which included the song for The Rugby World Cup) as an example, Haydn explains, "When the basic tracks are synthesiser based, as they were in our particular case, you are better off initially spending your money on good synth equipment and then doing all the groundwork at home. The thing is, we had to spend a lot of time programming, a lot of time getting the effects just right, and even more time just simply experimenting, and if we had done all that in a studio it would have just eaten up the budget. Once all that was done, we went into a small inexpensive studio to get those sounds down onto the multitrack, and then we came to Abbey Road to do the serious recording. We overdubbed the orchestra in Studio One, did the vocals in Studio Two and then mixed the whole thing in Studio Three. To me it makes sense to use, whenever possible, the best location to achieve the best results."

This sentiment is endorsed by musician and producer Rod Argent, who first found fame in the Sixties with The Zombies. Their song 'Time Of The Season' from the album *Odyssey And Oracle* was a multi-million selling world hit, and recorded at Abbey Road by Peter Vince. "In those days there weren't too many studios to choose from," says Rod, "but today the choice is enormous and bands will go where they feel most comfortable, or where their finances permit."

The recurrent criticism that Abbey Road is often too expensive for the more time consuming pop albums is a misconception rapidly put to right by Studio Operations Manager, Colette Barber: "We are in fact extremely competitive with our rates. All right there is no way we can compete with the small specialist budget studios, but as far as the majority of the established studios are concerned, we are either the same or in some cases even cheaper. Perhaps we no longer attract quite as many big names here to record their albums as we used to, but over the years an awful lot of them have come here to overdub orchestras or choirs or anything else that we are renowned for doing so well." And there is no disputing that statement; artists like Howard Jones, Aha, Bronski Beat, Chris Rea, Gary Moore, Deacon Blue, Paul McCartney, Sade, Joan Armatrading, Take That, Blur and Sting are just a few who have chosen Abbey Road when they need to add that extra special something to their recordings. Colette is also keen to point out, "There are a lot of new, as well as established international groups, who now want to record here. Names such as Nick Cave and The Bad seeds; Bush, a British band who have become hugely successful in America; Hotei, one of Japan's biggest ever groups; as well as Lightning Seeds, Reef, Vent, and with their 1996 British chart success, Manic Street Preachers."

Since 1982 Abbey Road has had its fair share of eminently successful artists through its doors. Among those who've been more than happy to make their albums at the studios are Terrorvision, Ian Anderson, Adam Ant, David Coverdale and Jimmy Page, Mark Knopfler, Paul Young, Queen, David Essex and as solo artists in their own right, Paul Simon and Art Garfunkel.

Mark Owen (Ex-Take That) has recorded his first solo album at the studios with producer and ex-Abbey Road Engineer John Leckie. John, like so many of his counterparts, admits that whenever the budget permits he will always come to Abbey Road. "This place is like family, once you've worked here and you come back for the mastering, or to do another session, or simply pop in for lunch and a drink, you feel so comfortable, it's like visiting your granny. I certainly don't get that feeling anywhere else." When asked to what does he attribute his continued success (Simple Minds, XTC, The Stone Roses, Radiohead and Ride to name but a few), John's unhesitating reply is fascinating in today's world of high technology. "I don't do anything different in the studio today to what I did 20 years ago.

Above: **Members of Radiohead Colin Greenwood (left) and Thom Yorke (seated) are joined by Abbey Road engineer Chris Brown in number three control room where they were working on their album The Bends.**

I always get the bands to perform live in the studio, I use the same old mic's and layouts, and only add the fewest number of overdubs and effects possible. The whole thing sounds so much more natural, and I find the bands perform better too. I can't believe more people don't work this way."

American engineer Steve Albini is a new convert to Abbey Road. Steve has worked with Nirvana, The Pixies and P.J.Harvey, although he now tends to spend most of his time with the lesser known 'alternative' bands. He echoes John Leckie's feelings totally, and feels that recording sessions should simply be an extension of the band's normal live performances. He always insists on being involved with the complete process, unlike some engineers who are happy to hand their recordings over to someone else to remix. He is justly adamant that the 'natural' aspect should be maintained throughout, and not as he puts it, "transformed into a Speilbergian special effect." Bearing in mind that so much of his work involves strong monetary restrictions, how does he manage to persuade his artists to use Abbey Road. "The first full length thing I did here was The Auteurs album *After Murder Park*, which we did in Studio Two. It was so productive that now whenever I come over I try to encourage people to come here, even if it's only for string overdubs. Quite honestly, there aren't that many places you can go to and feel that you are getting your money's worth. I find that I am more productive in a fully staffed and 100% reliable studio like this, and I get twice as much done here as I would in a studio that doesn't charge as much. And the accommodation next door is a genius idea, if you need to go somewhere quiet for a while, you can go to the flat and sit on a comfortable sofa and read a book or watch TV, or take a long hot bath – that sort of thing is head and shoulders above pretending you're alone in a quiet corner of the studio. So I really do feel that although you're paying full whack, you are getting value for money, which is rare at any price."

Above: **Mark Owen with producer/engineer John Leckie in Studio Three during the recording of his first solo album, following the break-up of the highly successful band Take That.**

Paul Carrack seen here during the recording of the pilot for the TV programme Live at Abbey Road, *was to return shortly afterwards to record his album* Blue Views *with producer Peter Van Hooke.*

Peter Van Hooke, drummer, producer, manager, is a man totally in love with Abbey Road. In fact if he had enough money he'd buy the place. Peter's latest projct has been a pilot for a possible future television series entitled *Live at Abbey Road*. It was filmed over two days, and featured performances from Paul Carrack, Marcella Detroit, Marc Almond, Irish guitarist Brian Houston and a new band called Cast who coincidentally recorded their first album with John Leckie. All the live musical items were linked together with a host of interviews which on this occasion included George Harrison, who just happened to be in Abbey Road at the time. The object of the exercise was to show the artists performing live in a real studio situation, rather than the somewhat sterile environment of the television studio, where as Peter puts it, "Because of the limitations imposed upon them, the sound engineers just can't do justice to the sound. The difference achieved by doing it in a real studio is for me like Coca-Cola – you can't beat the real thing !"

Despite two absolutely hectic days, Peter's engineer Simon Smart, assisted by Abbey Road's Paul Hicks, was extremely impressed with the sound he was able to get from Studio Two. He was further delighted when Peter decided to make Paul Carrack's new album in the same studio and once again record the whole thing live – vocals and all. "To me that room is a freak," confesses Simon. "I will never understand how things can sound so good when you just plug in a microphone, go straight through the desk and it sounds fantastic. It needed very little work from me, and although there was spill on to the other mic's, it was always friendly spill." With no element of surprise, Peter's only comment is, "I've always known that this is a great place, for me it's simply the best."

On Tuesday 22 October 1986, fourteen children from Dunblane Primary and High schools travelled down from Scotland to attend a session at Abbey Road Studios to record a special version of Bob Dylan's 'Knockin' On Heaven's Door'. Its purpose was to raise money for the Dunblane Fund, following the massacre of so many helpless children and their teacher at the school earlier in the year. Dire Straits' Mark Knopfler felt "honoured" to help with this anti-gun anthem by coming to the studios and adding guitar to the recording. For such a worthy cause Abbey Road had no hesitation in offering their services, including those of engineer Peter Cobbin who also took on the role of producer.

It's important to point out at this stage that Abbey Road hasn't stood still over the last fifteen years – far from it. From the outside, little if anything about the 'residence' at Number 3 has altered, but once inside, any past recollections or preconceived images will probably fade into oblivion. From the spacious open-plan reception area to the 'Garden Restaurant', with every studio, post-production room and office in between, no location has been left untouched, hopefully for the benefit and appreciation of artists, clients and staff alike.

While many of the changes have been predominantly cosmetic, there were two major projects which are worthy of special mention. The first was the construction of a brand new control room for Studio One. "Ever since the arrival of stereo recording back in the late Fifties, the original control room ceased to be really suitable," confesses Ken Townsend, "and with the ever increasing size of mixing consoles, and the eventual arrival of film work, the situation became quite embarrassing." After careful consideration to find a suitable alternative location, and then a lengthy battle for planning permission, building work eventually began. It was a long and difficult process, which involved re-routing the whole of the incoming electricity supply to the studios, but finally in the spring of 1985, after a few minor teething troubles, the new control room was opened. Not only was it considerably larger, with a panoramic view of the studio and the projection screen, but it was also fitted with a brand new 56 channel, E Series Solid State Logic (SSL) mixing console, with 4-channel surround sound monitoring facilities (this was in fact Abbey Road's second SSL/E, the first being installed some 18 months earlier in Studio Two). As Neil Aldridge, Manager of Technical Operations, explains, "The SSL was chosen primarily for its automation facilities, which were a considerable asset to both classical and film engineers alike. With clients having to grab any studio time as it became available, the SSL, with its computer control, offered the ability to recall any previously stored desk settings to a very high degree of accuracy. This enabled a complete classical work, for example, to be recorded over several non-consecutive days with comparative ease."

The second and even more ambitious project was the complete rebuilding of Studio Three. As Ken is once again ready to admit, "Ever since the arrival of pop music, the situation with 'noise' breaking through into Studio One had been an ongoing problem." With the advent of high quality digital recording during the early Eighties, things were only getting more serious, a solution just had to be found. When EMI eventually gave the go-ahead to what would be Abbey Road's biggest expense since its original construction in 1931, one big question had to be put to designer and acoustician Sam Toyashima. "Sam," Ken asked tentatively, "can you assure me that we are going to get no sound interference at all with Studio One?"...."No problem Ken, no problem!" was Sam's reply. Ken continued, "I don't want to have to sue you afterwards if it doesn't work Sam,"... "You won't have to sue me Ken, it will work, I promise," was Sam's confident reply. "Well it did work," admits Ken, "and to this day I have nothing but respect for that man."

The revolutionary new Number Three complex, constructed under the watchful eye of Abbey Road's much respected recording engineer Mike Jarratt, has a studio with adjustable acoustics, various isolation booths and a 'live' mirrored drum room. Above the control room, and overlooking the studio, is a lounge with en-suite kitchen and bathroom facilities, and the huge control room itself houses a massive customised G-Series SSL, with 72 channels, and monitoring capabilities for full 8 channel surround sound, a requirement for many of today's film scores. Truly a studio within a studio, where clients can shut themselves away, if they so wish, and remain totally self sufficient. By a unique and totally unplanned coincidence, the first artists to work in the new Studio Three complex were Pink Floyd, who just happened to be the first people to use the studio on its two previous rebuilds – a strange but welcomed omen.

Although little has been done to Studio Two, for fear that its historic acoustics might be affected, the control room has been both enlarged and updated, with much approval from all its loyal clients. "We've upgraded the desk to a Neve VRP – 64 channel," confirms Neil Aldridge, "while Studio One now has a Neve VRP – 72 channel (64 fitted) desk, to replace the original SSLs, which were now some twelve years old."

Another big change over the last 15 years, has been the enormous increase in the number of freelance engineers who now work at Abbey Road, particularly on pop recordings. As Colette Barber readily admits, "When you think in the early Eighties we had eight or nine well established pop engineers, now we have just one – Chris Brown, although assistant engineers Paul Hicks and Guy Massey are rapidly learning the ropes, and standing in the wings waiting for their golden opportunity to come along." Mind you there have been some magic moments along the way, as Paul and Guy will readily admit. Paul has had the

Noel Gallagher, Paul McCartney and Paul Weller in Studio Two during the recording of 'Come Together' for the charity album Help.

unique opportunity to work with the three remaining Beatles on the Anthology project, while Guy's association with Paul McCartney is another story altogether. "It was 4th September 1995," reminisces Guy, "a date engraved on my memory. The occasion was the recording of the Lennon and McCartney song 'Come Together' with ex-Jam star Paul Weller. It was to be a track for a special charity album called *Help*, which was being released to raise money for the orphans of the war in former Yugoslavia."

Not only was this the fulfilment of a dream for Weller, to make a record in the same studio that The Beatles recorded *Sgt. Pepper* (the first album he ever bought), but incredibly it was 33 years to the day that his heroes themselves first came to Abbey Road to record their debut single 'Love Me Do'.

"The band assembled for the session were Paul on guitar, Steve

Craddock also on guitar, Damon Minchella on Bass and Steve White on drums," continues Guy, "and they effortlessly breezed through five takes of the track, with take three being chosen as the master. Paul Weller was so relieved that the track had been recorded quickly, because he was filled with complete nervous excitement, when he heard that Paul and Linda McCartney had turned up with their daughters Stella and Mary. A young lady by the name of Pippa, Paul Weller's publicity manager, then informed me that as if the arrival of the McCartney family wasn't enough, she had just heard that her heart-throb Johnny Depp had arrived, and she needed to go for a lie down. When Mr. Depp walked through the door I noticed he was accompanied by the gorgeous Kate Moss. Now I needed to go and lie down. Noel Gallagher from Oasis, and singer Carleen Anderson also turned up to add their musical contributions to the song, and the paparazzi had an absolute field day. When the track was finished, engineer Max Heyes and Producer Brendan Lynch got on with the mix, while everyone else was jamming in the studio. I just stood entranced at the top of the stairs for about half-an-hour; after all it's not often you get a chance to see three of the most influential musicians of the last 30 years playing together and enjoying themselves in such an historic location – it just made me realise how lucky I was to be working at Abbey Road."

But how did the two Pauls feel about the event? "Amazing!" recalls Paul McCartney, "although it was a rush job, everyone treated it as a party and we just enjoyed ourselves, it was great."

"That day was unreal," reflects Paul Weller,"it was like being in a dream." Well in a way it was, but this time a dream come true.

Paul McCartney is one of numerous pop and film composers who have made successful ventures into the classical world. EMI's Director of Recorded Productions and Senior House Producer John Fraser, has formed a close working relationship with Paul in respect of his new found talent. "Since the success of his first composition *Liverpool Oratorio*, Paul has become increasingly active in 'classical' composition," says John. "Most recently, Paul's collection of short pieces for solo piano, *A Leaf*, has been published, and a mobile recording, with Abbey Road's John Kurlander engineering, has been made with pianist Anya Alexeev performing live at St. James's Palace."

Mariss Jansons (left) presents Richard Hale with his twenty year award whilst on a mobile recording in Philadelphia to record the 'Shostakovich's Symphony No 10'.

The Abbey Road Mobile Recording Unit, in the capable hands of Graham Kirkby and Richard Hale, has served to maintain the tradition of location recording excellence. Over the last 15 years they have travelled as far afield as the USA, Israel, Poland, Italy, Norway, France, Austria, Spain and the former Soviet Union. The creation of the European Community, and the unification of East and West Germany, have now made journeys throughout Europe virtually trouble free by removing the time consuming delays at all the various border checkpoints.

Mike Sheady, Abbey Road's most senior classical engineer, who incidentally started his career in the pop world, has spent most of the last decade 'on the road' with the mobile units, working with such prolific artists as Riccardo Muti, Mariss Jansons, Wolfgang Sawallisch, Zubin Mehta, Bernard Haitink, Sir Charles

Mackerras and Sir Simon Rattle. In fact Mike's recording of Mahler's 2nd Symphony with Rattle and the CBSO in 1988 subsequently won for him the prestigious Gramophone Engineering Award.

Although the Abbey Road Mobile has been responsible for hundreds of recordings over the last 15 years, undoubtedly its most memorable has to be the album made in the Ballroom at Buckingham Palace on August 2, 1990, simply titled *A Birthday Concert For My Grandmother*. The recital was con-

Above: **During one of the many mobile recordings with the City of Birmingham Symphony Orchestra, conductor Sir Simon Rattle called a halt to procedings in order to present 20 year service awards.(Left to right, Graham Kirkby, Mike Sheady, Sir Simon Rattle and Ken Townsend).**

ceived and co-ordinated by HRH the Prince of Wales as a special tribute to Her Majesty Queen Elizabeth the Queen Mother, to celebrate her 90th birthday. The recording, produced by George Martin and engineered by Abbey Road's Mark Vigars, contained performances by cellist Mstislav Rostropovich, violinist José-Luis Garcia and soprano Marie McLaughlin with the English Chamber Orchestra conducted by Raymond Leppard.

Since the arrival of the Compact Disc, classical recording both home and away has enjoyed a new lease of life. Along with their more established mentors, young engineers such as David Flower, Simon Rhodes, Jonathan Allen and Alex Marcou, who have grown up with the latest technologies, are continuing to produce recordings of the highest quality. Recordings such as the award winning *Show Boat*, which saw the start of a highly successful series of musicals conducted by John McGlinn, The Complete Beethoven Symphonies with the Concertgebouw Orchestra under the baton of Wolfgang Sawallisch, Grieg's Piano Concerto, performed by Dudley Moore, Barbara Hendrick's collection of songs from the films of Walt Disney, an album of popular Christmas songs from Kiri Te Kanawa, Roberto Alagna and Thomas Hampson, the award winning opera *Peter Grimes* with LPO conducted by Sir Bernard Haitink, and the hugely successful *Porgy and Bess* recorded by Sir Simon Rattle and the LPO, in the presence of the Duke of Kent, who is the President of the orchestra.

Studio One is not only popular with EMI's classical artists and producers, but also with the other international record companies, who no longer have custom classical studios of their own. Decca, Sony, Phillips and Deutsche Grammophon are regular visitors, particularly when they have need to record their major artists who happen to be in England.

Above: **H.R.H. The Duchess of Kent recorded a poem for the album** The Seven Ages of Man **with producer Sean Murphy.**

Studio One was certainly the most suitable environment for the unique project dreamed up by another ex-Abbey Road engineer turned producer, Jeff Jarratt and his partner Don Reedman. It was in fact 1979 when they first recorded the most successful hit tunes of that period in a pseudo-classical style. *Classic Rock* was born, and apart from a brief lull during the late Eighties, when

Left: **Pictured here in Studio One's old control room are classical producer John Fraser with Kiri Te Kanawa, during the recording of her album** Come To The Fair, *a selection of English folk songs.*

dance records were very much the order of the day (and rhythm became more important than melody), it has continued to prove popular, with *Classic Rock 10* bringing the sales figure to well in excess of 10 million. "Because the sound of *Classic Rock* is so dependent on Studio One," insists Jeff Jarratt, "one of our main criteria has been to check that the studio is available before we even approach the London Symphony Orchestra."

The successful team of Jarratt, Reedman and Studio One also brought us *Hooked On Classics*, popular classical items with a constant drum rhythm throughout (three albums, the first of which was number one in the charts around the world), and an album with the popular international performer Michael Crawford, performing the songs of Andrew Lloyd-Webber, which has become a double-platinum hit on both sides of the Atlantic.

Another visitor to these shores who was equally impressed with 'The Sound of Studio One', was Richard Carpenter, brother of the late Karen Carpenter. "In the August of 1984, I had the occasion to work with the late, great British arranger Peter Knight on some additional recording for the Carpenters' second Christmas album, *An Old Fashioned Christmas*. I had looked forward to, and subsequently greatly enjoyed the experience. I was fascinated by the smallness of both the control booth and its mixing console, compared to the enormity of the studio itself. But then an impressively sized booth and console do not automatically make for an impres-

Below: **In the original number one control room, from left to right, Eric Tomlinson, Richard Carpenter, Peter Knight and Allan Rouse, during sessions to complete The Carpenter's album, An Old Fashioned Christmas *following Karen Carpenter's untimely death.*

sive recording, as engineer Eric Tomlinson proved so outstandingly."

There is however, one major criticism about Studio One. "Because everyone agrees that it is simply the best," as engineer Haydn Bendall kindly puts it, "You can't get in the bloody place unless you book a year in advance, and even then, chances are one of EMI's 'classical boys' have probably got in before you. Still, I'll always try there first."

One of EMI's 'classical boys' who did book well in advance was producer David Groves, who in 1996 completed a somewhat unique version of Puccini's *La Bohéme*. With the Philharmonia Orchestra under the direction of Antonio Pappano, the featured soloists include Thomas Hampson, Leontina Vaduva and the man hailed to be the next Gigli, Roberto Alagna. The recording, the first to be issued in the new CD-Extra format, was different in as much as the singers were required to move around a specially constructed stage area, much in the same way as a live operatic performance. And when the score called for a discreet offstage band to be playing, David persuaded the producer and artists performing in the adjacent Studio Two, to take a short break, to enable the necessary musicians from the opera to play in that particular studio; thereby obtaining exactly the desired effect. Studio Two's occupants on that occasion just happened to be stars from the popular TV soap *Coronation Street*, who were recording songs for a special Christmas album. They were more than happy to oblige, on the condition that they could sit in Studio One while the recording took place. The mutual arrangement proved a great success for both parties, once again confirming that today 'The twain shall meet', and long may it continue to do so.

Conductor Lorin Maazel and tenor Placido Domingo are joined in Studio One by composer and producer Andrew Lloyd-Webber during the recording of his work, Requiem.

Despite the undisputed increase in the number of new classical recordings that have taken place over the last ten or fifteen years, there is no denying that the greatest source of product and income has been from the re-issue of EMI's back catalogue. In the very early days of compact disc, the policy was simply to transfer the old tapes in their original form. However since the arrival of computerised systems dedicated to improving the quality of old recordings, the process has become a complete new art form. In the hands of Abbey Road's specialists, software programs such as CEDAR (Computer Enhanced Digital Audio Restoration) and Sonic Solutions 'No Noise', can be used to such great effect that old recordings can be improved beyond all recognition, as far as their sound quality is concerned. Peter Mew who, along with Michael Gray and Peter Vince, was one of the pioneers of compact disc premastering during its very early days, has become the man responsible for the Sonics System at Abbey Road since its arrival in 1988. Although originally designed as a system for the removal of unwanted background noise, Sonics has proved to be the ultimate editing system, facilitating previously undreamed of editing procedures, and not a razor blade in sight.

Abbey Road now has ten Sonics Systems (running on the Apple Macintosh), operating on a dedicated network which links the editing, remastering and CD premastering rooms together. In addition there is an abundance of additional Mac's and PCs scattered around the rest of the studios. "It's fascinating to note," remarks Peter Mew, "back in 1982 there wasn't one computer in the building, now the only rooms that don't have them are the toilets, and I guess that's just a matter of time!"

Another fascinating change has been in the number of people working in post production. Manager of the Post Production department, Chris Buchanan, explains, "During the Eighties there was a gradual change over to shift working, with two people sharing most rooms. Whereas in '82 we had five disc cutting rooms, three editing rooms and one or two general purpose copying rooms, we now have two disc cutting/mastering rooms, three CD preparation rooms, three copying rooms, one dedicated cassette copying room, three digital remastering rooms, two editing rooms and a multimedia suite. This restructuring relates to an increase of staff from 10 in 1982, to 30 in 1996. Although disc cutting, since the arrival of CD, has got less and less, limited to just promotional 12 inch singles, and the occasional special project, such as The Beatles' *Anthology*, in recent months there has been a noticeable increase in demand for disc cutting, and the few remaining manufacturers of vinyl discs (EMI included), have seen an increase back to the figures of some eight or nine years ago, with a particular resurgence in albums – it really is a funny old world."

One area of post production that receives more recognition than any other is in the digital remastering of those recordings made before the arrival of tape. Andrew Walter is responsible for compiling albums of material first recorded on 78's (both acoustically and electrically) by the legendary artists of days gone by. This particular facility has existed at Abbey Road for some 30 years or more, when in the days of analogue all extraneous clicks were removed by literally cutting them out of the tape, and justifiably, each successive engineer has received awards for the restorations he has performed. Andy is no exception, having received more awards than the entire 1996 British Olympic Team, but unlike his predecessors he is up against stiff competition from around the world, as the necessary technology becomes cheaper and more readily available. However, it must be said that Andy has two big things in his favour. Firstly EMI, in its various guises, is one of the oldest surviving record companies, with probably the biggest and most prestigious back catalogue in the world. Secondly, Andy is a most meticulous engineer and musician, who is not satisfied with simply copying the product with the minimum of treatment. He will always endeavour to obtain the best original source, having access to shellac and metal parts, and then insuring that all pitch

Left: **Clearly happy to have received discs commemmorating six months at number one and sales of over 225,000 for his recording of Vivaldi's Four Seasons, Nigel Kennedy is still blissfully unaware that TV presenter Michael Aspel is about to say to him... 'This Is Your Life'. Left to right: EMI's Rupert Perry, John Stanley (Kennedy's manager), Kennedy and Aspel.**

On a recent visit , cellist and conductor Mstislav Rostropovich is joined in Studio One by Andrew Walter.

correction, noise reduction and equalisation is performed with the best possible taste. "I hope what I am doing," reflects Andy, "is stopping people forgetting, and helping to perpetuate musical history. If nothing else, at least I'm maintaining an archive on what is hopefully an indestructible medium."

Well Andy's 'archive' includes some notable highlights, including *The Elgar Edition* – nine including everything by Elgar that was electrically recorded (winner of a Gramophone Award), *Composers In Person* – a series in which the original composers were either conducting, playing or in attendance at the recordings, and a six CD set of the complete works and performances of Noel Coward, which was nominated for a Grammy Award. Andy's most recent epic has been with Mstislav Rostropovich, who with the blessing of his good friend Boris Yeltsin, the Russian President, has brought to EMI a treasure trove of unique, live concert recordings previously unheard outside Russia. "They are absolute gems," reveals Andy. "Yes the odd little glitch here and there, but the performance, the feeling and the soul are second to none – the *crème de la crème* you might say." That simple phrase just about sums up Abbey Road – the *crème de la crème* Studio, with the *crème de la crème* staff, recording the *crème de la crème* artists.

'SIMPLY THE BEST'.

13
The Never Ending Story

In the four seemingly short years since the last edition of this book, Abbey Road Studios has continued to grow from strength to strength. Whether it's Classical, Film, Pop, Post-Production, Multimedia or even the very building itself, every aspect of the studios has been an ongoing story of success.

Classical

EMI Classics has continued to share Studio One with the worlds of film and MOR, along with clients from other international classical record companies. But as EMI's Stephen Johns explains, "We, like everyone else are very much artist led, and need to follow them to record their performances wherever they might be." This single overriding factor has resulted in the Abbey Road Mobiles being in constant demand, recording major artists at locations worldwide.

Stephen Johns, EMI's newest recruit to the classical production team, is in fact no stranger to Abbey Road. He first worked at the studios in 1988, when, as a young, fresh faced post-graduate, he was employed by Ken Townsend as a classical editor. He readily admits, "I was incredibly lucky to be able to learn every aspect of classical recording from some of the most respected names in the industry." However, in 1991 Stephen was seconded by a small independent company, where he was given the added opportunity to gain experience in record production. This new talent held him in good stead when in 1998 EMI Classics urgently required the services of a new producer in their ranks. Stephen was the obvious choice, and since his arrival has shared incredible success with colleagues John Fraser and David Groves.

On the artist front, stalwarts such as Placido Domingo, Nigel Kennedy (or simply 'Kennedy' as he now prefers to be known), Vanessa Mae, Kiri Te Kanawa, Roberto Alagna and his wife, Angela Gheorghiu continue to reap regular acclaim.

One major achievement, which involved closely co-ordinated teamwork between David Groves, The Abbey Road Mobile and Abbey Road's editors, was the Millennium New Year's Concert in Vienna, conducted by Riccardo Muti. The album was recorded, edited, pressed and released within days, and received a platinum disc within weeks, in Austria alone.

But there is one artist who perhaps deserves more than just a passing mention. Sir Simon Rattle's 20 years of loyal partnership with EMI has culminated in so many successes and accolades that he is now internationally respected as one of the greatest conductors of all time. It is fitting that his recording of Mahler's 10th Symphony with the Berlin Philharmonic Orchestra, won the prestigious Gramophone Award for the 'Record of the Year'. The album, produced by Stephen Johns on location in Germany with the Abbey Road Mobile, also won the Classical Brits Award for 'Best Orchestral Recording', and a Grammy for 'The Best Orchestral Recording of the Year'.

But the Simon Rattle story doesn't end there. Whilst his forte is classical music, his heart is also in the world of jazz, and in the autumn of 1999, he was given the chance to fulfil a dream – to record an album with a symphony orchestra and a jazz band playing together. This, coincidentally, had also been a dream of the late Duke Ellington, who, like Simon, firmly believed that 'music has no frontiers, and is beyond category'. With this thought in mind, it seemed only right to choose a selection of 'The Duke's' compositions for the occasion. Lady Rattle's uncle, Luther Henderson, who had at one time arranged compositions for Ellington, was thrilled when asked to supply the arrangements for Simon's recording. The outcome was a musical triumph, with the City of Birmingham Symphony Orchestra sharing the stage with a selection of the finest jazz musicians from America, and the addition of vocals by the incomparable Lena Horne.

Above: **Sir Simon Rattle** *(left) with Luther Henderson (centre) during* Classical Ellington *sessions in October 1999, with EMI producer Stephen Johns.*

Although Studio One is in constant use for both classical and film recording, August 2000 saw the two come uniquely together for the recording of Puccini's *Tosca*. Unique, because not only was the recording used for both soundtrack and CD, but the sessions were also filmed, and the studio footage cleverly edited into the final screen production. EMI's David Groves, a respected master of opera production, confesses, "This was an immense task from start to finish, and was undoubtedly one of the most demanding operas that the studios and I have ever experienced."

The recording, engineered by Simon Rhodes with the invaluable assistance of Bill Thwaites and the technical team, took over 17 sessions to complete, compounded by the need for both musical and visual perfection. As well as utilising Studio 2 for simultaneous recordings of offstage instruments and vocals, it was necessary to overdub further effects including numerous canons and church bells.

Following the initial recording, which was made onto Sony Digital 48-Track, (occasionally up to 54 tracks with the addition of further synchronised machines for the effects) the opera was mixed down to the 32 tracks of the Sonic Solutions System for editing. This process involved the whole of the editing department at Abbey Road and the team led by Senior Editor Simon Kiln began work a week after the recording started, and continued unceasing, for another six weeks.

"This job really pushed all the barriers," admits David Groves, "It was a great success and pioneered elements of multi-track editing probably beyond any international comparison. In fact, the successful outcome of this whole project was due entirely to an incredible team effort, which ended up utilising every department at Abbey Road."

The film was previewed at the Venice and Toronto Film Festivals, where everyone was totally overwhelmed by the performance. The final words are best left to the critics, when they wrote in Toronto's *Daily Star,* and Italy's *Corriere della Sera*, 'Thanks to director Benoît Jacquot's imaginative approach, Tosca has turned out to be a breakthrough movie, with a new way of presenting opera.' – 'Angela Gheorghiu is a fiery Tosca, Roberto Alagna is a fantastic Mario and Ruggero Raimondi a terrific Scarpia. This Tosca is packed full of new ideas, and saw a fabulous performance from Antonio Pappano and London's Royal Opera House Orchestra and Chorus.'

Because of the successful techniques employed with *Tosca*, David subsequently went on to record Verdi's *Il Trovatore* directly to a 32-track hard drive, eliminating tape completely.

Meanwhile, EMI Classics maintained its links with the pop world, with the John Fraser and Paul McCartney association. John's initial involvement was as producer for Paul's first classical work, *Liverpool Oratorio*. In 1997 he was delighted when Paul asked him to produce his second major classical composition, *Standing Stone*, commissioned by EMI to celebrate their centenary. "The album which was recorded in Studio One at Abbey Road, with engineer John Kurlander, called for huge orchestral and choral forces," recalls John, "so we used the full London Symphony Orchestra and Chorus, conducted by Lawrence

Below: **Sir Paul McCartney working with the orchestra in Studio One during the recording of his work Standing Stone.**

Foster. The recording was a great success, as was the subsequent first public performance at London's Royal Albert Hall, where it received a 10 minute standing ovation from a capacity audience."

Following the sad death of his wife Linda, Paul wrote the deeply personal choral piece entitled, 'Nova', which was included on an album called, *Garland For Linda – An Album to Commemorate the Life of Linda McCartney*. The recording, which also contained original music from other contemporary composers, featured The Joyful Company of Singers under the baton of Peter Broadbent. It was Recorded in All Saints Church, Tooting, London, by Engineer Arne Akselberg with the Abbey Road Mobile.

Paul's third album for EMI Classics, *Working Classical*, included three new short orchestral works, 'A Leaf', 'Spiral' and 'Tuesday', as well as several of the songs which Paul wrote for Linda, played by the Loma Mar String Quartet. The album was recorded in Studio One, again with Abbey Road's Arne Akselberg engineering. It was later launched by a live performance in Liverpool, with the quartet and The Royal Liverpool Philharmonic Orchestra conducted by Andrea Quinn.

Film

Since the early Eighties, when film music came to the rescue of an ailing Studio One, there hardly seems to have been a single month go by without some aspect of film scoring taking place, either in the studios or on location. Wherever it might be, regular clients such as John Barry, Gabriel Yared, Michael Nyman, James Horner and Michael Kamen continue to add their own particular music styles to a wide variety of films. However, a glance at the studio diary would suggest that Trevor Jones might consider taking up residency. Just a few titles from the ongoing list of films for which he has written scores include *G I Jane*, *Desperate Measures*, *The Mighty*, *Merlin*, *Thirteen Days* and his Music Award winning *Notting Hill*.

Below: Following the Abbey Road mobile recording in Berlin of his score for the film I Dream of Africa, *Maurice Jarre returned to the Penthouse studio with engineer Jonathan Allen to complete the project.*

Other film score successes at Abbey Road include *Captain Corelli's Mandolin* with music by Stephen Warbeck and Nick Park's latest contribution to the world of cinema animation, *Chicken Run* composed by Harry Gregson-Williams and John Powell whose music for the film *Shrek* was also recorded in Studio One.

As well as the host of new film scores, Abbey Road also has a working association with the American record label Varèse Sarabande, who regularly add re-recordings of original soundtracks to their catalogue. Most recently they have completed an album of the award winning score *To Kill A Mockingbird*, with the celebrated composer Elmer Bernstein. Elmer who has also re-recorded his scores for *The Great Escape* and *The Magnificent Seven*, worked with engineer Jonathan Allen, who has been responsible for many of these projects, mostly on location with The Abbey Road Mobile – do these chaps ever get to go home?

But in this category, special mention must be given to what had become one of the most eagerly awaited films for many decades. Following the phenomenal successes of its predecessors, *Star Wars: Episode One – The Phantom Menace* had sci-fi fans the world over drooling in anticipation. Such was the fanaticism

Left: *George Lucas and John Williams were re-united at Abbey Road Studios to record the score for the* Star Wars *prequel* The Phantom Menace. *Among the team were, left to right: Ken Wannberg (music editor), Randy Kerber, Rick McCallum (producer), Shawn Murphey (engineer), George Lucas, John Williams, Andrew Dudman and Jonathan Allen (assistant engineers), Dave Forty (technical engineer); kneeling: Joseph Williams (John's son) and Jamie Richardson (John's assistant).*

that people were buying tickets at movie theatres, watching the brief Star Wars trailers, and then leaving before the main feature.

When it came to recording the score, producer Rick McCallum together with George Lucas, John Williams and sound engineer Shawn Murphy, came to the unanimous choice of Studio One at Abbey Road. "I think to us it was partly like coming home, and partly an adventure to come here," recalls Rick McCallum. "The people at Abbey Road are extraordinary, nothing is too much trouble, and nothing is a problem. Not only that, but Studio One has such a history, the very atmosphere is just wonderful."

It had been 20 years since the last *Star Wars*, and John Williams confessed to finding the initial challenge quite daunting, but was pleasantly surprised how quickly the old inspiration came back. George Lucas had always had a vision of how the music should compliment the pictures, but as he is more than happy to admit, "It took the genius of John Williams to fully realise this vision. Once again this man has exceeded my expectations and produced a lavish, rich, moving and thrilling score. Every fan of *Star Wars* and great music alike is in his debt."

Shawn Murphy, assisted on this project by Abbey Road Engineers Jonathan Allen, Andrew Dudman and Dave Forty, is no stranger to the studios. He had previously worked on such successes as *Man Without A Face*, *Braveheart* and later, *Sleepy Hollow*. He is not only a fan of Studio One, but also of the large compliment of old valved microphones that Abbey Road possesses. It is a fact recognised by the majority of established engineers

Below: *During the* Star Wars *sessions both Ewan McGregor and Stephen Spielberg visited George Lucas at Abbey Road. Here Spielberg and Lucas discuss the new epic.*

that the warm and full sound that those vintage microphones can produce is still difficult to replicate with today's modern equivalents.

From one trilogy to another... After nearly one and a half years of filming in New Zealand – possibly the longest consecutive principal photography shoot for any film – all three stories of J.R.R. Tolkien's towering epic *The Lord Of The Rings* were completed. Composer Howard Shore, Executive Music Producer Paul Broucek and Supervising Engineer John Kurlander (ex–Abbey Road) had decided to put a team together in London to record, mix and master the music for the first of the films: *The Fellowship Of The Ring.*

Having started their sessions elsewhere, they came to complete their recording at Abbey Road. As Paul explains, "We knew the place had a world class scoring stage and could handle the size of orchestra and choir that we required – six sessions with a 96 piece London Philharmonic Orchestra, and three choir sessions. And we also knew that they had the capability to enable us to complete an immense amount of editing and mixing for this project."

Three editors worked simultaneously; Simon Kiln worked on all the two-track mixes on Sonic Solutions both for evaluation of the film mixes and also for the soundtrack album, whilst two 5.1 Protools set-ups were being used by Andrew Dudman and Michael Price. Engineers Peter Cobbin and Jonathan Allen, along with assistant Mirek Styles, were mixing music continuously in the Penthouse.

As Paul Broucek emphasises, "Everything was being used from the moment we started to the moment we left and then some. We were keeping it all going like a small factory operation."

The project was co-ordinated for Abbey Road by Peter Cobbin with the dedicated assistance of the whole team. A monumental 160 minutes worth of music was produced for this film – an epic amount for a world famous epic story.

Pop

Peter Cobbin came to Abbey Road back in 1995, at a time when The Studios had lost several of its established and experienced engineers, particularly in the area of large orchestral recordings. Martin Benge, who by that time had become Vice President of the EMI Studios Group, had made Peter's acquaintance some time before, when he was manager at Studios 301 in Sydney, Australia. Peter was not only an accomplished engineer at the time, but was also achieving some success as a producer and composer. Martin eventually persuaded Peter to bring his wife and family over to England, for a two-year trial period. Six years later they are still here.

Apart from an early association with John Yap, recording many of his musicals, Peter has had the opportunity to work across all fields of music, with such artists as U2, Cher, Janet Jackson, P.J. Harvey, Air, Luciano Pavarotti and Andrea Bocelli. One of his most recent projects was to record a number of tracks for the tribute album *Good Rockin' Tonight (The Legacy of Sun Records).* The individual sound of the Sun Studio in Memphis, immortalised by Elvis Presley, was an enormous influence on so many artists and musicians the world over. In the UK Mark Knopfler, Bryan Ferry, Brian May, Jools Holland and John Paul Jones were among those who came to Abbey Road and performed on various titles, alongside musicians Scotty Moore and D.J. Fontana (Elvis's original guitarist and drummer).

Meanwhile, one major technical advancement that has affected many people at Abbey Road is '5.1 Surround Sound'. Peter Cobbin, now Abbey Road's Senior Engineer, aptly sums up this new phenomenon: "There is no doubt that, over the last three years, surround sound has been the one single thing to shape the way we now think and work at The Studios. Be it on the original sessions or any subsequent post-production 5.1 is very much a guiding factor, and the enormous potential for pop music to be mixed in 5.1 is now being realised."

However, as Peter is quick to point out, "The art of good mixing is to use this new system in such a way as to create interest and excitement, without destroying the general listening enjoyment." And in all fairness Peter should know, for it was he that was given the enviable task of remixing the music soundtrack for The Beatles film *Yellow Submarine* in 5.1.

Peter worked closely with engineers Paul Hicks and Guy Massey, along with Allan Rouse, who is responsible for co-ordinating Beatles' projects. This new team was given almost complete freedom to do whatever they felt necessary to create a whole new listening experience, without destroying the original concept, and thereby upsetting the plethora of Beatles audiophiles world-wide.

One of the great plus points when it comes to working on any Beatles'

Introduced to Abbey Road by Mike Hedges, Travis are seen here during a session break in Studio One; from left: Andy Dunlop, Douglas Payne, Fran Healy and Neil Primrose.

related project is that the engineers have access to every original master tape, together with its associated paperwork. This fact combined with today's technology and engineering expertise, opens up a complete new realm of possibilities. The most exciting thing as far as the 5.1 mixes were concerned was the facility to create completely new multitracks for a number of the songs. On some of the original sessions four tracks were sufficient, and naturally these masters were used for the new mixes. But for many of The Beatles arrangements, four tracks simply weren't enough, and as a result it was necessary to mix down the four initial tracks onto one track of a fresh new tape, thereby creating three more tracks for recording. As Peter discovered, "For the more adventurous songs they would repeat the process yet again. And for the really adventurous songs there might even be a fourth tape!" The remix would be done using that final 4-track tape, which despite the best will in the world would have suffered to some degree from the effects of all those mixdowns.

Below: **Texas returned to their 'lucky' studios to overdub and mix tracks for their number one best selling album Greatest Hits.**

Above: **Manic Street Preachers were regular visitors to Abbey Road during the Nineties. This Is My Truth Tell Me Yours *was one of many albums worked on at the studios.***

Allan Rouse was able to undo all those remixes, and by syncing each 4-track tape with its predecessor, was able to create a whole new multitrack master, the likes of which George Martin and The Beatles could only have dreamed about back in the Sixties. Whilst having this unique master opened up a complete new world of possibilities, the inherent problems didn't stop there. When each of the original mixdowns took place it was necessary to add any effects that might be required, as in most cases they quite simply couldn't be added at a later date (are you still with me?). This meant long and careful assessment of the original masters, and then deciding how to duplicate the sounds. "Fortunately," recalls Peter, "Abbey Road has retained most of its ancillary equipment from those early years, and together with the detailed information written on the tape boxes and recording session sheets, all helped enormously in making the job that much easier."

The final result of this historic and groundbreaking project, which took many arduous months to complete, was a triumph for the whole team. But despite the acclaim that each and every member received, there was one extra magic moment in Peter's memory. "Undoubtedly, the highlight for me was to sit in on the playbacks with Paul, George and Ringo, and experience their total excitement, enthusiasm and utter delight for the whole thing."

The many clients who have worked at Abbey Road over the last decade, might well be forgiven for thinking that one man, Mike Hedges was just another member of the studio staff. The truth is that Mike is actually a client who simply loves Abbey Road, and that's why he spends so much time there. He started in the business as a trainee at Morgan Studios in London, back in the Seventies, but rapidly progressed to the role of freelance engineer/producer. In a relatively short time his credit list has evolved into a veritable Who's Who of the pop world. It encompasses such acts as The Undertones, The Beautiful South, Everything But The Girl, Siouxsie And The Banshees, The Cure, Travis and Manic Street Preachers. Sharleen Spiteri, lead singer of the phenomenally successful Scottish band Texas, was delighted to get an opportunity to work at The Studios. "I'll always have great memories of first working at Abbey Road, Texas were in with producer Mike Hedges, and he told us all of the great old stories. The thing is though, despite its illustrious past, Abbey Road today is a very under-stated studio; that's its great strength for me. Having recorded part of the *White On Blonde* album there, we returned last year (2000) to record and mix for the Texas *Greatest Hits* release. It's my lucky studio now."

Above: **Dr John, The Night Tripper,** pictured during the recording of **Anutha Zone,** while (below) Micky Quinn (left) and Gaz Coombes (right) of Supergrass record his song 'Voices In My Head' in Studio Two.

Mike's association with the studios goes much deeper than engineering and production. The one thing that initially endeared him to Abbey Road, apart from the magic of Studio Two, was the old EMI mixing desks. When in 1989 he acquired a large chateau in France, and installed a recording studio for his own personal use, he was overjoyed when he found himself able to purchase one of the old mixing consoles. EMI had put it in storage after it was removed to make way for a Solid State Logic desk back in 1983. "It's the biggest, and one of the best desks they ever made," boasts Mike. "It's a Mk.IV, TG12345 model with 40 inputs, each with its own limiter and compressor, and most importantly a simple but effective EQ which is the very essence of its unique sound. This particular desk came out of Studio Two, which makes it really special, when you remember albums like Pink Floyd's *Dark Side Of The Moon* were recorded on it."

Mike, along with engineer/co-producer Ian Grimble (an ex-Abbey Road engineer), likes to work in the same way as the John Leckies of this world, with as much of the basic track being recorded in one go. "I always get the bands to play live," says Mike, "because in that way, as long as they're well rehearsed, you get a nice tight performance, which hopefully is as close to the finished thing as possible."

Although they often use other studios to record their basic tracks, Hedges and Grimble continue to do much of their overdubbing and mixing at Abbey Road. They, like John Leckie, are regularly assisted by Guy Massey, who has progressed most successfully since those earlier days as an assistant engineer. Guy has been involved in the engineering of hit albums for the likes of Manic Street Preachers and most recently Spiritualised's critically acclaimed album *Let It Come Down*.

Another project involving Guy's engineering, and John Leckie's production, was Dr John's album *Anutha Zone*. For this 'retro album' as Dr John (real name-Mac Rebennack) called it, he enlisted the help of Paul Weller, Jools Holland, Portishead, Supergrass, Ocean Colour Scene, Spiritualised and members of Primal Scream. The result is reported as being 'an amalgam of Creole Funk,

Right: *Following the phenomenal worldwide success of The Spice Girls during the Nineties, the remaining four members of the group returned to work in Studio Three. Sitting on the front steps of The Studio are, left to right, Victoria Beckham, Emma Bunton, Mel B and Mel C.*

straight-up Britpop and Space Rock'. Whatever you want to call it, it certainly worked and the album subsequently became an international success.

Paul Hicks, like Guy Massey, has also been rewarded for his hard work and patience as an assistant and has already had his own fair share of success as a fully-fledged engineer. It all started back in 1997, when The Spice Girls came in to record a jingle for Pepsi Cola. They enjoyed the session so much, that they chose to return to Abbey Road to record their album *Spice World*, and the single 'Too Much', which gave Paul his first UK Number One as an engineer.

"It was during the height of their fame," recalls Paul, "and we were recording the album at the same time as they were involved in *Spiceworld – The Movie*, so they were in and out of the place all the time. It was all quite hectic, but there was a great buzz on the sessions." Since that pleasurable 'baptism', Paul has gone on to work with such artists as Jamiroquai, Toploader, Gomez, Jimmy Page and Robert Plant (Led Zeppelin) on the reunion album *Walking Into Clarksdale*, and with Sir Paul McCartney.

Paul returned to 'The Old Place' to record his album *Run Devil Run*. He too wanted to record in the Hedges/Leckie tradition, which of course was the way The Beatles had worked on their early albums, hence Paul's wish to 'Do It In The Road' (Abbey Road that is.). His band, for this occasion, comprised David Gilmour (Pink Floyd) and Mick Green (Johnny Kidd & The Pirates) on guitars, Ian Paice (Deep Purple) on drums, Pete Wingfield on keyboards and of course the man himself on bass and vocals.

They recorded the whole album in Studio Two, with tracks to spare, in just one week, with engineers Geoff Emerick and Paul Hicks. "It was very hard work, but equally it was very satisfying," admits Paul (M). At the end of each day at 5.30 p.m. the sessions stopped and the musicians went home, something unheard of in the music business these days, but it meant the recordings sounded fresh because the band was fresh and rested too. It was a very demanding week for everyone concerned, but it all worked well because Paul wanted it to be right first time, as he says, "Apart from a little 'fixing' here and there, what you hear is basically what happened that week."

The album was produced by Chris Thomas, who got his big break shortly after managing to get a job as an assistant to George Martin during the very early days of AIR London. He had been sitting in on a Beatles' recording for the *White Album*, when quite unexpectedly, George, who was going on holiday, left him to produce the remaining sessions. It was a somewhat rocky start, as Chris is more than ready to admit, but The Beatles soon warmed to him, and since then he's never really looked back. In fact Chris's subsequent and enviable success list includes, five albums for Roxy Music, The Sex Pistols' *Never Mind The Bollocks*, Wings' *Back To The Egg* and a dozen albums with Elton John.

Above: **Paul McCartney, David Gilmour and fellow members of Paul's 'Rock'n'Roll Band' during the** Run Devil Run *sessions in Studio Two.*

Following the recording sessions, the band performed a live gig at The Cavern in Liverpool. This concert, broadcast by BBC Television, was also mixed and edited by Geoff Emerick and Paul Hicks back at Abbey Road, and Paul has since re-remixed the performance in 5.1 for release on a DVD produced by Abbey Road Interactive.

Post Production/Multimedia.

With the arrival of new systems such as 5.1 Surround Sound, Abbey Road has readily adapted to these new trends and technologies. One major feature, as Neil Aldridge, Manager of Technical Operations, has been only too aware, was the need to update every studio and selected post production rooms to provide those full surround sound capabilities, together with all the very latest in ancillary equipment.

The Audio Restoration Suite, which has been responsible for so many award winning 78 rpm and early tape remastering projects, has had to be completely relocated, and is now additionally capable of remastering in surround sound. The soundtrack for the DVD release of *The Graduate* was just one of the many fruits of their labours. Likewise, remastering Room 4, which coincidentally was the room where 'Quadraphonics' first saw the light of day, has also been completely refitted, to facilitate its new association with surround sound for DVD, and SACD.

Although most of the original equipment has remained in the post production rooms, new items such as the Protools Hard Disc Recording and Editing System, and Sadie Computer Editing Systems have now joined the ranks of their Sonic Solutions forerunners. The hard disc, now commonplace in all home computer systems, has been a great boon to the areas of recording and editing, where it is often replacing tape as the main recording medium, because of the speed and versatility it offers in operation.

Gimme Some Truth, the documentary film about the making of John Lennon's legendary Imagine *album, won a Grammy in 2001 for Best long Form Video.*

Meanwhile, the remaining remastering rooms have all undergone extensive technical and structural upgrades, and as Senior Digital Remastering Engineer, Peter Mew is proud to acknowledge, "The quality of product we produce on such a constant basis is quite unsurpassed." Apart from the many achievements of his colleagues, Peter alone has been responsible for such projects as the 10 CD set and 2 DVD's for Freddie Mercury's *Solo Collection*, 17 CDs from the David Bowie catalogue, and the 6 CD set to celebrate 50 years in recording *Produced By George Martin*. This series encompasses his work from the early days with the likes of accordionist Jimmy Shand, Matt Monro and Rolf Harris, the comedy era with Peter Sellers, Spike Milligan and the *Beyond The Fringe* team, the Sixties and the Seventies with The Beatles et al, and finally to the Nineties with Celine Dion, Sting and Jose Carreras.

In June of 1998, when Yoko Ono visited the Studios, she was presented with a Double Platinum Disc for the remastered album *Lennon Legend*. During her visit she was invited to listen to an experimental surround-sound mix of the track, 'Imagine', in order to obtain her approval to proceed with further mixes for a documentary and DVD about John Lennon. Such was Yoko's enthusiasm that she not only approved the track, but returned the following year to join Peter, Allan, Paul and Guy when they worked, not only on the 5.1 mixes for the project, *Gimme Some Truth*, but also on new stereo remixes of the albums *Imagine* and *Plastic Ono Band*. "Just to sit with Yoko was an incredible experience," reflects Peter, "because she was so conversant with John's work, she was

able to help in deciding what was correct, sonically, for each song. It really helped to remind me that so much of what we do as engineers, isn't just about what we do technically, but how we work with people. It's our place to get to know and understand what it is that they want, and then how we can help them to achieve it." 'The Team' obviously succeeded in this quest, for as Yoko herself is more than ready to admit, "I will never forget my experience of working on the *Gimme Some Truth* DVD at Abbey Road Studios. People were sensitive to my particular needs, while the engineers exercised their utmost expertise, precision and patience with their work. We clicked, so-to-speak, so much so that I find myself looking for an excuse to work there again."

The DVD went on to win the Grammy for Best Long Form Video. At the same awards Radiohead's *Kid A*, mastered by Abbey Road's Chris Blair, won a Grammy for Best Alternative Album.

The increased demand for DVD product has been a contributing factor to the rapid growth in the Interactive department at Abbey Road. The outcome is that Creative Director Samantha Harvey's team has risen in 5 years from 2 to 21.

As Samantha explains, "High quality audio is an important feature of DVD Video, and nowadays 5.1 is vital on all DVD's. As a result, there has been a growth in the close alliance between the main Studios and the Interactive department. We have been working together to master ECD's (Enhanced CD's) for several years, our first DVD release where the music had been remixed in 5.1 by Abbey Road engineers was the highly acclaimed *Gimme Some Truth*. This subsequently led to

Above: **Yoko Ono is presented with a commemmorative disc to recognise UK sales exceeding 600,000 of Lennon Legend,** *in the Abbey Road garden in 1998. Left to right: Senior EMI executives* **Mike Heatley, Rupert Perry and Tony Wadsworth.**

the same policy being adopted for our next production, Eurythmics *Peacetour*, which has been reported as the most technically advanced music DVD yet released. Our other successes include Robbie Williams' *Where Egos Dare* and, in conjunction with BBC Television, *Gormenghast*. Hopefully we can maintain this precious relationship, with many more successes to come."

Another aspect of Abbey Road Interactive is to design and provide high quality websites, and without doubt the most successful to date has to be the site set up to coincide with the release of The Beatles' *1* album. Samantha, justly proud of her team's success, explains, "The site, which was a joint venture between Apple Corps Ltd and EMI Music, featured interactive sections for each of the 27 tracks, and was viewed by over 130,000 people in the first four hours. It was subsequently nominated for 'Best Online Design / Online Promotional Campaign', by the Music Week Online Awards, and was also a nominee for the BAFTA 'Interactive Best Entertainment Website'". The album itself went on to sell in excess of 22 million copies world-wide, topping the charts in no less than 34 countries.

The Building.

As mentioned previously, all post production rooms have been updated, structurally and technically, but some of the biggest changes have been in the Studios themselves. The Penthouse Studio was gutted, and replaced with a spacious control room, and the newly updated Neve Capricorn Digital Console was reinstalled. This studio, now with surround sound facilities, serves primarily as a mixdown suite, much frequented by the classical and film fraternity, although

Right: **Taken in 1981, this shot illustrates the enormity of the studios behind the original house. Studio Three is just visible behind the house, and the air conditioning ducts on the roof of the penthouse are to the right. The roof of the huge Studio One dominates the rear while the world famous Studio Two can be seen to its right.**

it does have a small en suite lounge, which aptly doubles as an isolation room for the occasional overdub.

Studio Three now has as its centrepiece a Solid State Logic, J Series Console, with no less than 96 channels. At the time of its installation (early 2001), it was confirmed as being the largest desk in the country.

But without doubt the most startlingly impressive change has to be the control room of Studio One. This was a monumental challenge from start to finish, but what was achieved in the four months of its closure has to be seen to be believed, a true credit to everyone involved.

The structure of the existing control room was completely demolished to allow it to be extended considerably. Although the popular Neve VRP Legend console with VSX film panels and an additional 8 channels was re-instated, everything else was new. The surround sound monitoring is capable of handling every type of format used by the cinema industry. There is now a huge, triple-glazed, multi-faceted control room window, which gives visibility to virtually every part of the studio, and its 44-foot projection screen. There has also been the addition of two separation booths (one with live acoustics, and one damped) adjacent to, and both visible from, the control room and the studio. Above this impressive nerve centre, and accessible from the studio or the control room, there is now a large lounge area with a viewing window looking down into the studio. In addition, the lounge has its own independent audio system, together with a 50-inch Plasma screen on which to watch film playbacks. A private greenroom and office, together with full bathroom facilities, complete this truly remarkable transformation.

Below: **Versatile composer Lalo Schifrin,** *responsible for more than 100 scores including the theme from* **Mission Impossible,** *in the new Studio One control room with engineer Peter Cobbin and assistant Chris Clark.*

As Colette Barber, Abbey Road's Operations Manager will proudly tell you, "We have listened very closely to what our clients want, and have improved every area of the control room. Despite the alterations the unique acoustics of the studio itself have remained unchanged. Our first priority is to ensure that our facilities are as comfortable and as flexible as possible. Our customers expect a high calibre of service, both in terms of our engineers' experience and our technical facilities. We now know that we meet those expectations. All in all, we believe we provide the ultimate inspirational environment in which to work."

For that never-ending entourage of fans and tourists who besiege the studios on a daily basis, there is one other small building, some 400 metres from the studios, which is also worthy of a mention. The Abbey Road Café, by the entrance to St John's Wood Underground Station, has been set up with Abbey Road's blessing and co-operation by Jeff Jarratt, whose success story is told in Chapter 12. The café got a licence to trade under its historic name, and subsequently opened on April 30, 1999. "We always have some of the great music associated with The Beatles or Abbey Road playing in the background," says Jeff. "Apart from being the official stockists of all the Abbey Road merchandise, we've also acquired the rights for the UK and Europe to manufacture and sell a range of Beatles related products. We've got a great team of staff working for us, and it's all credit to them that we have been voted 'One of the Best Coffee Shops in London'. Oh, and by the way, apart from the *Abbey Road* book, we also sell a great cappuccino, so do pop in if you're passing."

'Abbey Road has managed to survive a number of difficult periods during its history, but in the last four years we have successfully refurbished almost every studio and room in the building, creating a most impressive environment in which to face the 21st Century. But most importantly we have continued to employ some of the best people in the industry.'

CHRIS BUCHANAN
Director of Operations, October 2001.

And so, in the year of Abbey Road's 70th Anniversary, let us raise a glass and drink a toast to:

THE GREATEST STUDIOS IN THE WORLD... EVER'

Glossary

Acoustics—1 The science of sound. 2 The natural sound within a studio which can be altered by changing the coverings and textures of walls, ceilings and floors.

ADT (automatic double tracking)—An electronic means of duplicating a voice or instrument track with a fraction of a second delay to simulate the effect of more performers and thus enhance the sound. This developed from the original artificial double tracking.

Ambiophony—Refer to page 49.

Amplifying channels—Because the volume of sound from microphones is very low, amplifiers in the mixing console boost the sound up to an acceptable level.

A&R (artists and repertoire)—The original term applied to a record producer, his job being to find suitable repertoire for the artist to record.

Baffle boards—In this context, refers to four large sound-absorbing panels, some 15 feet wide by 20 feet high, which can be opened out from the studio walls, thus creating separate isolated areas within a large studio.

Balance engineer—The person responsible for the positioning of musicians, microphones and operating the mixing console.

Basic rhythm track—The least number of instruments that are able to be recorded before subsequent instruments and/or vocals are overdubbed.

Column amps—Amplifiers of the type used by 'pop groups', usually taking the form of tall cabinets containing several loudspeakers.

Crossed pairs—Two identical microphones mounted adjacent to each other, and at such an angle that a natural stereo recording can be made.

Cutter head—The electrical device which, by means of a sapphire or diamond stylus, actually cuts the groove on the lacquer disc.

Dash—A replacement lacquer. The lacquers supplied from one recording are termed, for example, dash 2 or dash 35, depending on the number of replacements required.

Decibel (dB)—A widely used term relating to the power of sound levels.

Demo—A simple, basic recording of a new musical work literally a demonstration.

DVD—Digital Versatile Disc

Disc cutting—The process of cutting the groove in the lacquer disc.

Drop-in—The ability to change instantly from replay to record on one or more tracks of a multi-track machine, enabling the replacement of a particular section of music.

Dubbed—Copying from a disc or pre-recorded tape on to another tape, or the combining of two or more of such recordings into a composite.

Dynamic peaks—Sudden large increases in sound levels, the loudest points during a recording.

Echo chamber—A large room of non-uniform shape with numerous reflective surfaces and containing a loudspeaker and microphone. Any sounds routed through the loudspeaker will create an echo effect similar to a tiled bathroom, these are then received by the microphone and combined with the original sound source.

Editing—Cutting the recorded tape and joining together chosen sections to form a complete and faultless work.

EMT plates—A widely accepted form of artificial echo, patented and manufactured by the West German company, EMT. It comprises a large thin steel plate, some 8 feet by 5 feet, suspended in a framework. This plate is made to vibrate in much the same way as a loudspeaker cone. The vibrations are received by two pick-ups fixed at the boundaries of the plate. The duration of the vibrations can be varied by a mechanical damping device.

Equaliser—A sophisticated form of tone control which has the facility to be able to raise or lower the levels of selected frequencies.

Faders—Sliding volume controls, as distinct from the conventional rotary type.

5.1—One of the surround sound formats, 5.1 comprises 3 speakers in the front: left, centre and right, 2 speakers in the rear: left and right and the '.1' refers to the effects channel that provides extremely low end frequencies (sub-bass).

Frequencies—Vibrations creating low to high pitch sounds, depending on the number of such vibrations per second, usually referred to as Hertz (Hz), eg, 50 Hz creates a low bass sound, 10,000 Hz a high treble sound. The response of the human ear is approximately 20-20,000 Hz.

Gofor—A title once given to junior recording assistants, derived from, 'Gofor some coffee' . . . 'Gofor some tea', etc.

Hertz—Unit of frequency (= 1 cycle per second).

Lacquer disc—A high quality aluminium disc coated with a thin layer of black acetate, used in the cutting process.

Limiter—An electronic device which restrains sudden increases in volume, thus preventing possible overloading.

Loop—A length of tape joined to form a continuous Loop so that when it is played on a tape machine it repeats the recorded signal ad infinitum.

Magnetic delay drums—A motorised rotating drum which has its outer face coated (as with magnetic tape) to allow recordings to be made on it. These recordings are reproduced via numerous playback heads placed strategically around the drum's circumference, thus delaying the recorded signal by varying amounts.

Master—That which is decided as being the best version of a particular recording.

Mastering—The act of cutting the master disc.

Micro groove record—The original term given to the LP disc.

Mixing (or Re-mixing)—Combining together the various tracks of a multi-track recording, to produce a mono, or more commonly, stereo master tape.

Mono (Monophonic)—Single channel reproduction.

MOR—Literally means 'middle of the road', a term used to describe music that is neither pop nor classical.

Moving coil microphone—A type of microphone where sound striking a diaphragm causes a coil to vibrate within a magnetic field, thus creating an electrical impulse. This is basically the reverse operation of a loudspeaker.

Moving coil recorder—Similar in operation to a loudspeaker except that the coil is attached to a cutting stylus rather than a diaphragm; the forerunner of today's cutter head.

Multi-track—This applies to any form of recording other than mono or stereo and it can refer to any one of 3, 4, 8, 16, 24 or 48 tracks. The width of tape used varies according to the number of tracks, and is usually 1 inch for 4 and 8 track, and 2 inch for 16 or 24 track (½ inch for both 24 and 48 track digital formats).

Muting—The facility to switch off any incoming signal to a mixing desk. In the case of computerised mixing desks this can be programmed to occur at any pre-determined point.

Non-directional—A term applied to a microphone which receives sounds from all directions, as distinct from a cardioid microphone, which will receive sounds on one side only, and a figure of eight microphone, receiving sounds on two opposite sides.

Overdubbing—The addition of instruments and/or vocals to an unfinished multitrack recording.

Pre-mix box—A box containing four fader volume controls which could accept four microphones, the output of this box being fed into one input of a mixing console effectively increasing its recording capabilities.

Ribbon microphone—A type of microphone in which electrical impulses are generated by the movements of sound waves on a metal ribbon suspended in a magnetic field.

Splicing—The joining of two pieces of recording tape as part of the editing process.

Stereo (Stereophonic)—Twin channel reproduction, creating the effect of space and depth between the two loudspeakers.

Stereo picture—The apparent positions of instruments and/or vocals at and between the two loudspeakers during a stereo playback.

Synthesized music—Not the natural sounds of musical instruments, but sounds that have been altered or totally created by electronic means.

Tape tension—That which ensures constant contact of the tape against the heads of the tape machine.

Test pressing—One of a few initial records which are manufactured for technical and artistic approval before mass production can commence.

Top—A reference to the treble or high frequencies.

Valve—A glass encased device which controls the flow of electrical current, subsequently replaced by the transistor.

Wound-up piano—Recording the lower notes of a piano at half speed so that when played back at normal speed an unusual but pleasing effect is created.

Acknowledgements

Thanks go to all those people who gave up their valuable time to be interviewed for this book and to those who kindly allowed me to use photographs from their own private collections. These include: Richard Langham, Leslie Bryce, Mark Vigars, Dezo Hoffman, EMI Records Ltd, Raymon Laurence, Doug McKenzie, Peter Vernon, David Sim, Brian Gibson, Paul Tomlinson, Alan Brown, Richard Young, John Dove, A.C.K. Ware, Reg Wilson, Gerry Kelly, David Farrel, Peter Mew, Angus McBeam, G. MacDominic, Axel Poignant, Francis Dillnutt, Thames Television Ltd, Harry Hands, Eddie Klein, Russell Baxter, Clive Barda, David Appleby, Mari O'Connell (PPS), England Records Ltd, John Price Photography, Peter Vince, Allan Rouse, Iain Macmillan, George Martin and Linda McCartney.

Thanks also to Janet Lord, John Evans, John Mouzoros and Kim Clark at Manchester Square; to my editor, Carole Drummond; to all those people at Abbey Road studios who have given their help and support to the compilation of this book.

To end on a personal note, I would like to thank Clive and Fenella for the country retreat; Diane Nicklin for diligently typing the manuscript; Paul McCartney for the Foreword; George Martin for his moving Preface; Brenda Jenkins for her perseverance; EMI Records (UK), Abbey Road and Patrick Stephens Limited for giving me the chance to put 'author' on my passport; and, finally, my wife, Pat, for her encouragement, patience and for reading, rereading and even re-re-reading the text and correcting my grammar.

BRIAN SOUTHALL
1982

Photo Acknowledgements: Van Anastasiou/Peter Van Hook, Apple Corps Ltd, Beat Publications Ltd, Clive Barda, Leslie Bryce, Buena Vista Television, Dan Broncks, Richard Carpenter, Jim Crone, Malcolm Crowthers, Phil Dent, John Dove, EMI Records, David Eustace, Robert Freeman, Brian Gibson, Mark Harrison, Dezo Hoffman, Michael Kamen, Alex Von Koettlitz, Nora Kryst, John Leckie, MPL Communications, Iain Macmillan, Elsa Murphy, News International, Mathew Joseph Peak/Varese Sarabande Records, Nat Peck, Brian Rasic, Brian E.Rybolt/Sonics Associates Inc., Esther Shafer, Lester Smith, Ringo Starr, Charles Sturge, Michael Le Poer Trench/Robert Macintosh, Peter Vernon, Lawrence Watson/Go Discs! Ltd and Reg Wilson.

Personal Acknowledgements: We would like to thank Ken Townsend for his faith in, and support for, the whole project. Also to Chris Charlesworth (Omnibus) for his continued enthusiasm, Imogen Burley for all her help and input, Mark Lewisohn, Neil Aspinall and Jeremy Neech (Apple Corps Ltd), Jude Conway, Mike Heatley, Phil Dent, David Hughes and Janie Orr (EMI Records), Lisa Pettibone, Janet Lord, John Mouzouros, Angela McNeice, and all our interviewees. Finally a very special thank you to Wendy and Fiona for so many years of patience and understanding.

PETER VINCE & ALLAN ROUSE
2001

www.abbeyroad.co.uk
www.abbeyroadcafe.co.uk

Abbey Road's Number Ones

Since the first pop singles chart appeared in 1952, Abbey Road has played a significant part in the recording of hundreds of hit records. It is impossible to catalogue the records which were in part recorded at the studio but the following are the 80 Number One singles which were recorded at Abbey Road studios or utilised Abbey Road's mobile recording studio.

1954	Oh Mein Papa	Eddie Calvert
1955	Softly Softly	Ruby Murray
1955	Cherry Pink and . . .	Eddie Calvert
1955	Dreamboat	Alma Cogan
1956	No Other Love	Ronnie Hilton
1959	Side Saddle	Russ Conway
1959	Roulette	Russ Conway
1959	Living Doll	Cliff & The Shadows
1959	Travellin' Light	Cliff & The Shadows
1959	What Do You Want	Adam Faith
1960	Starry Eyed	Michael Holliday
1960	Poor Me	Adam Faith
1960	Please Don't Tease	Cliff & The Shadows
1960	Shakin' All Over	Johnny Kidd & The Pirates
1960	Apache	The Shadows
1960	Tell Laura I Love Her	Ricky Valance
1960	I Love You	Cliff & The Shadows
1961	You're Diving Me Crazy	Temperance Seven
1961	You Don't Know	Helen Shapiro
1961	Reach For The Stars	Shirley Bassey
1961	Kon-Tiki	The Shadows
1961	Walking Back To Happiness	Helen Shapiro
1961	Moon River	Danny Williams
1962	The Young Ones	Cliff & The Shadows
1962	Wonderful Land	The Shadows

1962	I Remember You	Frank Ifield
1962	Lovesick Blues	Frank Ifield
1963	The Next Time/Bachelor Boy	Cliff & The Shadows
1963	Dance On	The Shadows
1963	Wayward Wind	Frank Ifield
1963	Please Please Me	The Beatles
1963	Summer Holiday	Cliff & The Shadows
1963	Foot Tapper	The Shadows
1963	How Do You Do It	Gerry & The Pacemakers
1963	From Me To You	The Beatles
1963	Do You Want To Know A Secret	Billy J. Kramer & The Dakotas
1963	I Like It	Gerry & The Pacemakers
1963	Confessin'	Frank Ifield
1963	Bad To Me	Billy J. Kramer & The Dakotas
1963	She Loves You	The Beatles
1963	You'll Never Walk Alone	Gerry & The Pacemakers
1963	I Want To Hold Your Hand	The Beatles
1964	Anyone Who Had a Heart	Cilla Black
1964	Little Children	Billy J. Kramer & The Dakotas
1964	Can't Buy Me Love	The Beatles
1964	World Without Love	Peter & Gordon
1964	You're My World	Cilla Black
1964	A Hard Day's Night	The Beatles
1964	Do Wah Diddy Diddy	Manfred Mann
1964	I Feel Fine	The Beatles
1965	I'll Never Find Another You	The Seekers
1965	The Minute You're Gone	Cliff Richard
1965	Ticket To Ride	The Beatles
1965	I'm Alive	Hollies
1965	Help!	The Beatles
1965	Tears	Ken Dodd
1965	The Carnival Is Over	The Seekers
1965	Day Tripper/	The Beatles
	We Can Work It Out	The Beatles
1966	Pretty Flamingo	Manfred Mann
1966	Paperback Writer	The Beatles
1966	Yellow Submarine/	The Beatles
	Eleanor Rigby	The Beatles
1967	All You Need Is Love	The Beatles
1967	Hello Goodbye	The Beatles
1968	Lady Madonna	The Beatles
1968	Congratulations	Cliff Richard
1968	Hey Jude	The Beatles
1968	Lily The Pink	Scaffold
1969	The Ballad of John and Yoko	The Beatles

1971	Grandad	Clive Dunn
1971	My Sweet Lord	George Harrison
1971	Ernie	Benny Hill
1975	January	Pilot
1975	Make Me Smile (Come Up & See Me)	Steve Harley & Cockney Rebel
1975	Whispering Grass	Don Estelle & Windsor Davies
1976	Combine Harvester	Wurzels
1977	Mull Of Kintyre	Wings
1982	Goody Two Shoes	Adam Ant
1988	The One and Only	Chesney Hawkes
1991	He Ain't Heavy, He's My Brother	The Hollies
1996	Knockin' On Heaven's Door	Dunblane

When Prime Minister Margaret Thatcher chose to visit Abbey Road Studios in May 1990, she was introduced to Alan Shacklock who was producing the soundtrack to the film Buddy's Song *starring Chesney Hawkes and Roger Daltrey. Chesney's song 'The One and Only' gave Abbey Road its 76th number one.*

As the list of Number Ones produced at Abbey Road seems to reduce rapidly through the years, we would like to point out that this is due to the different way in which music is recorded today. It is often the case that one song can have been worked on in many different studios – we can very rarely take full credit for a Number One single that has been recorded, mixed and mastered solely at Abbey Road. However, the studios continue to have a significant association with many Number Ones throughout the world, both in the single and album charts.

Index